California
HMH SCIENCE DIMENSIONS™
Volume 1

Grade 7
Units 1–3

Watch the cover come alive as you adjust factors for plant growth.
Download the HMH Science Dimensions AR app available on Android or iOS devices.

This Write-In Book belongs to

_____

Teacher/Room

_____

Houghton Mifflin Harcourt™

Consulting Authors

Michael A. DiSpezio

Global Educator
North Falmouth, Massachusetts

Michael DiSpezio has authored many HMH instructional programs for Science and Mathematics. He has also authored numerous trade books and multimedia programs on various topics and hosted dozens of studio and location broadcasts for various organizations in the United States and worldwide. Most recently, he has been working with educators to provide strategies for implementing the Next Generation Science Standards, particularly the Science and Engineering Practices, Crosscutting Concepts, and the use of Evidence Notebooks. To all his projects, he brings his extensive background in science, his expertise in classroom teaching at the elementary, middle, and high school levels, and his deep experience in producing interactive and engaging instructional materials.

Marjorie Frank

Science Writer and Content-Area Reading Specialist
Brooklyn, New York

An educator and linguist by training, a writer and poet by nature, Marjorie Frank has authored and designed a generation of instructional materials in all subject areas, including past HMH Science programs. Her other credits include authoring science issues of an award-winning children's magazine, writing game-based digital assessments, developing blended learning materials for young children, and serving as instructional designer and coauthor of pioneering school-to-work software. In addition, she has served on the adjunct faculty of Hunter, Manhattan, and Brooklyn Colleges, teaching courses in science methods, literacy, and writing. For *California HMH Science Dimensions™*, she has guided the development of our K–2 strands and our approach to making connections between NGSS and Common Core ELA/literacy standards.

Acknowledgments

Cover credits: (plant) ©HMH; (Earth at night) ©Nastco/iStock/Getty Images Plus/Getty Images.

Section Header Master Art: (machinations) ©DNY59/E+/Getty Images; (rivers on top of Greenland ice sheet) ©Maria-José Viñas, NASA Earth Science News Team; (human cells, illustration) ©Sebastian Kaulitzki/Science Photo Library/Corbis; (waves) ©Alfred Pasieka/Science Source

© Houghton Mifflin Harcourt Publishing Company • Image Credits: ©HMH

Michael R. Heithaus, PhD

Dean, College of Arts, Sciences & Education Professor, Department of Biological Sciences Florida International University Miami, Florida

Mike Heithaus joined the FIU Biology Department in 2003 and has served as Director of the Marine Sciences Program and Executive Director of the School of Environment, Arts, and Society, which brings together the natural and social sciences and humanities to develop solutions to today's environmental challenges. He now serves as Dean of the College of Arts, Sciences & Education. His research focuses on predator-prey interactions and the ecological importance of large marine species. He has helped to guide the development of Life Science content in *California HMH Science Dimensions™*, with a focus on strategies for teaching challenging content as well as the science and engineering practices of analyzing data and using computational thinking.

Bernadine Okoro

Access and Equity Consultant

S.T.E.M. Learning Advocate & Consultant Washington, DC

Bernadine Okoro is a chemical engineer by training and a playwright, novelist, director, and actress by nature. Okoro went from working with patents and biotechnology to teaching in K–12 classrooms. A 12-year science educator and Albert Einstein Distinguished Fellow, Okoro was one of the original authors of the Next Generation Science Standards. As a member of the Diversity and Equity Team, her focus on Alternative Education and Community Schools and on Integrating Social-Emotional Learning and Brain-Based Learning into NGSS is the vehicle she uses as a pathway to support underserved groups from elementary school to adult education. An article and book reviewer for NSTA and other educational publishing companies, Okoro currently works as a S.T.E.M. Learning Advocate & Consultant.

Cary I. Sneider, PhD

Associate Research Professor Portland State University Portland, Oregon

While studying astrophysics at Harvard, Cary Sneider volunteered to teach in an Upward Bound program and discovered his real calling as a science teacher. After teaching middle and high school science in Maine, California, Costa Rica, and Micronesia, he settled for nearly three decades at Lawrence Hall of Science in Berkeley, California, where he developed skills in curriculum development and teacher education. Over his career, Cary directed more than 20 federal, state, and foundation grant projects and was a writing team leader for the Next Generation Science Standards. He has been instrumental in ensuring *California HMH Science Dimensions™* meets the high expectations of the NGSS and provides an effective three-dimensional learning experience for all students.

Program Advisors

Paul D. Asimow, PhD
Eleanor and John R. McMillan Professor of Geology and Geochemistry
California Institute of Technology
Pasadena, California

Joanne Bourgeois
Professor Emerita
Earth & Space Sciences
University of Washington
Seattle, WA

Dr. Eileen Cashman
Professor
Humboldt State University
Arcata, California

Elizabeth A. De Stasio, PhD
Raymond J. Herzog Professor of Science
Lawrence University
Appleton, Wisconsin

Perry Donham, PhD
Lecturer
Boston University
Boston, Massachusetts

Shila Garg, PhD
Professor Emerita of Physics
Former Dean of Faculty & Provost
The College of Wooster
Wooster, Ohio

Tatiana A. Krivosheev, PhD
Professor of Physics
Clayton State University
Morrow, Georgia

Mark B. Moldwin, PhD
Professor of Space Sciences and Engineering
University of Michigan
Ann Arbor, Michigan

Ross H. Nehm
Stony Brook University (SUNY)
Stony Brook, NY

Kelly Y. Neiles, PhD
Assistant Professor of Chemistry
St. Mary's College of Maryland
St. Mary's City, Maryland

John Nielsen-Gammon, PhD
Regents Professor
Department of Atmospheric Sciences
Texas A&M University
College Station, Texas

Dr. Sten Odenwald
Astronomer
NASA Goddard Spaceflight Center
Greenbelt, Maryland

Bruce W. Schafer
Executive Director
Oregon Robotics Tournament & Outreach Program
Beaverton, Oregon

Barry A. Van Deman
President and CEO
Museum of Life and Science
Durham, North Carolina

Kim Withers, PhD
Assistant Professor
Texas A&M University-Corpus Christi
Corpus Christi, Texas

Adam D. Woods, PhD
Professor
California State University, Fullerton
Fullerton, California

English Development Advisors

Mercy D. Momary
Local District Northwest
Los Angeles, California

Michelle Sullivan
Balboa Elementary
San Diego, California

Lab Safety Reviewer

Kenneth R. Roy, Ph.D.
Senior Lab Safety Compliance Consultant
National Safety Consultants, LLC
Vernon, Connecticut

Classroom Reviewers & Hands-On Activities Advisors

Julie Arreola
Sun Valley Magnet School
Sun Valley, California

Pamela Bluestein
Sycamore Canyon School
Newbury Park, California

Andrea Brown
HLPUSD Science & STEAM TOSA
Hacienda Heights, California

Stephanie Greene
Science Department Chair
Sun Valley Magnet School
Sun Valley, California

Rana Mujtaba Khan
Will Rogers High School
Van Nuys, California

Suzanne Kirkhope
Willow Elementary and Round Meadow Elementary
Agoura Hills, California

George Kwong
Schafer Park Elementary
Hayward, California

Imelda Madrid
Bassett St. Elementary School
Lake Balboa, California

Susana Martinez O'Brien
Diocese of San Diego
San Diego, California

Craig Moss
Mt. Gleason Middle School
Sunland, California

Isabel Souto
Schafer Park Elementary
Hayward, California

Emily R.C.G. Williams
South Pasadena Middle School
South Pasadena, California

VOLUME 1

UNIT 1 Science and Engineering   1

Lesson 1 • Science, Engineering, and Resource Use are Related 4

Hands-On Lab Investigate the Influence of Decisions on Resource Use 11

People in Science Shreyas Sundaram, Electrical Engineer 17

Lesson 2 • Engineer It: Using the Engineering Design Process 22

Hands-On Lab Design a Bicycle Helmet Model 30

Careers in Engineering Civil Engineering 37

Unit Review 43

ENGINEER IT **Unit Performance Task** 47

UNIT 2 The Structure of Matter   49

Lesson 1 • Patterns Can Be Observed in Organisms and Nonliving Things 52

Hands-On Lab Model Particles in Objects 63

People in Engineering Gianluca Cusatis, Civil Engineer 65

Lesson 2 • Matter Exists in Different States 70

Hands-On Lab Observe States of Matter 73

Lesson 3 • Changes of State Are Caused by Changes in Thermal Energy 84

Hands-On Lab Investigate a Change of State 87

Careers in Science Forensics 99

Lesson 4 • Organisms and Nonliving Things Are Made of Atoms 104

Hands-On Lab Model Molecules 114

Unit Review 127

Unit Performance Task 131

VOLUME 1

UNIT 3 Chemical Processes   133

Lesson 1 • Matter Changes Identity in Chemical Reactions..........................136

Hands-On Lab Observe Substances Before and After a Change 147

Lesson 2 • Chemical Equations Model Chemical Reactions..........................154

Hands-On Lab Observe a Chemical Reaction 163

Lesson 3 • Engineer It: Using Thermal Energy in a Device 174

Hands-On Lab Choose a Chemical Process 185

People in Science   Fritz Haber and Carl Bosch, Chemists.............................189

Lesson 4 • Synthetic Materials Are Made from Natural Resources..................194

Hands-On Lab Make a Synthetic Material 208

Careers in Engineering   Biomass Engineer 213

Unit Review 219

ENGINEER IT Unit Performance Task 223

This is a crystal of progesterone, an important hormone in the human body. It can be synthetically produced from plant materials using a series of chemical reactions known as the Marker Degradation.

© Houghton Mifflin Harcourt Publishing Company • Image Credits: ©Arthur Siegelman/Visuals Unlimited/Getty Images

VOLUME 2

UNIT 4 Matter and Energy in Organisms and Rock   225

Lesson 1 • The Flow of Energy Drives the Cycling of Matter in Organisms 228

 Hands-On Lab Investigate Decomposition 238

Lesson 2 • Chemical Reactions Provide Energy for Cells 248

Hands-On Lab Investigate the Effect of Sunlight on *Elodea* 254

Lesson 3 • The Flow of Energy Drives Weathering, Erosion, and Deposition 266

Hands-On Lab Model Erosion and Deposition 277

Lesson 4 • The Flow of Energy Drives the Rock Cycle 284

Hands-On Lab Model Crystal Formation 289

Unit Review 309

ENGINEER IT **Unit Performance Task** 313

© Houghton Mifflin Harcourt Publishing Company • Image Credits: ©Bret Edge/AGE Fotostock/Getty Images

Mountain goats feed and play on the rocky peaks formed by Earth's processes.

VOLUME 2

UNIT 5 Earth's Resources and Ecosystems

315

Lesson 1 • The Movement of Earth's Plates Affects Earth's Surface 318

 Hands-On Lab Model the Movement of Continents 330

People in Science   Doug Gibbons, Research Scientist Engineer 335

Lesson 2 • Natural Resources Are Distributed Unevenly 340

Hands-On Lab Model Recharge and Withdrawal in an Aquifer 353

Lesson 3 • Resource Availability Affects Organisms 360

Hands-On Lab Investigate Effects of Limited Resources 371

Lesson 4 • Patterns Can Be Observed in Interactions between Organisms 382

Hands-On Lab Simulate Feeding Relationships 386

Lesson 5 • The Flow of Energy Drives the Cycling of Matter in Ecosystems 400

Hands-On Lab Model Energy Flow in an Ecosystem 405

People in Science   Charles Elton, Ecologist 411

Unit Review 417

ENGINEER IT   **Unit Performance Task** 421

We depend on forests for many resources, including paper, furniture, medicines, and biofuels.

© Houghton Mifflin Harcourt Publishing Company • Image Credits: ©GarysFRP/iStock/Getty Images Plus/Getty Images

VOLUME 3

UNIT 6 **Earth's Surface and Society** 423

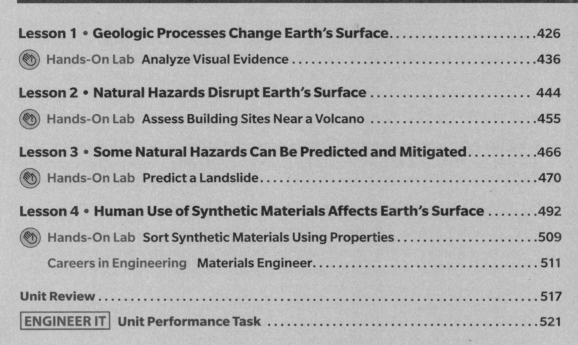

Lesson 1 • Geologic Processes Change Earth's Surface........................426

Hands-On Lab Analyze Visual Evidence 436

Lesson 2 • Natural Hazards Disrupt Earth's Surface 444

Hands-On Lab Assess Building Sites Near a Volcano 455

Lesson 3 • Some Natural Hazards Can Be Predicted and Mitigated..........466

Hands-On Lab Predict a Landslide...470

Lesson 4 • Human Use of Synthetic Materials Affects Earth's Surface 492

Hands-On Lab Sort Synthetic Materials Using Properties 509

Careers in Engineering Materials Engineer....................................511

Unit Review 517

ENGINEER IT **Unit Performance Task** 521

UNIT 7 **Biodiversity and Ecosystem Dynamics** 523

Lesson 1 • Biodiversity Indicates Ecosystem Health...........................526

Hands-On Lab Measure Biodiversity..530

Careers in Science Restoration Ecologist 539

Lesson 2 • Ecosystems Can Stabilize in Response to Change 544

Hands-On Lab Identify Factors That Influence a Population Change 554

People in Science Rodolfo Dirzo, Terrestrial Ecologist 557

Lesson 3 • Engineer It: Maintaining Biodiversity and Ecosystem Services ...562

Hands-On Lab Model Habitat Fragmentation..................................572

Careers in Science Ecotourism...583

Unit Review 589

ENGINEER IT **Unit Performance Task** 593

© Houghton Mifflin Harcourt Publishing Company • Image Credits: (t) ©Will Schmidt/YAY Micro/age fotostock; (b) ©Scott T. Smith/Corbis Documentary/Getty Images

Claims, Evidence, and Reasoning

Constructing an Argument

Constructing a strong argument is useful in science and engineering and in everyday life. A strong argument has three parts: a claim, evidence, and reasoning. Scientists and engineers use claims-evidence-reasoning arguments to communicate their explanations and solutions to others and to challenge or debate the conclusions of other scientists and engineers. The words *argue* and *argument* do not mean that scientists or engineers are fighting about something. Instead, this is a way to support a claim using evidence. Argumentation is a calm and rational way for people to examine all the facts and come to the best conclusion.

A **claim** is a statement that answers the question "What do you know?" A claim is a statement of your understanding of a phenomenon, answer to a question, or solution to a problem. A claim states what you think is true based on the information you have.

Evidence is any data that are related to your claim and answer the question "How do you know that?" These data may be from your own experiments and observations, reports by scientists or engineers, or other reliable data. Arguments made in science and engineering should be supported by empirical evidence. Empirical evidence is evidence that comes from observation or experiment.

Evidence used to support a claim should also be relevant and sufficient. Relevant evidence is evidence that is about the claim, and not about something else. Evidence is sufficient when there is enough evidence to fully support the claim.

Reasoning is the use of logical, analytical thought to form conclusions or inferences. Reasoning answers the question "Why does your evidence support your claim?" So, reasoning explains the relationship between your evidence and your claim. Reasoning might include a scientific law or principle that helps explain the relationship between the evidence and the claim.

© Houghton Mifflin Harcourt Publishing Company • Image Credits: ©HMH

Here is an example of a claims-evidence-reasoning argument.

Claim	Ice melts faster in the sun than it does in the shade.
Evidence	Two ice cubes of the same size were each placed in a plastic dish. One dish was placed on a wooden bench in the sun and one was placed on a different part of the same bench in the shade. The ice cube in the sun melted in 14 minutes and 32 seconds. The ice cube in the shade melted in 18 minutes and 15 seconds.
Reasoning	This experiment was designed so that the only variable that was different in the set-up of the two ice cubes was whether they were in the shade or in the sun. Because the ice cube in the sun melted almost 4 minutes faster than the one in the shade, this is sufficient evidence to say that ice melts faster in the sun than it does in the shade.

To summarize, a strong argument:

• presents a claim that is clear, logical, and well-defended
• supports the claim with empirical evidence that is sufficient and relevant
• includes reasons that make sense and are presented in a logical order

Constructing Your Own Argument

Now construct your own argument by recording a claim, evidence, and reasoning. With your teacher's permission, you can do an investigation to answer a question you have about how the world works. Or you can construct your argument based on observations you have already made about the world.

Claim	
Evidence	
Reasoning	

 For more information on claims, evidence, and reasoning, see the online **English Language Arts Handbook.**

Whether you are in the lab or in the field, you are responsible for your own safety and the safety of others. To fulfill these responsibilities and avoid accidents, be aware of the safety of your classmates as well as your own safety at all times. Take your lab work and fieldwork seriously, and behave appropriately. Elements of safety to keep in mind are shown below and on the following pages.

Safety in the Lab

☐ Be sure you understand the materials, your procedure, and the safety rules before you start an investigation in the lab.

☐ Know where to find and how to use fire extinguishers, eyewash stations, shower stations, and emergency power shutoffs.

☐ Use proper safety equipment. Always wear personal protective equipment, such as eye protection and gloves, when setting up labs, during labs, and when cleaning up.

☐ Do not begin until your teacher has told you to start. Follow directions.

☐ Keep the lab neat and uncluttered. Clean up when you are finished. Report all spills to your teacher immediately. Watch for slip/fall and trip/fall hazards.

☐ If you or another student is injured in any way, tell your teacher immediately, even if the injury seems minor.

☐ Do not take any food or drink into the lab. Never take any chemicals out of the lab.

Safety in the Field

☐ Be sure you understand the goal of your fieldwork and the proper way to carry out the investigation before you begin fieldwork.

☐ Use proper safety equipment and personal protective equipment, such as eye protection, that suits the terrain and the weather.

☐ Follow directions, including appropriate safety procedures as provided by your teacher.

☐ Do not approach or touch wild animals. Do not touch plants unless instructed by your teacher to do so. Leave natural areas as you found them.

☐ Stay with your group.

☐ Use proper accident procedures, and let your teacher know about a hazard in the environment or an accident immediately, even if the hazard or accident seems minor.

Safety Symbols

To highlight specific types of precautions, the following symbols are used throughout the lab program. Remember that no matter what safety symbols you see within each lab, all safety rules should be followed at all times.

Dress Code

- Wear safety goggles (or safety glasses as appropriate for the activity) at all times in the lab as directed. If chemicals get into your eye, flush your eyes immediately for a minimum of 15 minutes.
- Do not wear contact lenses in the lab.
- Do not look directly at the sun or any intense light source or laser.
- Wear appropriate protective non-latex gloves as directed.
- Wear an apron or lab coat at all times in the lab as directed.
- Tie back long hair, secure loose clothing, and remove loose jewelry. Remove acrylic nails when working with active flames.
- Do not wear open-toed shoes, sandals, or canvas shoes in the lab.

Glassware and Sharp Object Safety

- Do not use chipped or cracked glassware.
- Use heat-resistant glassware for heating or storing hot materials.
- Notify your teacher immediately if a piece of glass breaks.
- Use extreme care when handling any sharp or pointed instruments.
- Do not cut an object while holding the object unsupported in your hands. Place the object on a suitable cutting surface, and always cut in a direction away from your body.

Chemical Safety

- If a chemical gets on your skin, on your clothing, or in your eyes, rinse it immediately for a minimum of 15 minutes (using the shower, faucet, or eyewash station), and alert your teacher.
- Do not clean up spilled chemicals unless your teacher directs you to do so.
- Do not inhale any gas or vapor unless directed to do so by your teacher. If you are instructed to note the odor of a substance, wave the fumes toward your nose with your hand. This is called wafting. Never put your nose close to the source of the odor.
- Handle materials that emit vapors or gases in a well-ventilated area.
- Keep your hands away from your face while you are working on any activity.

Safety Symbols, continued

Electrical Safety

- Do not use equipment with frayed electrical cords or loose plugs.
- Do not use electrical equipment near water or when clothing or hands are wet.
- Hold the plug housing when you plug in or unplug equipment. Do not pull on the cord.
- Use only GFI-protected electrical receptacles.

Heating and Fire Safety

- Be aware of any source of flames, sparks, or heat (such as flames, heating coils, or hot plates) before working with any flammable substances.
- Know the location of the lab's fire extinguisher and fire-safety blankets.
- Know your school's fire-evacuation routes.
- If your clothing catches on fire, walk to the lab shower to put out the fire. Do not run.
- Never leave a hot plate unattended while it is turned on or while it is cooling.
- Use tongs or appropriately insulated holders when handling heated objects.
- Allow all equipment to cool before storing it.

Plant and Animal Safety

- Do not eat any part of a plant.
- Do not pick any wild plant unless your teacher instructs you to do so.
- Handle animals only as your teacher directs.
- Treat animals carefully and respectfully.
- Wash your hands thoroughly with soap and water after handling any plant or animal.

Cleanup

- Clean all work surfaces and protective equipment as directed by your teacher.
- Dispose of hazardous materials or sharp objects only as directed by your teacher.
- Wash your hands thoroughly with soap and water before you leave the lab or after any activity.

Student Safety Quiz

Circle the letter of the BEST answer.

1. Before starting an investigation or lab procedure, you should
   - **A.** try an experiment of your own
   - **B.** open all containers and packages
   - **C.** read all directions and make sure you understand them
   - **D.** handle all the equipment to become familiar with it

2. At the end of any activity you should
   - **A.** wash your hands thoroughly with soap and water before leaving the lab
   - **B.** cover your face with your hands
   - **C.** put on your safety goggles
   - **D.** leave hot plates switched on

3. If you get hurt or injured in any way, you should
   - **A.** tell your teacher immediately
   - **B.** find bandages or a first aid kit
   - **C.** go to your principal's office
   - **D.** get help after you finish the lab

4. If your glassware is chipped or broken, you should
   - **A.** use it only for solid materials
   - **B.** give it to your teacher for recycling or disposal
   - **C.** put it back into the storage cabinet
   - **D.** increase the damage so that it is obvious

5. If you have unused chemicals after finishing a procedure, you should
   - **A.** pour them down a sink or drain
   - **B.** mix them all together in a bucket
   - **C.** put them back into their original containers
   - **D.** dispose of them as directed by your teacher

6. If electrical equipment has a frayed cord, you should
   - **A.** unplug the equipment by pulling the cord
   - **B.** let the cord hang over the side of a counter or table
   - **C.** tell your teacher about the problem immediately
   - **D.** wrap tape around the cord to repair it

7. If you need to determine the odor of a chemical or a solution, you should
   - **A.** use your hand to bring fumes from the container to your nose
   - **B.** bring the container under your nose and inhale deeply
   - **C.** tell your teacher immediately
   - **D.** use odor-sensing equipment

8. When working with materials that might fly into the air and hurt someone's eye, you should wear
   - **A.** goggles
   - **B.** an apron
   - **C.** gloves
   - **D.** a hat

9. Before doing experiments involving a heat source, you should know the location of the
   - **A.** door
   - **B.** window
   - **C.** fire extinguisher
   - **D.** overhead lights

10. If you get chemicals in your eye you should
    - **A.** wash your hands immediately
    - **B.** put the lid back on the chemical container
    - **C.** wait to see if your eye becomes irritated
    - **D.** use the eyewash station right away, for a minimum of 15 minutes

Go online to view the Lab Safety Handbook for additional information.

Science and Engineering

How do humans explore and design our world?

Unit Project 2
Lesson 1   Science, Engineering, and Resource Use Are Related 4
Lesson 2   Engineer It: Using the Engineering Design Process 22
Unit Review 43
Unit Performance Task 47

Many communities around the world face housing shortages. One of the goals of the CalEarth SuperAdobe project is to provide affordable and sustainable housing to these communities.

You Solve It How Can You Design a Ship to Carry Cargo?

Design container ships for different purposes, including carrying a large volume of cargo, traveling the fastest, being the most fuel efficient, and having the least environmental impact.

Go online and complete the You Solve It to explore ways to solve a real-world problem.

Develop a Solution

Waste management issues affect parks, schools, and businesses.

A. Look at the photo. On a separate sheet of paper, write down as many different questions as you can about the photo.

B. **Discuss** With your class or a partner, share your questions. Record any additional questions generated in your discussion. Then choose the most important questions from the list that are related to addressing and solving a problem in your community or school. Write them below.

C. Choose a problem in your school or community to research. Here's a list of problems you can consider:

Food Allergies   Bullying
Garbage and Waste   Accessibility
Food and Snack Options Transportation
Extracurricular Activities

D. Use the information above, along with your research, to develop a solution to the issue you chose to address.

Discuss the next steps for your Unit Project with your teacher and go online to download the Unit Project Worksheet.

Language Development

Use the lessons in this unit to complete the network and expand your understanding of these key concepts.

	Similar term
	Phrase
	Cognate
	Example
	Definition

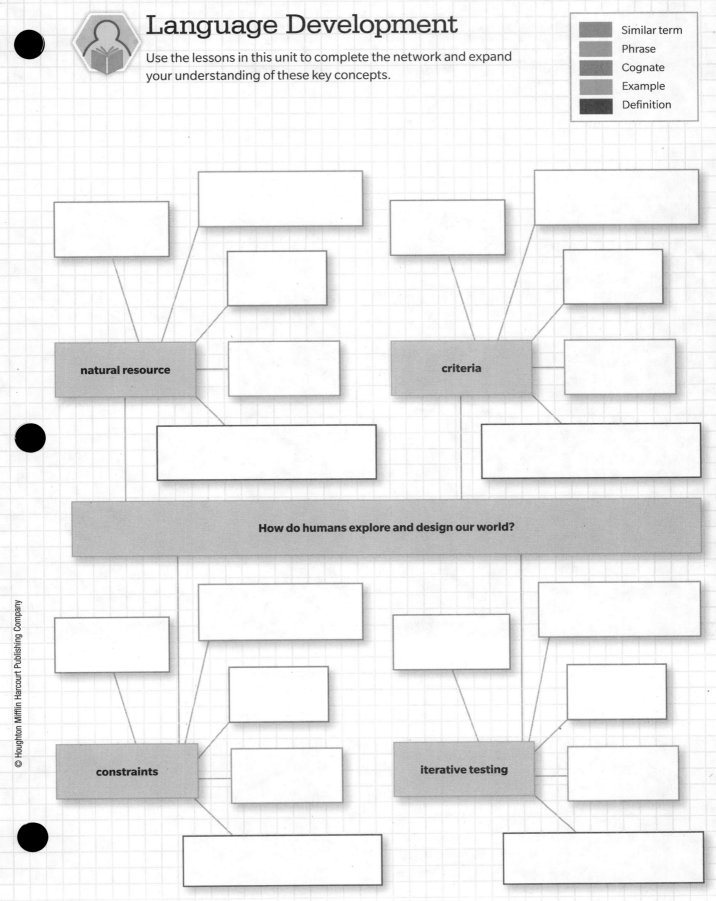

natural resource

criteria

How do humans explore and design our world?

constraints

iterative testing

Science, Engineering, and Resource Use Are Related

The Bixby Bridge, which is built of reinforced concrete, spans a steep canyon cut by Bixby Creek. The bridge offers dramatic views along California State Highway 1.

Explore First

Mining Clay Mix several beads into a ball of clay. Flatten the clay onto a small paper plate so it is about 3 cm thick. Try to get all the beads back out without moving or changing the shape of the clay. How does this constraint influence your mining method? Do you think minerals in Earth's crust can be mined without disrupting the land, soil, or plants?

CAN YOU EXPLAIN IT?

How could this construction boom in China be related to this flood in Indonesia?

As the human population increases, cities such as Chongqing, China are growing rapidly. As buildings, roads, and bridges are built, the demand for concrete skyrockets.

This is one of thousands of flooded homes along the Bengawan Solo River in Indonesia. Flooding in the region has increased due to sand mining activities along the banks of the river.

1. Chongqing is over 4,000 km from this flooded area in Indonesia. How might these two places be related?

2. How does each image relate to society's needs? Explain your answer.

EVIDENCE NOTEBOOK As you explore this lesson, gather evidence to help explain how a construction boom in China could relate to flooding in Indonesia.

Relating Natural Resources to Science and Engineering

Natural Resources and Society

All societies depend on natural resources for food, water, materials, and energy. A **natural resource** is any natural material or energy source that humans use. Examples include water, oil, minerals, plants, sunlight, wind, and animals. Societies use resources as a way of building wealth by mining, harvesting, and trading the resources with one another. It may be hard to imagine how products such as plastic or concrete come from nature. These kinds of products are made by processing natural resources.

Nonrenewable resources, such as sand, coal, and oil, are used more quickly than they can form. Renewable resources are replaceable in a relatively short time period. Plants are examples of renewable resources because they grow relatively quickly. Sunlight and wind are continually available as sources of energy, so they are also called renewable resources.

3. **Discuss** Could an object, tool, or structure be made without the use of a natural resource? Explain your answer.

Products Made Using Sand, a Nonrenewable Natural Resource

Silica, found in sand, is a major ingredient of glass, used for everything from windows to phone screens.

Without sand, concrete would not be available to make roads, sidewalks, bridges, or buildings.

Electronic devices contain silicon microchips made from the silica found in sand.

The Distribution of Natural Resources

Natural resources are part of the Earth system, which includes the hydrosphere, biosphere, geosphere, and atmosphere. For example, the water we drink comes from the hydrosphere. Food is part of the biosphere. Minerals are obtained from the geosphere. The air we breathe is in the atmosphere.

Most natural resources are concentrated in specific locations on Earth. The natural processes that lead to the formation or growth of a resource may occur only in specific locations under certain conditions. Citrus fruits grow best in warm, rainy climates. Coal forms in swamp environments. Sand forms as certain rocks are broken down into tiny pieces. Both sand and coal are formed by geologic processes that can take place over millions of years. One major factor that affects how accessible a resource is to people is location. For example, it is easier to mine sand from a beach than from the bottom of a deep lake.

Ecosystems and Ecosystem Services

An *ecosystem* is a community of organisms and the nonliving components in their environment. Natural processes in healthy, functioning ecosystems result in clean air and water, fertile soil, and other *ecosystem services* that benefit humans. Ecosystem services also include shade, recreation, the pollination of plants, and pest control. These services are essential to human societies and economies. For example, wetland ecosystems can prevent severe flooding when heavy rains occur.

Humans alter ecosystems to obtain and use natural resources. When native plants are removed to plant crops or mine minerals, the biodiversity of the ecosystem is negatively affected. This is because the number of plants—and any organisms depending on those plants—would decrease. *Biodiversity* refers to the number and variety of organisms in an ecosystem. Ecosystem processes and services are weakened or destroyed as biodiversity decreases. Humans also build over ecosystems. For example, covering wetland soils with asphalt and concrete makes the ground *impervious*, which means the ground cannot absorb water. Rainwater ends up collecting and flowing over the surface instead of soaking into the ground. This decreases the ability of the wetland to provide the ecosystem service of flood prevention.

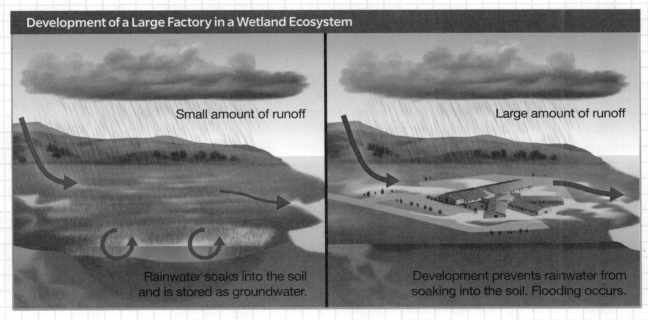

Development of a Large Factory in a Wetland Ecosystem

Small amount of runoff

Large amount of runoff

Rainwater soaks into the soil and is stored as groundwater.

Development prevents rainwater from soaking into the soil. Flooding occurs.

4. Engineer It The development of this factory resulted in frequent floods in the area, mostly due to the addition of impervious surfaces. The owners of the factory want to make changes to prevent future flooding. Help the owners brainstorm solutions for the flooding problem. Choose one solution and describe how you could test it.

The Roles of Scientists and Engineers in Society

Through science, we learn how the world works. *Science* is the practice of asking questions and developing explanations about how things work in both the natural world and the designed world. People are not only curious about how the world works, but they want to address needs and solve problems. This is what engineers do. *Engineering* is the practice of defining problems and developing solutions for those problems. Society's needs and desires have a major influence on scientific investigations, engineering, and the development of technology.

Scientists and engineers work together. Scientists use tools developed by engineers to investigate the world. Engineers use scientific knowledge while they solve problems. For example, scientists might discover a natural compound that kills infectious microbes, but the scientists would need to work with engineers to develop a way to manufacture medicine from this natural compound.

5. Complete the following description to differentiate between scientists and engineers.

A community was facing a problem with excessive waste from paper products. A group of scientists / engineers developed a simple recycling process to help solve the problem. A group of scientists / engineers then conducted an investigation to determine how much energy the recycling process took.

Science, Engineering, and Technology

Some of the first evidence of humans developing technology includes cutting tools that were made over 3 million years ago. *Technology* is any tool, process, or system that is made to solve a problem. Technology is usually the result of an engineering solution—that is, technology is developed to address a need. The use of technology in engineering and science has led to important discoveries about the natural world and led to the development of entire industries and engineered systems.

Ask Science and Engineering Questions

6. Discuss Scientists discovered that large termite mounds maintain an interior temperature that is cooler than the outside temperature. The cooling process within termite mounds could be used to generate ideas for ways to cool buildings in hot weather. With a partner, identify one question scientists might ask about this phenomenon to understand it. Then identify one question that engineers might ask to address the need for cooling buildings.

_____

_____

_____

_____

_____

_____

_____

_____

Describing Natural Resource Use

Resource Use Can Be Modeled as a Life Cycle

Each natural resource has a unique life cycle, beginning when it is grown or extracted and ending when it is thrown away. However, its story may continue if the resource is reused or recycled. For example, rocks containing aluminum are extracted from Earth's crust. The aluminum is separated from the rock by a series of chemical processes. The aluminum is then transported to factories to make products such as soda cans and aluminum foil. Products are transported to stores, sold to consumers, used, and then thrown away, recycled, or reused. Just as a rock does not look like a soda can, a raw natural resource does not always resemble the final product.

7. **Language SmArts | Draw** Identify a tool or object you use in school and think about its life cycle, from a natural resource to the final product. Draw a diagram of your object's life cycle and label each stage.

Obtaining Resources

A natural resource's life cycle begins when the resource is obtained. Natural resources can be collected, mined, or harvested in many ways. For example, fresh water is pumped for drinking. Lettuce is grown for food. Sand, gravel, and limestone are mined to make concrete. The sun's energy is collected and used to generate electrical energy.

Obtaining Natural Resources

drinking water extraction

sand mining

solar energy collection

vegetable farming

Production

While some resources can be used directly, others must be processed to make them usable. Production, or manufacturing, involves modifying a resource from its original state. Processing raw materials requires energy and technologies such as tools, equipment, and manufacturing processes. For example, vegetables are harvested, washed, and packaged. Water, cement, gravel, and sand are combined in large mixers to produce concrete. Fresh water is often filtered and treated to remove harmful substances and microbes, which makes it safe to drink. Once a product is made, it is prepared for distribution.

Concrete is a mixture of cement, which is a binder, water, sand, and a mix of fine and coarse pebbles called *aggregate*.

Distribution

After a product is made, it is distributed to the user or consumer. For example, concrete is used in the construction of buildings and roadways, so concrete is distributed to construction sites. Sometimes, the raw materials to make concrete are sent to construction sites and the concrete is produced on site. Drinking water is another resource that must be distributed. Water pumped from its source can go through treatment plants, reservoirs, and underground pipes before being used by a household. Drinking water is also bottled and distributed to stores for purchase. Some products must be transported long distances to get to consumers. Often, there are many steps involved in the supply chain that distributes a product to its users.

8. The city of Dubai is surrounded by desert sand, but it imports sand from Australia for construction. This is because the wind-blasted desert sand surrounding Dubai is too smooth to be used to make construction materials. Nearby marine sands were once used but the supply is now exhausted. How do you think Dubai's need for construction sand affects Australian societies? How might it affect Australian ecosystems?

These tall skyscrapers in Dubai include glass and concrete, both of which require large amounts of sand to make.

Hands-On Lab

Investigate the Influence of Decisions on Resource Use

With a partner, use the table to model scenarios in which two people share a limited resource. Each person chooses a low, medium, or high rate of use. Depending on their choices, each person will get a different benefit level, with 1 being the lowest benefit and 10 being the highest benefit. For example, if Person 1 chooses a low rate of resource use and Person 2 chooses a medium rate, you look at the first row and second column, which contains the numbers 1 and 9. The benefit level is 1 for Person 1 and 9 for Person 2.

Procedure

STEP 1 You and your partner live in a place with a limited supply of water to use each month. What are some ways you will need to use the water?

Person 1 \ Person 2	Low	Medium	High
Low	1 / 1	1 / 9	1 / 10
Medium	9 / 1	8 / 8	3 / 9
High	10 / 1	9 / 3	4 / 4

STEP 2 Model at least five scenarios with different combinations of each person's rate of use. For each scenario, record the rate of use and benefit levels for each person.

Analysis

STEP 3 What patterns do you observe from your results?

STEP 4 Does one person's choice affect the benefit the other person gets? Use evidence from your results to explain.

STEP 5 How does this model demonstrate the consequences of making choices about resource use?

© Houghton Mifflin Harcourt Publishing Company

Consumer Use

A product's life cycle includes its use by consumers. As the human population rapidly increases, so does the need for food, water, and shelter. Consumer use of technology such as cell phones and computers also increases. More roads, bridges, and buildings are constructed as well. Consumer preferences also drive the life cycle of different natural resources. For example, the demand for fruits and vegetables that are blemish-free means that growers will likely not have a market for fruits and vegetables that are slightly misshapen but otherwise perfectly edible.

Examples of Consumer Use of Natural Resources

Clean drinking water is a natural resource that is essential to a healthy life.

Concrete is a critical building material that is used for buildings as well as recreation areas, such as this skate park.

Solar panels similar to the ones on this boat reduce society's dependence on fossil fuels as an energy source.

Produce from farms provides food. Fresh fruits and vegetables are processed less than packaged foods.

EVIDENCE NOTEBOOK

9. How are the construction and technology industries driving the demand for sand? Record your evidence.

Disposal

There are several ways products can be handled after consumers use them. For example, plastic bags from a grocery store can be discarded by throwing them into the trash. They can be reused by taking them back to the store, or they can be recycled to make different plastic products. Concrete from an old building can be reused to make new concrete or other products. Recycled paper can be processed to make cereal boxes, paper towel rolls, and many other products.

10. Look back at your life-cycle steps and diagram from earlier in the lesson. How would reusing or recycling the product change the product's life cycle and the demand on resources used to make the product?

© Houghton Mifflin Harcourt Publishing Company • Image Credits: (tl) ©Houghton Mifflin Harcourt; (tr) ©Daniel Milchev/Stone/Getty Images; (bl) ©Wojciech Kozielczyk/Alamy; (br) ©fstop123/E+/Getty Images

Do the Math
Analyze Land Reclamation in Singapore

To address the growing population of the city state of Singapore, engineers have increased the island's land area using sand and other aggregate materials.

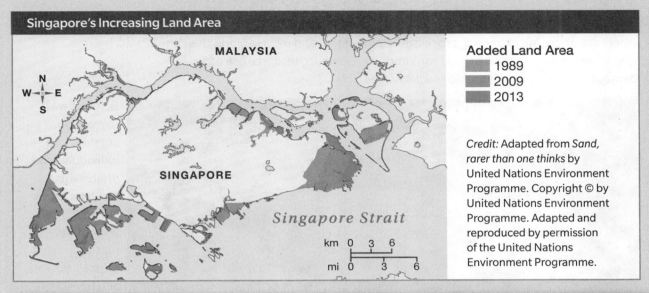

Singapore's Increasing Land Area

Added Land Area
- 1989
- 2009
- 2013

Credit: Adapted from *Sand, rarer than one thinks* by United Nations Environment Programme. Copyright © by United Nations Environment Programme. Adapted and reproduced by permission of the United Nations Environment Programme.

11. In 1989, the total land area of Singapore was 626.4 km². By 2013, it was 716.5 km². By how many square kilometers did Singapore grow from 1989 to 2013?

12. Calculate the percentage increase in land from 1989 to 2013. First, take the amount of added land over that time period and divide it by the original land area in 1989. Then, multiply by 100%.

13. Discuss Much of the sand used to increase Singapore's land area has been imported from other countries. Some sand has been dredged from the surrounding ocean floor, and some artificial sand has been made by crushing rock. With a partner, develop a scientific question regarding Singapore's use of sand.

Describing the Impacts of Resource Use

Impacts of Resource Use by Life-Cycle Stages

Natural resource use affects society in positive and negative ways. Jobs are created where resources are extracted, processed, transported, and recycled, and this can strengthen the economies of local communities. However, resource use can also damage the ecosystems on which society relies.

Before it was mined and crushed into individual sand grains, this sandstone was covered by a layer of soil that supported grasses, flowers, and trees.

14. Many organisms, such as birds, deer, and bees, depended on the vegetation and soil that was removed to mine sandstone here. Their populations have decreased dramatically since the mining operation started. How might the decrease in these populations affect humans? Explain your reasoning.

Obtaining Resources

Ecosystems are affected by the way resources are obtained. An area sustains physical damage such as erosion and the loss of vegetation when it is cleared to extract or harvest resources. Pollution caused by fuel spills and improperly stored waste can contaminate soil and water sources. Erosion can physically remove organisms. These negative impacts can decrease the biodiversity of ecosystems. When sand is mined from a river bottom, water can flow faster and erode the river's banks. Flooding can also occur, further disrupting the river ecosystem and any people who depend on or live near the river. In some countries, mining companies are required to follow strict laws that help control the damage that mining may cause. Careful selection of where to mine sand can reduce damage and allow time for affected ecosystems to recover from mining activities.

Production

Processing resources to make usable products requires energy and other resources. Fossil fuels are often burned to provide energy to processing facilities. Therefore, the production phase of a resource's life cycle can have negative impacts on the environment. Fossil fuels are nonrenewable and cause pollution when they are burned. The waste from processing resources must be properly handled to ensure that it does not pollute the soil, water, or air.

The Trans-Alaska pipeline transports crude oil from northern Alaska to refineries in Valdez, in southern Alaska.

Distribution

The impacts of resource distribution can negatively affect ecosystems and the people who depend on those ecosystems. Roads and other infrastructure built to transport resources divide habitats and disrupt migration patterns. Ships carrying consumer goods can cause changes to aquatic ecosystems. However, distributing natural resources is often necessary. For example, clean drinking water is a resource that is not equally distributed on Earth. Having better access to clean drinking water improves the health of individuals and raises the overall living standards in the society.

Consumer Use

As the human population increases, the need for resources increases. The negative effects of resource use can include depletion of nonrenewable resources and pollution. For example, coal is burned to provide energy, but this process pollutes the environment. Coal is also a nonrenewable resource. Wind turbines are a cleaner energy resource. However, producing and installing them requires changes to the environment, and using them can injure and kill birds.

Societies must weigh the advantages and disadvantages of resource use. This may involve a choice between renewable and nonrenewable resources. Additionally, consumers might choose to use products that take less energy or fewer resources to make, or they may choose to reduce their use of resources.

Urban Development in Shenzhen, Guangdong, China

As the population in this city grows, consumers use more resources for building and transportation.

1985

2016

15. As cities grow, why does the need for sand increase? Select all that apply.

   A. Technologies, such as solar panels and computers, are in higher demand.

   B. More roads must be constructed for transportation.

   C. More buildings must be constructed for homes and offices.

   D. More people require water and food.

Disposal

Discarding materials can have negative impacts on ecosystems. Discarded materials end up in landfills, where they may take hundreds or thousands of years to decompose. Discarded materials can also introduce pollutants into soil and water if the materials are not stored properly. Increased use and disposal of products by consumers increases demand for landfill space.

Recycling and reusing products reduces the demand on natural resources because fewer new products have to be made. Recycling and reusing products also reduces the demand for landfill space.

16. Discuss Compare and contrast ways to reuse and recycle a consumer product.

Old concrete is crushed into fine particles in order to be recycled to make new concrete items.

EVIDENCE NOTEBOOK

17. Describe the effects of using sand on both society and on ecosystems. Record your evidence.

Describe the Effects of Using a Resource

18. Humans depend on ecosystems for ecosystem services and resources. For example, this river ecosystem provides water, fish, and a place to swim. The forest ecosystem provides wood, shade, and erosion control. Choose a resource and describe the possible effects of its use on society and on ecosystems throughout its life cycle.

_____
_____
_____
_____
_____
_____
_____
_____
_____
_____
_____
_____
_____
_____

Continue Your Exploration

Name: _____   **Date:** _____

Check out the path below or go online to choose one of the other paths shown.

People in Science

• **Frac Sand Mining**
• **Hands-On Labs** 🖐
• **Propose Your Own Path**

Go online to choose one of these other paths

Shreyas Sundaram

Shreyas Sundaram was interested in science, engineering, and mathematics at an early age. He lived in India until age 10, when he moved to Canada. He earned degrees in computer engineering and electrical engineering.

Dr. Sundaram researches the design and resilience of national economies, power grids, ecosystems, and networks such as the Internet. *Resilience* is the ability of a system to function when it is being overused or disrupted.

Shreyas Sundaram (at right) and his PhD student Ashish Hota work together on Dr. Sundaram's prospect theory project.

Modeling Human Behavior

Several models have been developed to help predict what people will do in a given situation. Prospect theory describes how people make decisions when the likelihood of certain outcomes is known and the risks and rewards of each outcome are defined. For example, imagine this choice.

• **Option 1:** You are guaranteed to receive $5.
• **Option 2:** You have a 50% chance of receiving $10, and a 50% chance of receiving no money.

Which option would you choose? Not everyone will choose the same option, and most decisions will be based on how much a person values the money.

Game theory studies the ways in which one person's behavior and choices affect another's. Dr. Sundaram applies prospect and game theory to study how people use large-scale shared resources. He theorizes that while using shared resources, people may make decisions in their own best interest, even if it hurts the entire group. Shared resources such as forests, hiking trails, roads, and fresh air are used by everyone. The way that some people use shared resources affects other people's ability to use them. For example, a factory that produces a lot of air pollution affects the air quality for everyone in the community. According to prospect theory, the more people value something, the less likely they are to risk losing it. People who value a shared resource are less likely to

Continue Your Exploration

use it in a way that might harm or destroy it. People who value clean air may be more likely to use public transportation than to drive their own cars. Dr. Sundaram and others have shown that people's values have an effect on resource use. For example, people may value the freedom of driving their own vehicle over air quality.

1. Which of the following do you think would be a better situation? Use evidence from the graph to support your answer.

   • **Situation 1:** Everyone in a community values a forest a moderate amount.

   • **Situation 2:** 50% of people highly value the forest and 50% of people do not value the forest.

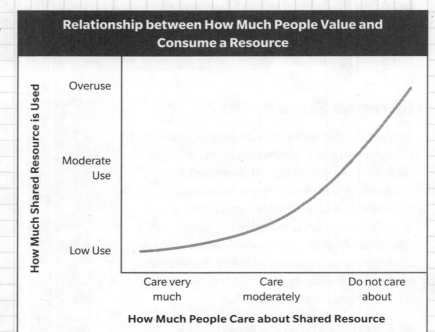

Relationship between How Much People Value and Consume a Resource

Credit: Adapted from "Fragility of the Commons under Prospect-Theoretic Risk Attitudes," doi.org/10.1016/j.geb.2016.06.003, from *Games and Economic Behavior,* Volume 98 by Ashish R. Hota et al. Copyright © 2016 Elsevier. Adapted and reproduced by permission of Elsevier.

2. Why is it important for scientists to understand how and why a population might use a shared resource?

3. How might a shared resource be protected from overuse? Use an example of a shared resource in your answer.

4. **Collaborate** Research a resource that has been overused in the past or is currently being overused. Present a poster to the class that describes the resource, how it has been used in the past and by whom, and goals for managing the use of the resource in the future. Explain why education can help manage the use of shared resources.

Can You Explain It?

Name: _____   Date: _____

How could this construction boom in China be related to this flood in Indonesia?

 EVIDENCE NOTEBOOK

Refer to the notes in your Evidence Notebook to help you construct an explanation for how a construction boom in China could relate to flooding in Indonesia.

1. State your claim. Make sure your claim fully explains the relationship between the construction boom in Chonqing, China, and the flooding near this river in Indonesia.

2. Summarize the evidence you have gathered to support your claim and explain your reasoning.

Checkpoints

Answer the following questions to check your understanding of the lesson.

Use the photo to answer Questions 3–4.

3. Sand is mined from this location in order to make concrete. Growing cities use large amounts of concrete to construct buildings and roads. Which of the following is something an engineer might ask about sand mining and concrete use? Select all that apply.

   A. What is an alternative material?

   B. What is the cost of concrete as compared to the alternative material?

   C. How does the strength and durability of concrete compare to the strength and durability of the alternative material?

   D. Why are cities growing so quickly?

4. People catch fish in this aquatic ecosystem and sell the fish to make a living. Why might these people be concerned about sand mining here? Select all that apply.

   A. Sand mining disturbs the habitats of the fish.

   B. Sand mining brings more fish into the area.

   C. Sand mining kills and drives away predators of the fish.

   D. Sand mining kills and drives away the organisms fish eat.

Use the photo to answer Questions 5–7.

5. Silicon is needed to make digital camera sensors such as the one shown. Silicon is obtained from silica, a mineral found in sand. Order the steps below to describe the life cycle of silica as a resource. The first and last steps are done for you.

   1 Sand is extracted from an environment by mining.

   ___ People buy cameras and use them.

   ___ The silica in the sand is processed to obtain silicon.

   ___ Digital camera sensors are made and put into digital cameras.

   ___ Digital cameras are distributed to stores for purchase.

   6 The camera stops working, and its parts are recycled.

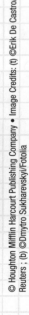

6. Consumer demand for digital cameras is related to sand mining. As consumer demand increases, the amount of sand mined increases / decreases / stays the same.

7. Scientists use technology to ask questions / solve problems about the world. Engineers develop and use technology in order to ask questions / solve problems to address the needs of society.

© Houghton Mifflin Harcourt Publishing Company • Image Credits: (t) ©Erik De Castro/ Reuters ; (b) ©Dmytro Sukharevskyi/Fotolia

Interactive Review

Complete this section to review the main concepts of the lesson.

Natural resources and ecosystem services are needed by humans. Scientists work to explain the world, while engineers work to solve problems.

A. Describe how both a scientist and an engineer could contribute to reducing the use of a nonrenewable resource.

The life cycle of a natural resource can include obtaining the resource, and resource production, distribution, consumer use, and disposal.

B. Identify one resource you use, and describe its life cycle.

Resource use affects both the environment and people. The effects can be positive and negative.

C. How would a solution allowing humans to grow more food crops on less land benefit humans and ecosystems?

Using the Engineering Design Process

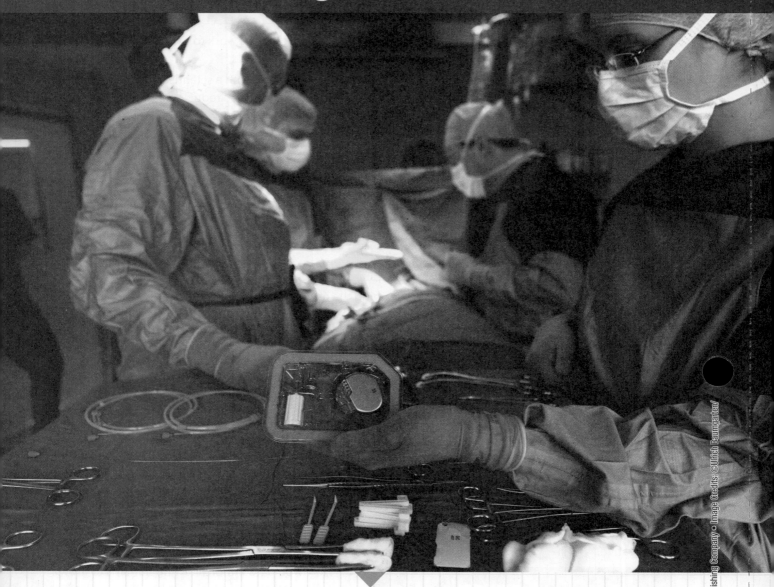

The function of the artificial heart pacemaker remains the same since the first one was developed in the 1920s, but its design has changed significantly since then.

Explore First

Modeling a Cargo Boat How might construction materials affect an engineering solution? Build boats out of a sheet of paper and an identically-sized sheet of aluminum foil. Place both boats in a tub of water. Slowly add pennies or other similar-sized weights to both boats. What do you observe as more weight is added to each boat?

CAN YOU EXPLAIN IT?

How is engineering related to this Plastic Bottle Village?

Builder Robert Bezeau addressed several engineering problems with one solution by developing the "Plastic Bottle Village" in Panama. This open wall shows how the plastic bottles are arranged within the walls. The walls of the finished homes will be plastered to insulate them further.

1. What problems do you think the plastic bottles embedded in these walls are intended to solve?

2. The Plastic Bottle Village is built on an island off the coast of Panama. Do you think this design solution could be used in other locations? Explain your answer.
What advantages are there to using old plastic bottles as building materials? Are there disadvantages? Explain your answer.

 EVIDENCE NOTEBOOK As you explore this lesson, gather evidence to help you explain how engineering is related to this Plastic Bottle Village.

Developing Engineering Solutions

You use many engineered objects and processes every day. Each of them was designed and built to help with a need. Cell phone cases and roller coasters are very different devices. However, they are both developed using engineering design processes. Designing useful tools, devices, objects, processes, and systems requires careful planning, testing, and manufacturing. The engineering design process has many steps. Although there is not a fixed order of steps, the processes engineers use to design a cell phone case and a roller coaster are very similar.

This chimp uses a stick to collect stinging ants from an ant colony so she can eat large numbers of them quickly.

 3. Language SmArts | Discuss Together with a partner, look at the photo of the chimpanzee eating ants from a stick. Chimps, unlike humans, are limited to using nearby natural materials to make tools to gather the stinging ants. In your own words, state the design problem faced by the chimp.

Every Solution Begins with a Design Problem

Engineers solve problems. In order to design a solution, engineers must start with a clearly stated problem. In engineering, the word *problem* does not mean that something is wrong. Instead, an engineering design problem is a statement that defines what solution is needed. The design problem must be stated in a way that describes what the solution needs to do and how it needs to do it. The problem does not have to be complicated for an engineered solution to work. The chimpanzees in the photo are not engineers, but they do have something in common with engineers. They are faced with a problem they need to solve.

© Houghton Mifflin Harcourt Publishing Company • Image Credits: ©National Geographic Stock

The Engineering Design Process

Engineering design has much in common with scientific practices. However, its purpose is different from that of scientific inquiry. The engineering design process involves defining and solving problems or meeting needs. Engineers must first define the design problem. They must identify features and qualities that a successful solution must have. Then they continue on in the engineering design process, which is shown in the diagram. Engineers do not always follow the design process steps in order. For example, it is common for engineers to go back and redefine the problem for which they've brainstormed several possible solutions. It is also common for design changes to be made after testing proposed solutions.

An Outline of the Engineering Design Process

Testing and data analysis are parts of the engineering design process. Developing the best solution to a problem is based on analyzing data that indicate how well each design solution works.

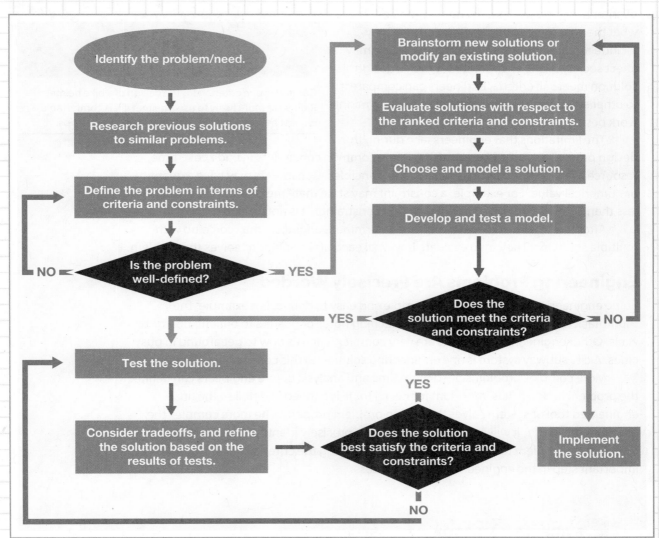

© Houghton Mifflin Harcourt Publishing Company

Identify Needs or Desires

An engineered solution begins with a need or desire for a solution. That desire or need may come from individuals, groups, or society.

Solutions to a need, for a safe and more comfortable way for people with Type I diabetes to take insulin or a desire or preference for a cell phone with a better camera, are the foundations of the engineering design process. Precisely identifying and defining the problem that needs solving is a first step to building its solution.

Define Engineering Problems

The **criteria** of a design problem are the features or qualities the solution should have. Examples of criteria include who needs the solution and what the solution should do. Other criteria may include requirements about ways the solution may affect society or the environment. When a design solution meets all criteria, engineers can compare it to other solutions and evaluate which solution might work best.

Comfort is one criterion for the design of a bike helmet. Riders are more likely to use a helmet if it is comfortable. The earliest helmets were made of padded leather strips.

The limitations that engineers face during the design process are called **constraints.** Some common constraints include cost, time, resource availability, and scientific laws and principles. Constraints may have a quantity, or numerical value. For example, a constraint may state that "the product must weigh less than 95 g." If a design does not meet the constraints, it is not acceptable.

After the criteria and constraints are determined, engineers may come up with multiple solutions. They then evaluate how well each of the solutions solves the problem.

Engineering Problems Are Precisely Worded

Some engineering problems are very simple and easy to define. For example, the thumbtack was created as a solution for attaching notes or posters to bulletin boards or walls. Other engineering problems are very complex, such as how to get around in busy cities. A city subway system is one engineering solution to this complex problem.

More complex problems need more time and analysis before engineers can define the problem in detail. It is important for needs to be identified in detail so the final engineered tool or system solves the design problem properly. The more complex the problem, the longer it will likely take engineers to precisely identify needs and criteria. Defining the problem to be solved by clearly identifying the criteria and constraints is an important step in the engineering design process.

EVIDENCE NOTEBOOK

4. What needs are addressed by using old plastic bottles as building materials? Are they the needs of individuals, a group of people, or an entire society? Record your evidence.

Case Study: Bicycle Helmets

The idea of using a head covering to protect a bicyclist during a fall began more than a hundred years ago, due to concerns about head injuries to riders. As more people began to ride bikes, more head injuries from falls occurred. It was a long time before helmets began to look like the ones you wear today. One of the earliest designs was made of simple strips of leather stitched together. While this design was light and comfortable to wear, it offered little protection to the rider. Bike riders also used motorcycle helmets, mountain climbing helmets, and construction hardhats. However, none of these helmets were designed specifically for the type of fall a bicyclist might have.

More and more injuries occurred for two main reasons: more people were cycling, and riders were either not wearing helmets or were wearing helmets not designed for biking. Society needed a safety tool to help bicyclists protect their heads in falls from their bikes. A helmet designed specifically for biking conditions needed to be designed to provide protection.

Components of a Bicycle Helmet

The components of bicycle helmets are designed to meet the following criteria: reducing the impact forces to a rider's skull from a fall or collision, keeping the helmet secure on the wearer's head, and being lightweight and comfortable. Many components have changed over time due to changes in legal requirements and new scientific research.

 The shiny, flat covering on the outside of the helmet reduces the frictional forces on the helmet that would occur if the expanded polystyrene shell were bare. The smooth covering reduces the possibility of the soft polystyrene interior snagging on a rough surface and causing a severe neck injury.

 The expanded polystyrene shell provides protection by absorbing the energy of an impact. The foamy material absorbs the kinetic energy of the impact, collapses, and may crack. It also cushions the head from the sudden acceleration change that would happen if the skull were in direct contact with a hard surface such as asphalt or cement.

 Fitting pads work along with the straps to keep the helmet stable on the rider's head.

 A helmet that moves or falls off during a collision does not protect. Adjustable straps are needed for a good fit.

Do the Math
Calculate the Amount of Material Needed

When determining the manufacturing cost of a design, one of the most important factors is the price and amount of materials that are needed to build it.

Explore Online

The airbag helmet was developed by design students Anna Haupt and Terese Alstin. It is made of nylon fabric that inflates when sensors in the collar detect a fall. Anna is showing how the collar is worn.

5. It takes a 1.5 m length of 137 cm-wide fabric to make the collar of an airbag helmet. The manufacturer is making 250 special-order collars. One morning, a technician finds they have only 65% of the length of fabric they need to make the collars. How many more meters of fabric are needed to be able to make all 250 collars? Show your work.

Brainstorm, Develop, and Test Solutions

When it came to developing a bike helmet, many designs were looked at and tested. Some ideas worked. Some did not. The process of identifying which designs work and which do not is similar for all engineering design challenges.

After a design problem is defined, a team comes up with as many solutions as possible. Some ideas may seem silly. However, starting off with many solution ideas is better than starting with only one idea. Each idea is compared to see how well it meets the criteria and constraints of the problem. The ideas that meet the criteria and constraints the best are kept. The other ideas are set aside. The most promising ideas are then rated. The rating is based on how well parts of each design meet the criteria and constraints. This rating step is helpful because some parts of a solution might be very successful. Other parts of the same solution might not solve the problem as well. If no single design idea addresses the problem well, the best features of each design may be combined into one best idea.

Consider Tradeoffs

To work within the constraints of a design problem, engineers often make tradeoffs. A *tradeoff* is the act of giving up one design feature in order to keep another, more desirable one. A tradeoff may also be agreeing that a given criterion is not as highly rated as another criterion. For example, keeping costs low is important in any design project. However, using stronger, more expensive materials means the product is less likely to break and will last longer. For modern bike helmets, a light bike helmet design was preferred over a thicker, full-face-covering design. Even though a thicker helmet that covers the face offers more protection, cyclists would be less likely to wear such a helmet because it would be heavier. Therefore, maximum protection was traded for a lighter design that more people would be more likely to wear. For this bike helmet design, the criterion that the helmet is comfortable is more important than the criterion that the helmet offers the maximum protection to the rider.

This spork design includes a cutting edge along one of the fork prongs and a spoon on the other end.

This spork design has a combination of a spoon and fork in one and a traditional full handle.

6. Sometimes, the best parts of different solutions can be combined to create a solution that is better than any solutions that came before it. Is making design tradeoffs the same as, or different from, the practice of combining the best parts of different solutions? Explain your answer.

Optimize Solutions

After proposed solutions are selected and tested, the solution that performs the best in tests is chosen. Additional tests are done with this possible solution. A test model of the best solution is built, and tests are carried out on this model. Design improvements are made to the model as a result of repeated, controlled tests. For example, after repeated tests, the many-layered design of bicycle helmets was identified as the best way to protect bicyclists from head injury. Tests continued on helmet solutions to maximize bicyclists' safety. Tests were done to identify the density of foam that absorbs energy the best during a fall. Based on the test results, changes were made again to the helmet design. Its overall performance was improved due to this additional testing.

Design testing that is repeated many times is called **iterative testing.** The iterative design process involves testing, analyzing, and refining a product, system, or process based on test results. During the iterative design process, changes are made to the most recent version of the design based on test results. The purpose of the iterative design process is to improve the quality and usefulness of a design. The results of iterative tests help engineers develop the best solution possible.

EVIDENCE NOTEBOOK

7. Would it be better to start the design process for plastic bottle homes by working with one building design idea or with four different building design ideas? Record your evidence.

Hands-On Lab
Design a Bicycle Helmet Model

Design and test a bicycle helmet model based on specific criteria and constraints.

Criteria are the features a design solution should have. *Constraints* are the limits designers have to work within and can be thought of as the "must haves" of a design solution.

MATERIALS
- aluminum foil
- bubble wrap with small bubbles
- duct tape or reinforced strapping tape
- egg (raw)
- flexible foam sheeting
- newspaper
- paperboard strips
- scissors
- string or yarn

Procedure and Analysis

STEP 1 The table on the next page is a decision matrix. A *decision matrix* helps engineers determine which design solutions best fit the criteria and constraints of the problem. Review and discuss the criteria listed in the decision matrix. Add at least two more criteria that you would like your bicycle helmet model to have. Add at least one more constraint.

STEP 2 In the 2nd column, rate each criterion from 1–3, depending on how important you think it is. Use 1 to represent "not very important," 2 to represent "somewhat important," and 3 to represent "very important."

STEP 3 Brainstorm design solutions. Choose two of your solutions to evaluate using the decision matrix. Describe these solutions.

Design A:

Design B:

STEP 4 In the table, evaluate Design A. For each criterion, the design can be scored up to, but not more than, the rating given to the criterion in Step 2. Constraints should be rated as either "yes" (it will meet the criterion) or "no" (it will not and should be rejected). Total the number of points. Next, evaluate Design B.

STEP 5 Total the points for each design. A decision matrix is a good way to compare different designs and determine which best fit the criteria and constraints of the problem, but it does not make the decision for you. If you favor a design that did not get the maximum number of points, there may be a criterion you are using that is not listed. If so, redefine the problem by adding this criterion to your matrix.

STEP 6 Decide which is the best solution, and explain your reasoning.

© Houghton Mifflin Harcourt Publishing Company

Criteria	Rating (1–3)	Design A	Design B
The helmet protects the egg from cracking when dropped from a height of 1.5 m.			
The helmet is as small as possible, no more than twice the width of the egg.			
The egg can easily be placed in the helmet and removed.			
Total Points for Each Design			

Constraints	Design A	Design B
Use only the materials provided	Yes / No	Yes / No
	Yes / No	Yes / No
	Yes / No	Yes / No

STEP 7 Test the model by dropping your helmet (open side up) with a raw egg inside. Describe the effects on the egg.

STEP 8 A large chicken egg weighs about 56.7 g. A human head weighs about 4.5 kg. In what ways is an egg a good model for a human head in this test? How is an egg not a good model? Explain your answers.

© Houghton Mifflin Harcourt Publishing Company

Define a Real-Life Design Problem

A working fire alarm can double the chances of surviving a house fire. Fire alarms generally attach to a ceiling. As a result, they can be hard to reach. Their loud, shrill sound can be very annoying, especially when the cause is burnt toast. However, these annoying aspects are actually important to the design. Because smoke rises, an alarm should be located high on a wall or ceiling to quickly and reliably detect smoke. The piercing sound may be needed to wake up sleeping people during a fire. The location and types of sound that are most effective have been determined by many years of research, testing, and analysis.

Fire alarms are designed specifically to sound shrill and annoying. Lives may depend on a fire alarm's alerting people in the event of a fire.

8. It is important to define the criteria and constraints of a design problem to come up with a successful solution. Choose whether the following points are criteria or constraints. Place a check mark in the correct column.

Requirements	Criterion	Constraint
According to a government regulation, the alarm must produce a signal of at least 65 decibels at a distance of 10 feet.		
The battery compartment should be easy to open.		
The alarm should have a signal for alerting users that the battery is low.		
The alarm should weigh less than 225 g (about 9 oz).		
For safety, lithium ion batteries cannot be used. Only larger 9V batteries may be used.		
The design should have as few moving parts as possible.		

9. **Write** Add one other criterion or constraint that would be appropriate for a fire alarm design. Compare your criterion or constraint with a partner's.

_____

_____

_____

_____

_____

Comparing Engineering and Science Practices

Science and engineering are related to one another. However, they have different purposes. Science asks questions about phenomena and how the universe works, then attempts to develop explanations based on evidence. Engineering is the systematic practice of solving problems with designed solutions. New technologies are developed when engineers use scientific knowledge to develop solutions to problems.

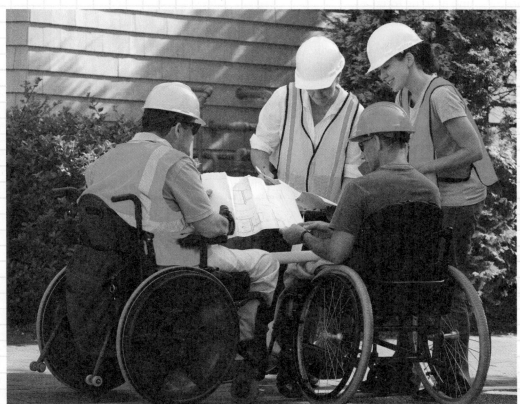

Buildings, roads, bridges, and parks are designed to meet people's needs and solve community problems. Teams of engineers and others combine their practical experience with knowledge of mathematics and science. This team is discussing engineering drawings at a construction site.

Investigations in Science and Engineering

Science and engineering practices involve investigations. In science, the purpose of investigations is to explore phenomena and learn about how and why things work the way they do. In engineering, the purpose of investigations is to define and solve problems. Both science and engineering use investigative processes that depend on the results of tests and data analysis.

10. Read each of the following questions and decide whether it most likely would be asked by a scientist or by an engineer. Write your answer beside the question.

A. What tectonic processes lead to the formation of sandstone? _____

B. What is the most effective glass thickness for a small greenhouse? _____

C. What fuel-to-air ratio in a car engine produces the most power? _____

D. What type of drill is the best to use for a sand mining operation? _____

E. What is the minimum diameter of wire needed for a 150,000-volt transmission line? _____

Ask Questions and Define Problems

Scientists ask questions and seek answers in a systematic way. Engineers define a problem and look for a solution in a systematic way. For example, consider an investigation of *tensile strength*, the amount of force that a material can tolerate before it breaks. As a measured mass is added below the strip of material, the force exerted on the material increases. The material will stretch and eventually break. The amount of stretching and the force needed to cause a break depend on the property of the material known as tensile strength.

A tensile strength test could be used to investigate a science question, such as how the chemical properties of a material relate to its ability to withstand being pulled out of shape. The same test could be used to solve an engineering question, such as what material could be used to manufacture a part that must stretch less than 1% of its length when a certain-sized load is applied to it.

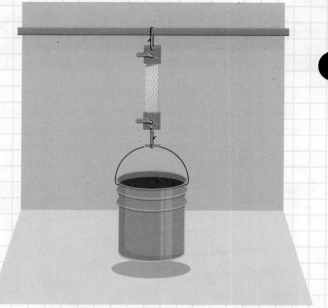

Tensile tests are commonly used to test how a material will react to pulling forces (forces being applied in tension). Here, a strip of bubble packaging is being tested to see how well the material withstands pulling and tearing.

EVIDENCE NOTEBOOK

11. What types of questions might be useful to ask about materials when designing a home for the plastic bottle village? Record your evidence.

Develop and Use Models

In a scientific investigation, a model might be used to make a prediction. For example, a mathematical model might predict how a new material will stretch, based on its chemical composition and its physical structure. A computer model of the atmosphere could forecast weather and climate changes. A physical model can show how atoms form molecules. Models are designed to account for many variables that affect the real-life object or phenomenon, but models cannot account for all variables. These differences are considered when analyzing data generated by the model.

Engineers also use models, but in a different way. Engineering models are generally built to test a solution to a problem or to determine whether a proposed solution will work. Models known as *prototypes* are often used to test a design. Prototypes can be physical models. They are used to communicate ideas about design solutions to other people. Prototypes are also tested to improve the design of the solution. They can also be a smaller model of the object or a component of a larger object. For example, a prototype of a bridge part might be built and tested to find out whether it can withstand forces without stretching or breaking.

© Houghton Mifflin Harcourt Publishing Company

Plan and Carry Out Investigations

In a scientific investigation, planning means asking a question and determining a way to investigate the question that will result in data that could help answer the question. For example, a scientist may ask how chemical structure affects tensile strength and then test materials with different chemical structures to measure the tensile strength of each material. In an engineering investigation, planning means clearly defining a need and the criteria and constraints of the solution. For example, an engineer defines a need for an inexpensive packing material that does not stretch more than a certain amount under a specific load. During the planning process, it is determined whether the material is too expensive to be used in the solution. The engineer will only test materials that meet the cost constraints. Being able to apply prior knowledge to novel situations that can arise during investigations is an important skill for scientists and engineers to have. So is the ability to break a problem down into smaller parts and organize and analyze data.

Strength testing of models is an important part of many engineering design projects.

Analyze and Interpret Data

The results of tests are useful because they can provide answers to questions or solutions to problems. Results of tests often include measurements that provide data. These data are analyzed then evaluated to help answer the question or solve the problem. For example, data from a tensile strength study can be analyzed and evaluated by plotting the data on a graph. Graphing data like these allows an engineer to compare the amount of mass supported by the part to how much the material stretched.

 12. Do the Math In the first part of the graph, the steep curve indicates elastic deformation of the material. If the load is removed now, the material will return to its original shape. Notice how the curve levels out toward the right. This indicates plastic deformation. Applying this much mass to the material changes its structure and causes it to stretch permanently. The point at which the deformation changes from elastic (temporary) to plastic (permanent) is called the *yield point*.

Evaluate the graph. What would happen to the material if 2,000 g were applied and removed?

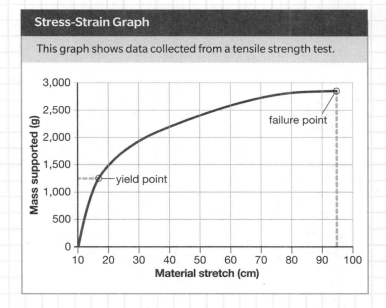

Stress-Strain Graph

This graph shows data collected from a tensile strength test.

Construct Explanations and Design Solutions

Scientists use data to develop explanations of why or how something occurs. For example, they may relate the yield point of a material to its structure in order to explain how chemical bonds affect stretching. Engineers use data to design solutions. The yield point of a material determines how it can be used in an application where a force might cause a part to stretch.

Engage in Argument from Evidence

Both scientists and engineers make arguments based on analyzed data. When the word *argument* is used this way, it does not necessarily mean that there is disagreement among people. Instead, an argument is a statement that explains something based on reason and evidence. Data are used to support the argument. Data show how the results match predictions or meet criteria and constraints.

Communicate Information

After results of an investigation or test are evaluated, they must be communicated clearly if they are to be useful to other scientists and engineers. Data communication means clearly stating the results of the investigation, arguing that the results provide an explanation or solution, and supporting the conclusion with evidence. Other people should be able to use the communicated information to repeat the investigation and obtain the same results.

Language SmArts
Outline Design Steps

There are several different types of sand. Not all sands are suitable for the same applications. The types of minerals that make up the sand and the size of the sand's particles determine what the sand is best suited for. For example, silica sand, which contains large amounts of silicon dioxide (SiO_2), is used to make glass and silicon components for electronics. Sand and other types of aggregate are used in mixtures to make concrete. Large-gravel aggregate is better for use in roads and other rough surfaces, while sand is better for concrete that needs to be smooth.

13. Outline what steps you would take in designing an experiment to determine which of the three types of aggregate shown in the photos would be best suited to make concrete.

_____

_____

_____

_____

_____

_____

_____

_____

gravel

desert sand

River sand

Continue Your Exploration

Name: _____ Date: _____

Check out the path below or go online to choose one of the other paths shown.

| Careers in Engineering | • **Earliest Examples of Technology**
• **Hands-On Labs** 🖐
• **Engineering Solutions for Organ and Tissue Transplants**
• **Propose Your Own Path** | *Go online to choose one of these other paths.* |

Notice the structures that have been built in your town, such as roads, bridges, and buildings. Civil and mechanical engineers work on those structures. *Civil engineers* design and maintain public facilities, including roads, buildings, railroads, and airports. *Mechanical engineers* design machines, such as elevators, that are used in these facilities. Civil engineers who work on improving and restoring natural systems (such as rivers, seashores, and forests) are called *environmental engineers*.

Civil Engineering

Civil engineers are involved at every step of construction projects. They oversee project design and construction and maintain the project once it is complete. They use all the tools and steps of the engineering process from determining the engineering problem, defining its criteria and constraints, brainstorming new ideas, modeling and testing the ideas, to working on the final design. Then they supervise the construction. There are many roles within civil engineering. Some of these include architectural, structural, and environmental engineering. Civil engineers also develop transportation systems and manage water resources.

Engineers from the Army Corps of Engineers inspect and secure a levee built across a roadway during a flood.

Continue Your Exploration

Army Corps of Engineers

While many people think of the army as being involved in military activities only, the Army Corps of Engineers includes units that are trained for nonmilitary responses as well. Natural disasters can occur anywhere in the world. The U.S. Army Corps of Engineers has teams of engineers who respond to disasters in the United States and elsewhere. These teams are made up of engineers and other specialists who have the training and knowledge to deal with the effects of hurricanes, floods, earthquakes, and other natural disturbances that disrupt communities. Each team includes engineers who can lead missions, such as removing debris so that traffic can begin to move, providing emergency power, and assessing bridges and other structures to determine whether they are safe. The Army Corps of Engineers also helps perform search-and-rescue operations during disasters. They help find survivors who may be trapped and unable to reach safety on their own. Army Corps of Engineers team members include electrical, civil, transportation, structural, and hydrological engineers.

1. Which of these activities would likely include the work of civil engineers? Choose all that apply.

   A. designing a new sports stadium

   B. testing concrete formulas to be used in a parking garage

   C. brainstorming improvements to plastics used in making toys

   D. rebuilding severely eroded banks of a river to reduce flooding

2. Which of these activities would most likely be carried out by a civil engineer who specializes in environmental engineering?

   A. testing steel beams for a large bridge

   B. brainstorming ways to prevent landslides on steep slopes

   C. designing a new system for unloading cargo from rail cars

   D. developing a robot to search for survivors of natural disasters

3. Explain why a response team that provides help after an earthquake would benefit from including civil engineers.

4. **Collaborate** Identify one or more natural disasters in which engineers were involved in a community's recovery. Identify the roles that engineers had in restoring the functions of the community.

© Houghton Mifflin Harcourt Publishing Company

Can You Explain It?

Name: _____ **Date:** _____

How is engineering related to this Plastic Bottle Village?

 EVIDENCE NOTEBOOK

Refer to the notes in your Evidence Notebook to help you construct an explanation for how engineering is related to this Plastic Bottle Village.

1. State your claim. Make sure your claim fully explains how engineering is related to this Plastic Bottle Village.

2. Summarize the evidence you have gathered to support your claim and explain your reasoning.

Checkpoints

Answer the following questions to check your understanding of the lesson.

Use the photograph to answer Questions 3 and 4.

3. Which of the items shown in the photo were developed using engineering design processes to develop a solution to a problem? Choose all that apply.

   A. computer

   B. coffee cup

   C. table

   D. pen

4. Match items shown in the photo with the problem statement they were most likely designed to address. Write the name of the object after each statement.

   A. Made of a type of ceramic that reduces the loss of thermal energy from a hot liquid over time. _____

   B. Writes clearly on paper without smudging or leaking ink. _____

   C. Portable loudspeakers that minimize sound leakage _____.

Use the photograph to answer Questions 5 and 6.

5. An engineer proposes that a newly developed chemical could be sprayed from aircraft to slow the rate of burning in a forest fire. What is the next step the engineer is likely to take to develop a solution to fighting forest fires?

   A. Test a number of similar chemicals.

   B. Spray and compare the effectiveness of each tested chemical to water.

   C. Add the chemical to all aircraft spray tanks.

   D. Design a spray system for the chemical.

6. Scientists and engineers study the effects of fires. Identify which of these questions would most likely be asked by a scientist, an engineer, or both. Write S for scientist, E for engineer, or B for both.

   A. Which materials are best for fighting fires? _____

   B. How does turbulence above a fire affect aircraft that drop water on a fire? _____

   C. What percent of fires have natural causes? _____

   D. How does the type of terrain affect the path of fires? _____

Interactive Review

Complete this interactive study guide to review the lesson.

The engineering design process identifies a problem and then proposes, tests, and optimizes a solution to that problem.

A. Explain why testing a solution based on the criteria and constraints of the design problem is a key part of the engineering design process.

Science and engineering are related fields, but they have different goals and purposes.

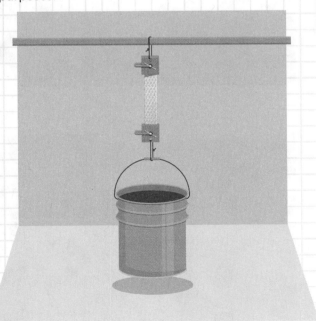

B. Models are important tools for both scientists and engineers. How do scientists and engineers differ in the way that they use models in their areas of study?

Choose one of the activities to explore how this unit connects to other topics.

People in Science

Nader Khalili Imagine living in a home that you built yourself out of affordable and easily-available resources. What would it look like? Would it stand up to the elements? Would it be comfortable? Nader Khalili was an Iranian-born architect who designed such homes, with the intent that they would be easy to construct. His design uses soil-filled sandbags and barbed wire to build stable, well insulated homes. The thick, curved walls are so stable they are earthquake resistant.

Research the use of this home design to help house war refugees and the homeless. Identify the features of the design that make it suitable for such uses.

Health Connection

Cholera Today Cholera, an often deadly intestinal infection, has long plagued societies. In 1854 in London, England, cases of cholera were linked to water pumps that were near sources of fecal waste. Water and sewage infrastructure in London were redeveloped as a result of these outbreaks. Today, the World Health Organization estimates there are roughly 1.4 to 4.0 million cases of cholera per year, resulting in 21,000 to 143,000 deaths worldwide.

Research a cholera outbreak and make a presentation about the causes of the epidemic. Describe how society and technology could prevent future outbreaks.

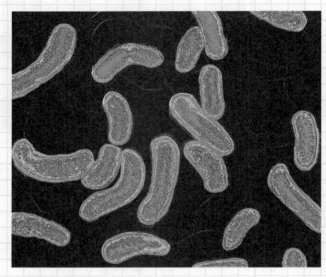

Technology Connection

Biomimicry Biomimetics, or biomimicry, is the imitation of nature to solve human problems. Studying nature can help produce better human-made technologies and structures. In a recent example, scientists studied the ability of geckos to climb smooth surfaces. This phenomenon inspired NASA to develop a material with small synthetic hairs that allow it to remain sticky after many uses.

Research another nature-inspired technology. Use the research to create a poster, visual display, or electronic image that explains the technology. Present your findings to the class.

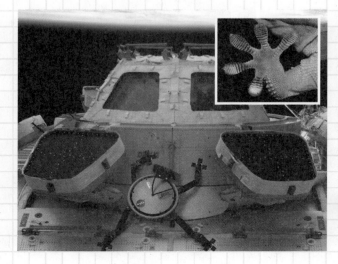

Name: _____   **Date:** _____

Complete this review to check your understanding of the unit.

Use the image of different wind turbine designs to answer Questions 1–2.

1. Wind is an important renewable energy resource. These wind turbine designs were developed by *scientists / engineers* in order to harness wind power in different environments. Each design has its own advantages and disadvantages. *Scientists / Engineers* investigated each type of wind turbine to answer questions about how the turbines affect migrating birds.

2. Using wind energy lessens air pollution and *benefits / harms* ecosystems.

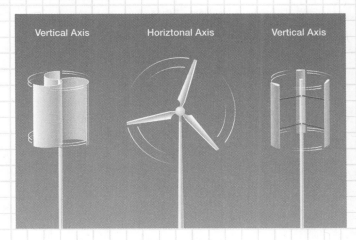

Vertical Axis   Horiztonal Axis   Vertical Axis

Use the graph to answer Questions 3–5.

3. *Diporeia* is a shrimp-like organism that is native to Lake Michigan. The quagga mussel was introduced to this aquatic ecosystem by humans in the late 1980s. As the graph shows, the *Diporeia* population *increased / decreased* as the mussel population *increased / decreased* .

4. Lake whitefish depend on *Diporeia* for food. Which of the following likely happened to the lake whitefish population over the time period shown on the graph?

   A. It decreased.

   B. It increased.

   C. It stayed the same.

5. *Scientists / Engineers* collected the data shown in the graph to answer the question "Is there a relationship between quagga mussel and *Diporeia* populations?" Together, scientists and engineers are working on understanding this relationship in order to solve problems related to the decline in the *Diporeia* population.

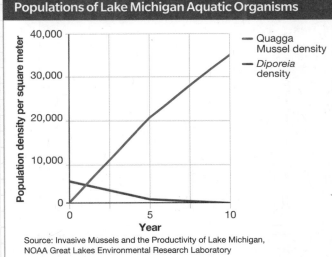

Populations of Lake Michigan Aquatic Organisms

— Quagga Mussel density
— *Diporeia* density

Source: Invasive Mussels and the Productivity of Lake Michigan, NOAA Great Lakes Environmental Research Laboratory

6. Complete the table by providing at least one example of how these engineering and science topics relate to each big concept.

Engineering and science	Energy and matter	Stability and change	Cause and effect
Natural resources	Natural resources are used to generate energy and to make materials. It takes energy to gather and produce resources and even to recycle them. Matter is conserved in a natural resource's life cycle.		
Impacts of resource use			
Technology			

Name: Date:

Use the diagram of the life cycle of a pencil to answer Questions 7–9.

The Pencil Production Process

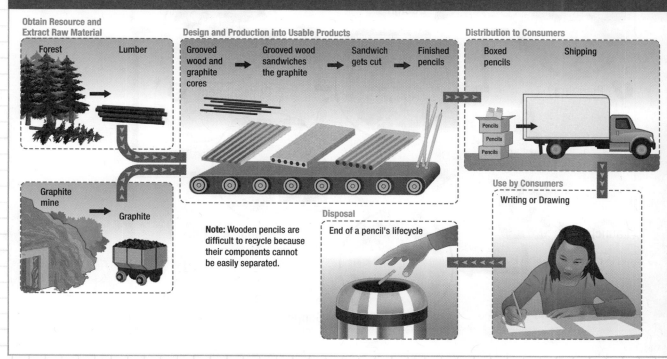

Obtain Resource and Extract Raw Material
Forest → Lumber
Graphite mine → Graphite

Design and Production into Usable Products
Grooved wood and graphite cores → Grooved wood sandwiches the graphite → Sandwich gets cut → Finished pencils

Note: Wooden pencils are difficult to recycle because their components cannot be easily separated.

Distribution to Consumers
Boxed pencils → Shipping
Pencils
Pencils
Pencils

Use by Consumers
Writing or Drawing

Disposal
End of a pencil's lifecycle

7. Identify one effect each step of the pencil's life cycle may have on society or the environment.

8. What are the inputs of the production stage? What are the outputs? How would a decrease in the outputs of the forest or graphite mine affect the production stage's inputs and outputs?

9. The pencil is a device that has been improved over time through the engineering design process. How do a pencil's design features satisfy the criteria and constraints for a writing tool? How could the design be improved?

Use the diagram of the web design process to answer Questions 10–12.

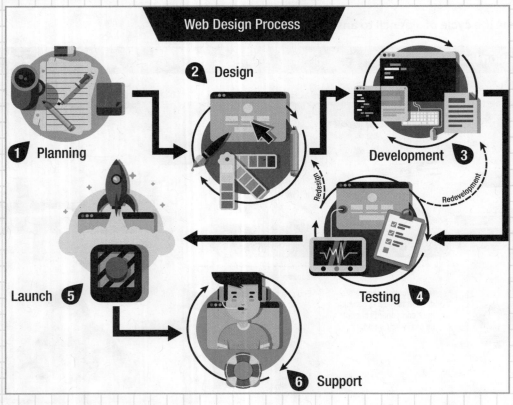

Web Design Process

1 Planning

2 Design

3 Development

4 Testing

5 Launch

6 Support

Redesign

Redevelopment

10. Recall the steps of the engineering design process. Compare and contrast the similarities and differences between the stages of the web design process and the engineering design process.

11. At what stage in the web design process are web designers most likely to return to planning with feedback for design improvement? What stage of the web design process most closely resembles the stage of the engineering design process at which the solution is implemented?

12. The engineering design process and the web design process both require the design teams to return to earlier stages and incorporate changes along the way. Why do these design processes involve multiple iterations of the design solution?

Name: _____   Date: _____

Which is the better water filtering solution for a village?

The water supply for a village in a developing nation is not safe to drink due to bacterial contamination. Your team has been asked to evaluate two purification systems to provide drinkable water. Identify and recommend which design best solves the problem.

Gravity filter

Filter straws

In this design, gravity pulls water from a large clay tank through filters with tiny pores that remove bacteria. This design can be used to provide enough clean water for a family.

These tubes contain fibers that trap bacteria as water passes through. This design allows individuals to drink freely using suction as clean water passes through the fibers.

The steps below will help guide your research and develop your recommendation.

Engineer It

1. **Define the Problem** Write a statement defining the problem you have been asked to solve. What are the criteria and constraints involved in selecting a water filtration method?

Engineer It

2. **Conduct Research** Describe the strengths and weaknesses of the solutions based on possible societal and environmental consequences of each design.

3. **Evaluate Data** Analyze each design's ability to meet the criteria and constraints of the problem. Is one solution more useful than the other? Which purification method will help the most people in the community?

4. **Identify and Recommend a Solution** Make a recommendation based on your research. Which design do you think the town should use? Explain your reasoning.

5. **Communicate** Present your decision to the community. Your argument should use evidence that supports the design that best meets the specified criteria and constraints. You should also describe the strengths and weaknesses of the design. Describe a situation where the alternate solution may be more useful.

✓ **Self-Check**

	I clearly identified the problem along with criteria/constraints for this problem.
	I researched design solution strengths and weaknesses.
	My solution is based on evidence gathered from my research.
	My recommendation is clearly communicated to others.

The Structure of Matter

How are the properties of matter related to its particles?

Unit Project 50

Lesson 1   Patterns Can Be Observed in Organisms and
Nonliving Things 52

Lesson 2   Matter Exists in Different States 70

Lesson 3   Changes of State Are Caused by Changes in
Thermal Energy. 84

Lesson 4   Organisms and Nonliving Things Are Made of Atoms 104

Unit Review 127

Unit Performance Task 131

Hot gases and molten rock from beneath Earth's surface ooze from Kilauea, a volcano in Hawaii.

You Solve It   How Can You Make a Synthetic Magnet?

Design cow magnets by selecting different combinations of metals, shapes, and sizes. Test your magnets to see which ones meet the given criteria.

Go online and complete the You Solve It to explore ways to solve a real-world problem.

Explore Disappearing Arctic Sea Ice

Large portions of ice in both Arctic regions of Earth are disappearing at alarming rates.

A. Look at the photo. On a separate sheet of paper, write down as many different questions as you can about the photo.

B. Discuss With your class or a partner, share your questions. Record any additional questions generated in your discussion. Then choose the most important questions from the list that are related to disappearing Arctic sea ice. Write them below.

C. Identify interactions in the Earth system that could be affecting the amount of Arctic sea ice.

D. Use the information above as you research Arctic sea ice and develop a model to show how sea ice is melting.

Discuss the next steps for your Unit Project with your teacher and go online to download the Unit Project Worksheet.

Language Development

Use the lessons in this unit to complete the network and expand your understanding of these key concepts.

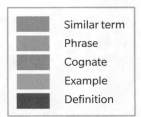

Similar term
Phrase
Cognate
Example
Definition

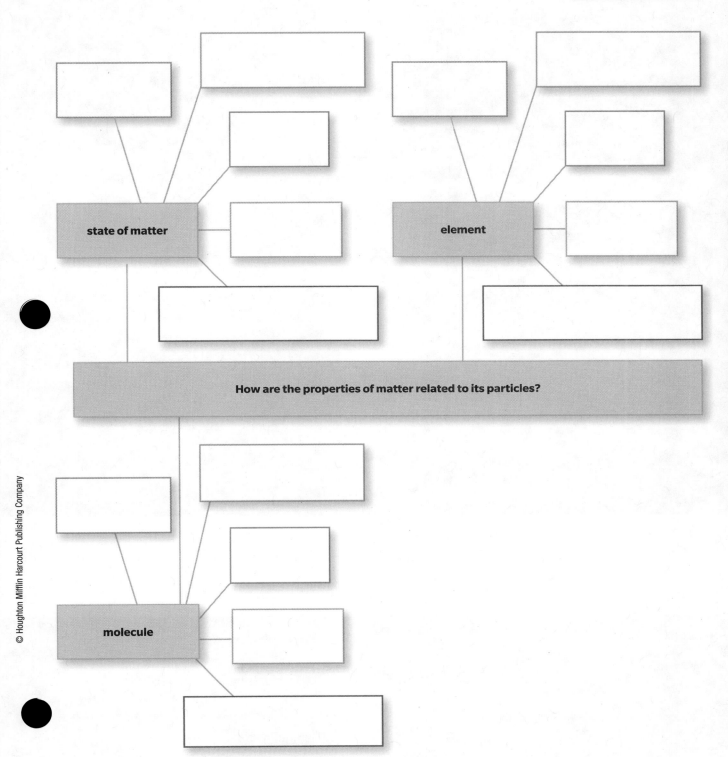

state of matter

element

How are the properties of matter related to its particles?

molecule

Patterns Can Be Observed in Organisms and Nonliving Things

Enormous gypsum crystals are found in the Cave of Crystals in Mexico. The shapes and properties of these crystals are determined by the particles that they are composed of.

Explore First

Describing Properties of Objects Place two objects in separate bags and trade bags with a partner. Reach into the bags and feel the two objects. Write down features of the two objects and try to identify them. Take both objects out of the bags. With your partner, discuss how well you were able to identify the objects. Which features were the best for identifying the two objects?

CAN YOU EXPLAIN IT?

Why do people choose wool as a material for warm clothing?

Wool is a type of fiber that comes from the coats of sheep and other animals. The first photo shows a sheep with a full coat of wool. The second photo shows clothing made from sheep's wool. Clothing such as jackets, socks, and scarves are often made from wool.

1. Humans make all sorts of objects and devices with many different purposes and made up of many different materials. How do people decide which materials to use for a specific purpose?

 EVIDENCE NOTEBOOK As you explore the lesson, consider the reasons why wool is used to make warm clothing.

Observing Patterns in Matter

Think about everything around you during your day. Your shirt, your desk at school, the water you wash your hands with, and the air blowing through your hair all have something in common. They are all matter. Matter is a word used to describe physical things. Most things you can see or feel are matter.

A basketball is made of matter.

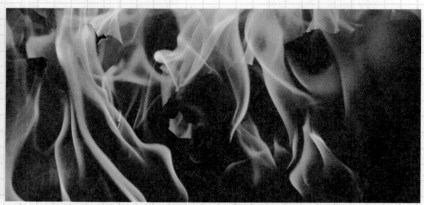

The light and heat that makes up fire are not matter.

2. A basketball is very different from a fire. What are some differences that might make a basketball matter, while light from a fire is not matter?

Matter

All matter, including basketballs and water, shares two properties. **Matter** is anything that has mass and volume. **Mass** is a measure of the amount of matter an object contains. **Volume** is a measure of how much space an object takes up. Both living and nonliving things are matter. Your body, a tiny ant, and the rocks and soil in a garden are all matter. Some things that you cannot see are also matter. Air is matter. It takes up space inside a basketball and its mass can be measured. However, the actual flame that you see in a fire is a combination of light and heat. Neither light nor heat has mass or takes up space. Because light and heat do not have mass or take up space, they are not matter.

3. Discuss Which of the following are matter? Select all that apply.

   A. light from the sun

   B. milk in a carton

   C. heat from a candle

   D. the sound of thunder

   E. a pebble on a beach

Everything that takes up space and has mass is matter. Even the air, which you cannot see, is matter.

Patterns and Categories in Matter

Many different patterns can be observed in matter. Samples of matter may have the same color, hardness, or smell. Some matter is liquid while some is solid or a gas. Looking for patterns in matter allows you to identify when two samples of matter share characteristics. If two samples show enough similar patterns, they could even be the same material. Recognizing patterns also allows you to categorize matter.

Placing things into categories can make them easier to interpret. Think about the grocery store. There is a section for fruits and vegetables, one for frozen food, and one for baked goods. Without these categories, going shopping would take you a lot longer. Some matter makes up living organisms and some makes up nonliving objects. Some objects that contain matter are made by humans and some occur naturally.

Language SmArts

Categorize Matter

4. In the first table, list at least three different patterns that you see in the matter in this photo. Identify objects that exhibit each of these patterns. In the second table, use your observations of patterns in matter to sort the objects into the categories *Living* and *Human Made*.

Pattern	Things That Exhibit the Pattern
white color	

Living	Human Made

> **EVIDENCE NOTEBOOK**
>
> **5.** Alpacas live on cold mountains and have coats similar to sheep. What patterns do you notice about these animals? Record your evidence.

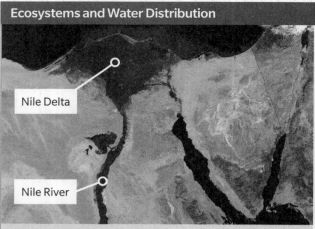

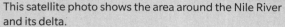

This satellite photo shows the area around the Nile River and its delta.

The lighter patches of sand are drier areas, while the darker patches are wet areas closer to the river.

6. What patterns do you notice in the plant growth shown in these two photos?

Patterns in Resource Distribution

In addition to the patterns between different samples of matter, there are patterns in the distribution of matter. These affect how living organisms interact with their environments. For example, all living things use water, so the distribution of water affects ecosystems. The distribution of water follows patterns, such as water flowing to lower areas. More living things will be in areas where more fresh water is available. Rainforests are dense with life compared to drier areas such as deserts. Droughts and human activity can affect the distribution of water, which then will affect ecosystems.

This rainforest has an abundant supply of water.

Observe Patterns in the World

Recognizing patterns can help scientists develop explanations of how the world works. They can then test these explanations to determine how specific patterns arise.

7. What are some questions that you could ask in order to determine more about why bears are drawn to rivers that salmon migrate through?

A bear catches salmon to eat in a river.

Analyzing Properties of Matter

Suppose you are playing a guessing game. You need to describe an object so someone can guess its identity. You might describe its size or weight, but the person guessing would likely need to know other properties of the object to guess what it is.

8. **Discuss** Identify three differences between the objects that you can see in the photo.

Notice how light reflects differently from the rock and the bell. Luster is a property that describes how light reflects off of and interacts with a substance.

Properties of Matter

Some patterns that you can identify matter with can be studied and formalized. An example of this was Friedrich Mohs' study of minerals in the early 1800s. After noticing patterns in how hard different samples were, Mohs developed a definition for *hardness* and the Mohs hardness scale. Mohs identified a property of matter.

Properties of matter are specific characteristics that matter exhibits. The mass of an object and the amount of space it takes up are both properties of that object. Other properties of matter can include how it looks, feels, or reacts to other matter. By observing patterns in matter, scientists can identify consistent properties. Properties of matter can be used to identify a sample of matter. They can also be used to tell the difference between two similar samples. For example, quartz and calcite are both white minerals. To correctly identify these minerals you must test other properties. Quartz is harder than calcite, and calcite will bubble when acid is placed on it.

Physical Properties

Physical properties are properties that can be observed without changing the identity of a sample of matter. You can see the color of a ball. You can measure the ball's mass. If you physically change a sample, its physical properties will change, but the identity of the sample will not. If you were to rip a piece of paper in half, it would change the mass, volume, and shape of the paper, but it would still be paper. If you were to take a piece of wood and use sand paper to make it smooth it would change the texture, but still be wood. Some other physical properties include thermal conductivity and flexibility. For instance, wool does not transfer heat well, allowing warm objects to stay warm. It is also flexible and can be bent into many shapes without breaking.

9. Some matter that undergoes changes to its physical properties can appear very different afterwards. You could crumple a can or melt ice. When wood burns, do you think its physical properties are simply changing or is something else happening to the wood? Explain your reasoning.

When wood burns, it turns to ash and energy is released.

Chemical Properties

Chemical properties are very different from physical properties. Just looking at or feeling an object will not tell you its chemical properties. A chemical property can only be identified during a chemical reaction or after one has taken place. An easy chemical property to observe is a substance's flammability, or the ability of a substance to burn. When a substance burns, it undergoes a chemical reaction and the identity of the substance changes. Wood can become ash, smoke, and carbon dioxide.

Some of the most easily observable chemical properties are a substance's ability to react with various other substances. Have you ever left apple slices out on the counter? The inside of an apple turns brown due to a reaction with oxygen. A piece of iron rusting is also a reaction with oxygen. The inside of an apple and iron both have the chemical property that they react with oxygen. Chemical properties govern how different substances will react with other substances.

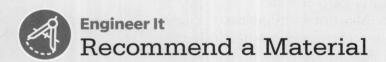

Engineer It
Recommend a Material

Electric conductivity, a physical property, is a measure of how well a material will transmit electric charges. Reactivity, a chemical property, refers to how likely a material is to undergo a chemical reaction. Knowing these two properties can allow you to choose what type of matter works best in a specific situation.

Material	Electric Conductivity	Reactivity
Gold	High	Low
Aluminum	Medium	Medium
Sodium	Low	High

10. If you were making an electric device and needed a piece that would easily transmit an electric charge and also not react with other materials, what material would you choose? Explain your choice.

© Houghton Mifflin Harcourt Publishing Company • Image Credits: ©ungyar/Fotolia

11. Label the following properties as either physical or chemical. Write a P next to physical properties and a C next to chemical properties.

  A. thermal conductivity—the rate thermal energy spreads through a substance _____

  B. flammability—the ability of a substance to burn _____

  C. magnetic attraction—whether a substance is pulled by a magnet _____

  D. melting point—the temperature at which a solid changes to a liquid _____

  E. reactivity with oxygen—the ability of a substance to chemically react with oxygen _____

Caves and Ecosystems

Limestone is a sedimentary rock that is formed primarily of calcium carbonate. Limestone is soluble in water. This solubility causes caves to form when water flows through large limestone deposits.

Some species of bat live in caves. They sleep hanging upside down from the ceiling of the caves.

Many species of cavefish are blind. Eyesight is not necessary to survive in their natural habitat, which is without light.

© Houghton Mifflin Harcourt Publishing Company • Image Credits: (t) ©Jeff Mauritzen/ National Geographic/Getty Images; (bl) ©ryzhkov_sergey/Fotolia; (br) ©wrangel/iStock/ Getty Images Plus/Getty Images

12. How would bats be affected if limestone were not easily dissolved by water?

  A. They would have fewer areas to use as shelter.

  B. Their food supply would diminish.

  C. They would be found in different areas around the world.

Properties of Natural Resources

The chemical properties of limestone shape the type of ecosystem that develops around it. Limestone caves often form as the limestone dissolves in water. These caves become habitats for organisms that would not be able to live in the area if these caves did not exist. The makeup of ecosystems are based on the properties of matter in the area. Animals that live in the Arctic tend to be white in color; they blend in with the snow that accumulates in that location. Fish have evolved gills and are able to breathe underwater.

Humans also interact with their environments based on the properties of matter that make it up. Farms tend to be in areas with nutrient–rich soil and flat land. Many cities are built on the coast or on rivers to make shipping easier. The types of rocks and soil in an area can determine whether or not basements are built in an area. When the properties of resources in an area change, human society is forced to change as well.

Do the Math
Calculate Salinity

Like pure substances, mixtures of different substances also have properties. Salinity is a property of matter that describes the salt content of a liquid mixture. Salinity is calculated by dividing the mass of salt in grams (g) by the mass of the solution in grams (g) that the salt is dissolved in. That result is multiplied by 1000 to give salinity in parts per thousand (ppt). A salinity of 40.0 ppt would mean that if you took 1000 g of a solution and evaporated all the water away, you would be left with 40 g of salt.

13. Calculate the salinity of the liquids in the table.

$$\frac{\text{mass of salt (g)}}{\text{mass of solution (g)}} \times 1000 = \text{salinity (ppt)}$$

Sample Solution	Mass of Salt (g)	Mass of solution (g)	Salinity (ppt)
A	27	1000	
B	15	850	
C	94	2355	
D	119	3796	

14. You are designing artificial plasma. The plasma must have a salinity between 30 ppt and 40 ppt. Which of the sample solutions from the table above fit this requirement?

EVIDENCE NOTEBOOK

15. Wool is often used to make cold–weather clothing. What are some properties of wool that make it a good coat for sheep and good for making clothing out of? Record your evidence.

Modeling Matter

Consider a thought experiment in which you tear a piece of paper in half. Then tear it in half again and then again. How many times could you continue this? Either you divide this piece of paper in half forever or you reach a point where it could no longer be divided in half and still be considered paper.

16. Do you think matter is continuous or made of tiny particles? Explain your answer and cite evidence from your life experiences.

17. Do you think water can be split into pieces? An electrolysis device uses electricity to separate water into oxygen and hydrogen. When separated, the oxygen always takes up about half as much space as the hydrogen. What might this tell you about the materials that make up water?

During electrolysis, water is separated into oxygen and hydrogen. The two gases are collected in separate tubes.

Evidence for the Particle Theory of Matter

Throughout history, philosophers and mathematicians have proposed many different models of matter. One hypothesis was that large pieces of matter were made up of many tiny particles.

Electrolysis of Water

The first convincing evidence for the particle theory of matter was discovered in 1803. That year, John Dalton separated some pure substances, including water, into their components. Dalton realized that when these pure substances were separated into their components, they always separated into the same ratios. This supported the idea that matter was made of building blocks that always combined in specific ways.

Brownian Motion

In the late 1820s, Robert Brown was studying the pollen of different plants by suspending pollen in water and looking at it under a microscope. During his research, he noticed that the pollen was moving. Brown decided to test if this motion only occurred with pollen. He did further experiments by placing different crushed materials in water and he saw the same random motion. This motion is now known as Brownian motion. There were several hypotheses for why these tiny, inanimate objects would move. One idea that seemed to explain the behavior well was that this motion was caused by microscopic particles colliding with the pollen.

18. How do the observations of Brownian motion help to reinforce or weaken the hypothesis that matter is made up of tiny particles?

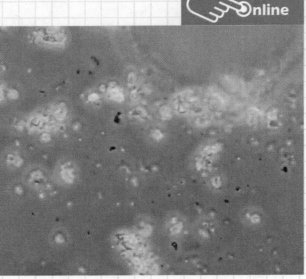

Particles of pollen suspended in water tend to move in random directions. This motion is called Brownian motion.

Evidence from New Technologies

New technologies have only provided more evidence for a particle theory of matter. In the 1980s, a very powerful microscope known as a scanning tunneling microscope was invented. Microscopes such as these have been able to generate images of individual particles of matter. Mass spectrometers are tools that can be used to determine the ratios of particles that make up a sample of matter. Mass spectrometers have also provided evidence that matter is made of particles. These new technologies provide direct evidence that further confirms ideas from hundreds of years ago.

19. If matter is made of many tiny particles, why does it seem to be continuous? Why doesn't water seem to behave like sand?

By using a scanning tunneling microscope, scientists are able to generate images of these gold particles.

Explore Online

Hands-On Lab
Model Particles in Objects

Use a variety of materials to develop several ways to model the particles that make up matter. Though all matter is made up of particles, different samples of matter still behave differently. Experiment with several ways to model different varieties of matter.

MATERIALS
- bags, plastic
- building blocks
- clay
- marbles
- paper
- pom poms, craft
- scissors
- straws
- string

Procedure

STEP 1 Pick a solid object in the room. Use the supplied materials to develop a model of the particles that make up that object.

STEP 2 Use the supplied materials to develop a model of the particles that make up a liquid, such as water.

STEP 3 Describe how you modeled the particles that make up the solid and the liquid. What similarities and differences were there in your two models? How are those related to the properties of the solid and the liquid?

STEP 4 **Draw** When table salt is separated into its components, equal parts sodium and chlorine are produced. Develop a model of salt that indicates the particles that it is made up of. Then, draw a diagram that also indicates the particles that make up table salt.

STEP 5 From your experience modeling particles, what are some conclusions you can draw?

Use Models to Understand How Particles Affect Properties

Does a house made out of wood have different properties than a house made out of mud? The properties of an object are affected by the particles it is made of. An object's color, mass, and density are just a few of the properties that are defined by its particles. Density is a measure of the mass of an object compared to how much space it takes up. The equation to calculate density is mass divided by volume.

Mercury is a metal that is in the liquid state at room temperature.

20. Which of the following would cause mercury to be denser than water? Choose all that apply.

   A. the particles that make it up have more mass

   B. the particles that make it up are closer together

   C. the particles that make it up move around faster

   D. the particles that make it up are a darker color

21. How do you think a substance's properties are affected by the properties of the particles the substance is composed of?

   _____

   _____

   _____

   _____

   _____

   _____

   _____

© Houghton Mifflin Harcourt Publishing Company • Image Credits: ©MarcelClemens/Shutterstock

Continue Your Exploration

Name: _____   **Date:** _____

Check out the path below or go online to choose one of the other paths shown.

People in Science & Engineering

- **Exploring Properties of Matter**
- **Hands-On Labs** 🖐
- **Propose Your Own Path**

Go online to choose one of these other paths.

Gianluca Cusatis, Civil Engineer

Gianluca Cusatis is a Civil and Environmental Engineering professor at Northwestern University. He is originally from Italy, where he earned his PhD. in Structural Engineering. Cusatis teaches structural and civil engineering courses, and researches how different materials behave. A large focus of Cusatis' work is modeling materials using computers. Recently, Cusatis has researched materials that could be used for construction on Mars.

Gianluca Cusatis has designed concrete that could be manufactured on Mars.

The idea of living on another planet has intrigued people for years, but many problems need to be solved before anyone can do it. One big problem with settling other planets is that astronauts will not have access to building materials normally used on Earth. People build many things out of concrete. Houses, sidewalks, and roads all use it. However, to make concrete, you need water, which is hard to get on planets like Mars. Cusatis and his PhD students conducted experiments and used computer modeling to explore ways to make concrete with materials found on Mars.

Cusatis' team realized that to make concrete on Mars, astronauts would need to use something other than water. They looked at the materials known to exist on Mars and realized that sulfur could be used instead. Sulfur is very abundant on Mars, and melting sulfur into a liquid allowed Cusatis' team to make concrete. Once this was determined, it was just a matter of determining the right recipe to make a useful concrete. Cusatis' team used computer models and physical tests to find a useful concrete recipe. What Cusatis' team ended up making was a recyclable construction material strong enough to withstand the impact of a meteorite. Their work takes us one step closer to making dreams of living on Mars a reality.

Continue Your Exploration

Scientists have been able to determine the types of matter present on Mars using instruments built into the Mars rovers and observations from telescopes.

1. Concrete is made up of three main components, water, aggregate (rocks), and cement, which is a powder. When the powder and water mix, they make a paste that hardens around the rock to form concrete. Why is concrete so useful in construction? Choose all that apply.

   A. It is easy to make and use.

   B. It lasts a long time.

   C. It is light and easy to move.

   D. It is fire resistant.

2. The waterless concrete Dr. Cusatis and his students developed is made using molten sulfur instead of water. Why would this concrete be useful on Mars?

3. Why might computer simulations be used to test the properties of different types of concrete? What would be the advantages of modeling these situations over making each type of concrete and then testing them?

4. **Collaborate** Research resources that are available on the moon. What obstacles would have to be overcome to live on the moon? What are some other technologies or materials that might need to be replaced if people wanted to settle Earth's moon?

Can You Explain It?

Name: _____ **Date:** _____

Why do people choose wool as a material for warm clothing?

 EVIDENCE NOTEBOOK

Refer to the notes in your Evidence Notebook to help you construct an explanation for why we use wool to make clothing.

1. State your claim. Make sure your claim fully explains why wool is chosen as a clothing material.

2. Summarize the evidence you have gathered to support your claim and explain your reasoning.

Checkpoints

Answer the following questions to check your understanding of the lesson.

Use the photo to answer Questions 3–4.

3. Which of the following features of the sulfur crystals are evidence that sulfur is composed of matter? Choose all that apply.

   A. It is yellow.

   B. It takes up space.

   C. It is visible.

   D. It has mass.

4. Which of the following properties of a mineral, such as sulfur, would help you identify it? Choose all that apply.

   A. hardness

   B. size

   C. color

   D. luster

Use the photo to answer Question 5.

5. The rocks in this photo are red. This is a chemical / physical property of the rocks. The red color of the rocks was caused by oxidation and rust. The ability of a sample of matter to rust is a chemical / physical property.

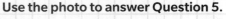

6. Which of the following would happen to the particles when you break a rock in half?

   A. Particles at the break would be destroyed.

   B. Particles at the break would detach from one another.

   C. All of the particles would be rearranged into new particles.

   D. New particles would be formed at the break.

Interactive Review

Complete this section to review the main concepts of the lesson.

Patterns of matter can be observed in both living and nonliving things.

A. How do patterns in different samples of matter help us categorize and study matter?

Properties of matter can be used to categorize and identify objects and substances. Matter has both physical and chemical properties.

B. Describe the differences between a chemical property and a physical property.

All matter is made up of very small particles. Before technology was developed to see particles, scientists found evidence that they existed.

C. Explain how the idea that matter is made up of particles is supported by a piece of evidence.

Matter Exists in Different States

Solid water provides an icy home to these penguins. They are also comfortable swimming in the liquid ocean water.

Explore First

Identifying States of Matter What makes an object a liquid, a solid, or a gas? Make a list of liquids, solids, and gases that you interact with daily. Make a list of the properties that all of the solids share. Do the same for liquids and gases.

Go **online** to view the digital version of the Hands-On Lab for this lesson and to download additional lab resources.

CAN YOU EXPLAIN IT?

How do the three forms of bromine differ from each other?

This container holds a single substance in three different forms at the same time. The light orange haze, the reddish-orange pool, and the bar are all forms of the element bromine.

1. Describe the differences in the three forms of bromine shown in the picture.

2. What could be the reason for these differences?

 EVIDENCE NOTEBOOK As you explore the lesson, gather evidence to help explain the differences you see in the three forms of bromine.

Observing Properties of Matter

Most of the matter around you is in one of three *states*, also known as *phases* of matter—solid, liquid, or gas. Each state can be described by the physical properties of volume and shape. You can observe shape by looking carefully at a material. There are many ways to measure volume, the amount of space matter takes up. For example, you might use a graduated cylinder to measure the volume of a liquid. To classify matter as a solid, liquid, or gas, you need to observe how the volume and shape of the sample can change.

3. Think of the solids and liquids that you encounter every day. In what ways are solids and liquids similar? In what ways are they different?

Explore Online

Liquid aluminum is poured into molds to make solid bars.

4. Why can the liquid metal be poured into a block-shaped mold? Describe what happens to the shape and volume of the liquid metal.

Observe States of Matter

Observe the shapes of a solid and liquid in different containers. Investigate how the volume of a solid, liquid, and gas may change and explain how the properties of each state of matter differ.

Procedure and Analysis

STEP 1 Draw 10 mL of air into the syringe. Record the initial volume in the table below.

STEP 2 Tighten the cap onto the end of the syringe, if one is available. Alternatively, you can press your finger against the end of the syringe to act as a cap. Push in the plunger. Record the final volume and any other observations. SAFETY NOTE: Always point the tip safely away from others when pushing in the plunger.

STEP 3 Observe the shape of the marbles in the cup. Remove the plunger and place the marbles in the syringe. Then replace the plunger so the bottom of the plunger touches the top of the marbles. Record the volume and observations.

STEP 4 Tighten the cap. Push in the plunger. Record the volume and observations.

STEP 5 Observe the shape of the water in the cup. Remove the marbles from the syringe and replace the plunger. Then draw 10 mL of water into the syringe. Record the volume and observations.

STEP 6 Tighten the cap. Push in the plunger. Record the volume and observations.

		Observations		
		Gas (air)	Solid (marbles)	Liquid (water)
	Initial shape	not visible		
	Shape in syringe	not visible		
	Initial volume			
	Final volume			
	Additional observations			

Do the Math How much did the volume of the samples change when you pushed in the plunger? Based on your results for the volume of air, what might you conclude about the shape of air in the syringe? Explain.

STEP 8 Which patterns did you observe that would help you classify any sample of matter as a solid, liquid, or gas? Compare the observations that you made for the solid, liquid, and gas samples of matter. Write *can* or *cannot* to make each statement true.

Gases _____ change shape and _____ change volume.

Liquids _____ change shape and _____ change volume.

Solids _____ change shape and _____ change volume.

Solids, liquids, and gases can be classified by whether or not their shape and volume can change. A **solid** is the state of matter in which the volume and shape of a substance are fixed. A **liquid** is the state of matter that has a fixed volume, but can change shape. A **gas** is the state of matter that can change both shape and volume. Liquids and gases take the shape of their container, while solids have a definite shape. Liquids and solids have constant volumes, while a gas can take up different amounts of space.

EVIDENCE NOTEBOOK

5. How do your observations of solids, liquids, and gases help you describe the differences in the three forms of bromine? Record your evidence.

Engineer It

Identify Patterns in Shape and Volume

6. Properties of matter affect how people handle different states of matter. Look at the tank of the truck in the photo. This tank is designed to carry propane gas. Why is this tank design useful for transporting a gas? Considering the volume and shape properties of each state of matter, how might the container on a truck carrying a liquid or solid be designed differently?

_____

_____

_____

_____

_____

Explaining States of Matter

Particles of Matter

All matter is made of tiny, moving particles. For any given substance, its solid, liquid, and gas forms are made up of the same kinds of particles. For example, water in any state is made up of the same type of particles. When water exists as a gas, the particles spread out. When water exists as a solid, the particles are arranged into a more structured pattern and cannot easily be rearranged.

In each state of matter, the particles that make up a substance move differently. Particles are generally attracted toward one another. When particles are not moving very much, the attractive forces between particles hold them close to one another. When particles are moving a lot, these attractive forces cannot hold the particles together and they spread out. A substance's state of matter depends on the motions of its particles.

The hardened, black lava and the flowing, red lava are both made of the same kinds of particles.

7. What states of rock can you see in the photo?

8. Discuss Think about the properties you have observed for solids, liquids, and gases. How might the arrangement and motion of the particles in each state result in these properties? Together with a partner or small group, describe or draw how you would model the particles of one substance as a solid, a liquid, and a gas.

Model Particles in Solids, Liquids, and Gases

Kinetic energy is the energy of motion. The kinetic energy of an object depends on its mass and speed. A moving car's kinetic energy increases as its speed increases.

The particles that make up matter also have kinetic energy. In all states of matter, even solids, the particles are in constant motion. However, the particles move in different ways in each state. As the motion of the particles increases, their kinetic energy also increases. Look at each model below to see how the particle spacing and motion differ in each state of matter.

9. Write gas, liquid, or solid to label the state that each model shows.

Particles are closely spaced and in contact with each other in a structured pattern. Particles vibrate in place without changing their positions in the structure.

_____

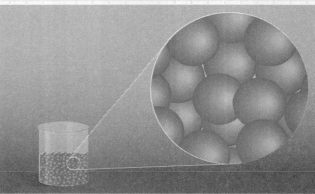

Particles are closely spaced and in contact with each other. Particles move past and around each other, so they change relative positions as they move.

_____

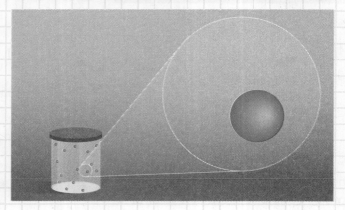

Particles are spaced far apart and only occasionally collide with each other. Particles change position relative to each other constantly because they are moving quickly.

_____

EVIDENCE NOTEBOOK

10. How do kinetic energy, particle motion, and particle attraction help explain the differences in the forms of bromine? Record your evidence.

11. Language SmArts Use what you have observed and learned about each state of matter to describe the characteristics of a solid, liquid, and gas. Write *yes* or *no* to complete the table.

	Characteristics	Solid	Liquid	Gas
Shape	fixed shape			no
	shape changes to fit container			
Volume	fixed volume	yes		
	volume changes to fit container			
Particle motion	vibrate in place		no	
	slide past each other, change position			
	move freely, change position			
Kinetic energy	has a low kinetic energy			
	has a medium kinetic energy	no	yes	no
	has a high kinetic energy			

12. Attractions between particles hold the particles of liquids and solids close together. Why is the attraction that particles have for each other not enough to keep gas particles close together?

13. Use what you have learned about particle attraction and kinetic energy. Write *increases* or *decreases* to label each arrow.

kinetic energy _____

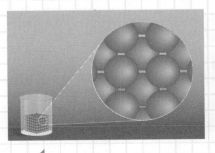 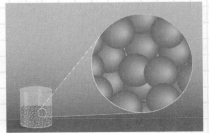 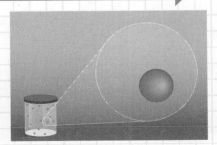

influence of particle attraction _____

Particles in Motion

The particles in matter are always moving, which means that the particles have kinetic energy. In a gas, the particles of a substance are far apart, move in all directions, and constantly change their relative locations. The attraction between particles has the least influence on gas particles because they have the most kinetic energy. In a liquid, the kinetic energy is less. The influence of particle attraction is greater in a liquid than in a gas. This means that liquid particles can change position, but stay close together. Particles in a solid are held close together and can only vibrate in one position. These particles vibrate in position because they have the least kinetic energy, and so they are most influenced by particle attraction.

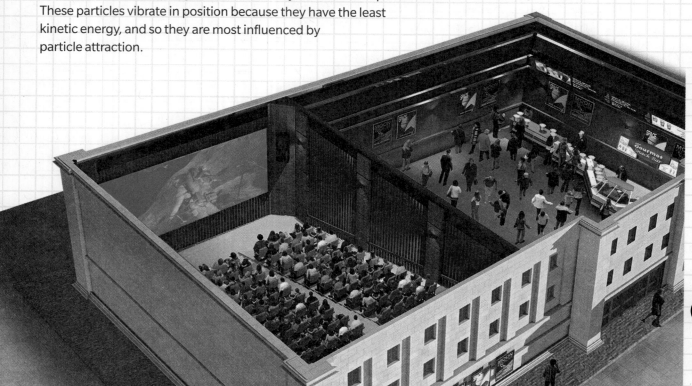

Make Analogies for Particles in Motion

14. Consider what you know about the motion and spacing of the particles in each state of matter. How can the illustrations of people watching a movie, getting concessions, and walking outside be used as models for different states of matter? Explain which group best represents the particles in a solid, liquid, and gas.

_____

_____

_____

_____

_____

_____

_____

15. Act Together as a group, act out a scenario to model how the arrangement of particles differs between solids, liquids, and gases.

Continue Your Exploration

Name: _____ Date: _____

Check out the path below or go online to choose one of the other paths shown.

Why Does Ice Float?

- **Plasma—A Fourth State of Matter**
- **Hands-On Labs** ✋
- **Propose Your Own Path**

Go online to choose one of these other paths.

Most Liquids and Solids

Particles that make up solids have attractions to each other that hold the particles very close in fixed positions. Particles in liquids have more kinetic energy, so they are able to move around more, but they are still held very close. In most substances, the particles in a liquid state are a bit farther apart than they are in a solid state. Because liquid particles are not packed as tightly together, the liquid state of a substance takes up more space than the same mass of the solid state. This difference in density means that a piece of solid will generally sink to the bottom of a liquid of the same substance.

A solid cube of oil sinks to the bottom of liquid oil. The solid is denser than the liquid.

Ice floats in liquid water. Unlike most materials, the solid is less dense than the liquid.

1. Why are most substances denser in the solid state than in the liquid state?

   A. Particles in a solid are smaller.

   B. Particles in a solid have more mass.

   C. Particles in a solid have no kinetic energy.

   D. Particles in a solid tend to be arranged into a smaller space.

Continue Your Exploration

Liquid and Solid Water

Water does not follow the predicted pattern of density that is found in most other substances. Remember, the ice cube floats in water, while the oil cube sinks in oil. If the solid ice were more dense than liquid water, it would sink. But it does not sink, which means that ice is less dense than liquid water.

As with other substances, the water particles vibrate in place in ice and slip past one another in liquid water. Ice is similar to many solids because water particles are arranged in a specific pattern that repeats throughout ice. However, this pattern differs from the pattern of particles in most solids because the spacing between water particles in ice is greater than the spacing between water particles in liquid water. As a result, fewer water particles in ice are packed into the same amount of space compared to liquid water. So, ice is less dense than liquid water.

2. These two particle models show water particles in ice and in liquid water. Write solid water or liquid water to label the models.

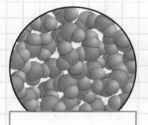 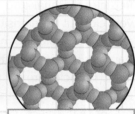

Water on Earth

The lower density of ice compared to liquid water does not only mean that ice cubes float in your water cup. This property of water is important for life on Earth because both liquid water and ice are part of Earth's hydrosphere. The hydrosphere, which contains all the water on Earth's surface, is an essential part of the Earth system. It interacts with the atmosphere and biosphere in many ways. For example, large pieces of floating ice provide penguins, polar bears, and walruses with a resting place as they look for food in the ocean.

3. Think about what happens in the hydrosphere and biosphere when ice forms at the top of a lake. What might happen instead if ice were denser than liquid water?

4. **Collaborate** With a partner, discuss your ideas about what would happen to an icy lake in the winter if ice were denser than liquid water. Come to an agreement about what would happen and draw a model of the lake with ice that is denser than liquid water. Then share your ideas and model with the class.

Can You Explain It?

Name: _____ **Date:** _____

How do the three forms of bromine differ from each other?

EVIDENCE NOTEBOOK
Refer to the notes in your Evidence Notebook to help you construct an explanation for the differences seen in the three forms of bromine.

1. State your claim. Make sure your claim fully explains why the three forms of bromine are different.

2. Summarize the evidence you have gathered to support your claim and explain your reasoning.

Checkpoints

Answer the following questions to check your understanding of the lesson.

Use the photo to answer Questions 3–4.

3. Write shape or volume to complete each sentence.

   The photo demonstrates that liquids can change _____.

   The _____ of the spilled milk is the same as the _____ of the milk that was in the glass to start.

4. Why does the milk flow out of the glass and spread out into a thin puddle rather than staying in the glass or spreading out more across the floor?

   A. The particles can break apart but cannot move.

   B. The particles can slide past each other, but attractions hold them close together.

   C. The particles cannot move, but they can grow in size.

Use the photo to answer Questions 5–7.

5. How can the volume of gas in the balloons be greater than the volume of the cylinder used to fill them?

   A. A gas has a fixed shape.

   B. A gas expands to fill its container.

   C. The volume of the container does not depend on the gas.

6. How can the properties of the particles in a gas explain why the volume of the balloons is greater than the volume of the container?

   A. The gas particles are bigger in the balloons.

   B. The distance between the gas particles is greater in the balloons.

   C. The gas particles are locked in place in the cylinder, but can move in any direction inside the balloons.

7. If the gas cylinder is empty after all of the balloons are filled, how does the total number of particles in all the balloons compare to the total number of particles that were in the cylinder?

   A. There are more particles in the balloons than were in the cylinder.

   B. There are fewer particles in the balloons than were in the cylinder.

   C. The number of particles in the balloons is the same as the number of particles that were in the cylinder.

8. A student drew a model showing particles that are close together in a regular pattern. Which sample has the student most likely drawn a model of?

   A. a bar of gold   **C.** an air sample

   B. molten aluminum   **D.** water vapor

Interactive Review

Complete this section to review the main concepts of the lesson.

Solids, liquids, and gases can be classified by their abilities to change their shapes and volumes.

A. What properties do liquids share with solids? What properties do liquids share with gases?

Differences in particle energy, particle motion, and particle arrangement explain the observed differences in the properties of solids, liquids, and gases.

B. Complete the chart to describe differences in a solid, a liquid, and a gas.

	Solid	Liquid	Gas
Particle arrangement			
Particle motion			
Particle energy			

Changes of State Are Caused by Changes in Thermal Energy

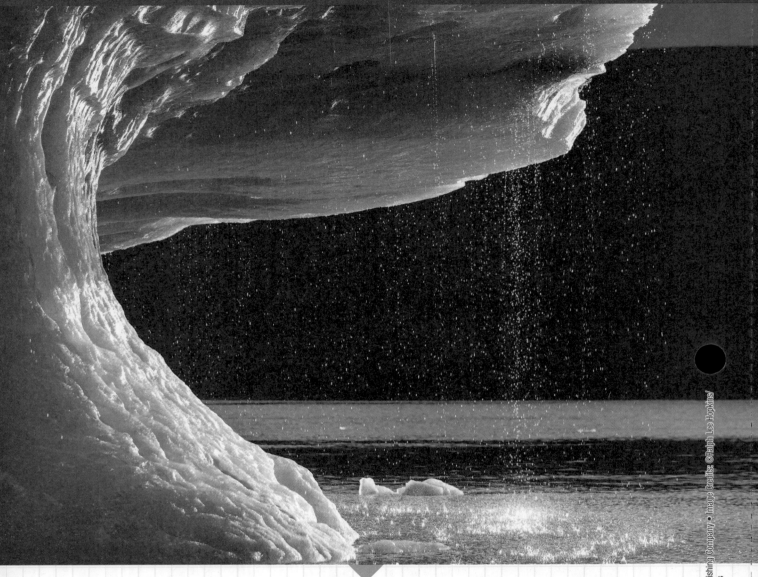

As outdoor temperatures rise, icebergs may start to melt.

Explore First

Categorizing State of Matter Changes What causes matter to change state? With a partner, make a list of at least eight instances of matter changing state. Sort the state changes by what they have in common. What are some common features of state changes?

CAN YOU EXPLAIN IT?

What could cause a piece of metal to melt in a person's hand?

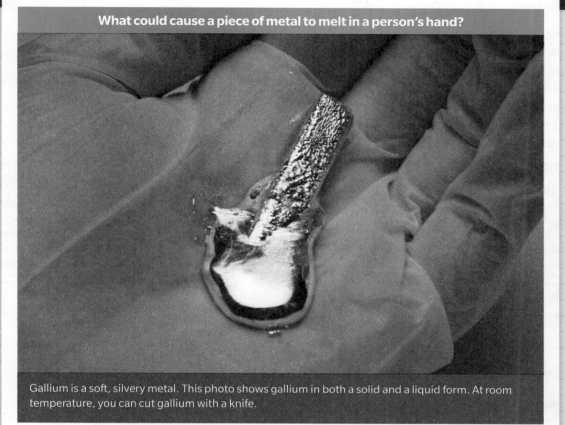

Gallium is a soft, silvery metal. This photo shows gallium in both a solid and a liquid form. At room temperature, you can cut gallium with a knife.

1. Think about some times you have seen a substance melting. What explanation can you suggest for how the gallium could melt in someone's hand?

 EVIDENCE NOTEBOOK As you explore the lesson, gather evidence to help explain how a piece of metal could melt in someone's hand.

Analyzing How Energy Influences a Change of State

Changes of State

All matter can exist in three common states, or phases—solid, liquid, and gas—and can change from one state to another. The process by which matter changes from one state to another is called a **change of state**. A change of state is a physical change, because the identity of a substance is the same regardless of the state it is in. For example, water is still water whether in an ice cube or after the ice melts into liquid water.

During a change of state, matter is neither created nor destroyed and the same number of particles make up a substance before and after a change of state.

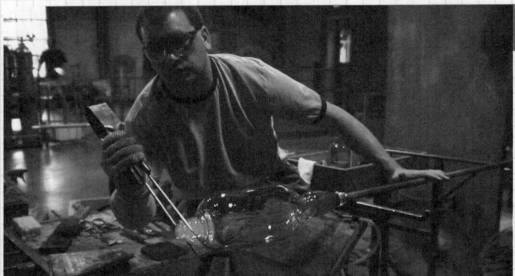

Explore Online

A professional glassworker creates a vase by changing the shape of the glass.

2. **Discuss** Together with a partner, determine the change of state that is shown in the photo. What observations led to your conclusion?

3. Think about what takes place when the change of state shown in the photo occurs. How does that change relate to the chemical identity and physical properties of glass?

Hands-On Lab
Investigate a Change of State

Predict ways in which you can make a change of state happen more quickly as an ice cube melts. Then plan and carry out an investigation to test your predictions.

MATERIALS
- cups, clear plastic
- ice cubes, small (4)
- paper towels

Procedure

STEP 1 Work with a partner or small group to list ways that you might make an ice cube melt faster than it would melt if you left it sitting in a cup on your desk. You may only use items in your classroom.

STEP 2 For your investigation, choose three of the methods your group discussed. Write each method in the table.

STEP 3 Gather the ice cubes. Place one ice cube in a cup on your desk. Use the methods you chose in Step 2 to melt the other three ice cubes.

STEP 4 Observe the ice cubes until one of them melts completely.

STEP 5 Record your observations in the table.

What did you do?	What were the results?
ice cube in a cup, on desk	

Analysis

STEP 6 Circle the best word to complete each sentence.

In this activity, energy was *added / removed* to make the ice cube melt faster.

The ice cube that received the *most / least* energy melted fastest.

STEP 7 Describe two actions that are different from what you did in this activity that might make the ice melt more quickly. Explain your reasoning.

EVIDENCE NOTEBOOK

4. How does energy relate to the question of how a piece of metal might melt in someone's hand? Record your evidence.

Identify a Change of State

5. This glass of ice water shows two changes of state happening:

- The solid ice in the glass is melting to form liquid water.
- Water vapor in the air is changing to liquid water on the surface of the glass.

Write *gaining* or *losing* to complete each sentence.

The ice is melting in the glass because it is _____ energy as it changes from solid to liquid.

Water drops form on the surface of the glass because water vapor is _____ energy as it changes from gas to liquid.

Modeling the Addition of Thermal Energy to a Substance

Energy Gain and Change of State

Each particle in a substance is moving in some way, so each particle has *kinetic energy*. **Thermal energy** is the total kinetic energy of all the particles in a substance. Adding thermal energy to a substance increases the kinetic energy. This increase in kinetic energy means the particles move faster. **Temperature** is a measure of the average kinetic energy of the particles.

6. Discuss Explain what is happening to the movement and kinetic energy of the water particles shown in the photo.

A flame adds energy to the water in this flask. As a result, the water temperature increases.

Change of State: Solid to Liquid

Adding enough thermal energy to a substance can cause a change of state to occur. The change of state from a solid to a liquid is called *melting*. When energy is added to an ice cube, the ice particles begin to vibrate more as energy is absorbed. Eventually, the solid ice melts and becomes liquid water. The temperature at which melting begins is called the *melting point*. Every substance has a specific melting point. This melting point will always be the same for that substance under the same conditions no matter the amount of the substance. The temperature at which ice melts and becomes liquid water is 0 °C at sea level.

Change of State: Liquid to Gas

If enough energy is added to a liquid, the liquid will turn into a gas. A change of state from a liquid to a gas is called *evaporation*. Water in a gas state is called water vapor. Adding thermal energy to liquid water particles causes them to move more quickly. When enough energy is added, the water changes to the gas state, forming bubbles, as the liquid water turns to water vapor. This process is called *boiling*. Boiling and evaporation both involve the same change of state: liquid to gas. The difference is the location of the change. Evaporation takes place at the surface of the liquid and can occur over a wide range of temperatures. Boiling occurs throughout the entire liquid and takes place at a specific temperature. Each substance has its own *boiling point*, the temperature at which the substance begins to boil. The boiling point of water is 100 °C at sea level.

7. Write *melting*, *evaporation*, or *boiling* to label each photo.

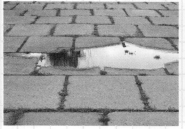

© Houghton Mifflin Harcourt Publishing Company • Image Credits: (t) ©E+/ElementalImaging/Getty Images; (bl) ©iStockPhoto.com; (bc) ©ntstudio/Shutterstock; (br) ©Houghton Mifflin Harcourt

Change of State from Solid to Liquid

The particles of a solid vibrate in place, held together by forces of attraction. Particles in a liquid remain close, but they have more kinetic energy, and they have more freedom of movement.

Change of State from Liquid to Gas

  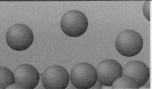 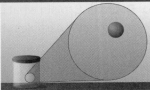

The particles in a gas have enough energy to overcome attractive forces, so they move about freely.

Explore Online

8. Describe the relationship between thermal energy and change of state. Write solid, liquid, or gas to complete each sentence.

If enough thermal energy is added to a liquid, it will change to a

_____.

If enough thermal energy is added to a _____, it will change to a liquid.

Energy Gain and Particle Motion

The particles of a solid are held together by strong forces of attraction. These forces hold the particles of a solid in a definite shape. As thermal energy is added to a solid, the kinetic energy of its particles increases. The particles vibrate faster until they can move more freely and slide around each other, and the substance becomes a liquid. This freedom of movement allows a liquid to flow and take the shape of its container.

When thermal energy is added to a liquid, its particle movement increases until the particles have enough energy to overcome the attractive forces. They completely break away from each other, and the substance becomes a gas. The movement of the gas particles not only allows the gas to take the shape of its container, but the gas particles will also move about and fill the entire space within its container.

© Houghton Mifflin Harcourt Publishing Company

Do the Math

Analyze Temperature During a Change of State

Think about warming a piece of ice. The ice gains energy and its temperature rises as the motion of the particles increases. The rise in temperature causes the ice to melt and eventually causes the resulting liquid water to boil. This is true for water just as it is true for any substance. What would the graph of temperature change over time look like?

You might think that the temperature would steadily increase as energy is added to a substance at a constant rate, but that is not the case. The graph actually shows two time periods where the temperature does not change even though energy is being added. The first time period corresponds to the temperature at which the solid is changing to a liquid, or melting. The second time period corresponds to the temperature at which the substance is changing to a gas, or boiling. The horizontal lines indicate that, during these times, energy transferred to the particles contributes to changing the state of the substance, instead of raising the substance's temperature.

9. Which statements correctly describe what is happening during the two flat-line periods in the graph? Select all that apply.

  A. Between points A and B, the solid substance is changing to a liquid.

  B. Between points A and B, the substance is losing energy.

  C. Between points C and D, the liquid substance is changing to a gas.

  D. Between points C and D, the substance is gaining energy.

10. You are warming a pot of ice. Explain what happens to the temperature when the water reaches its melting point and boiling point.

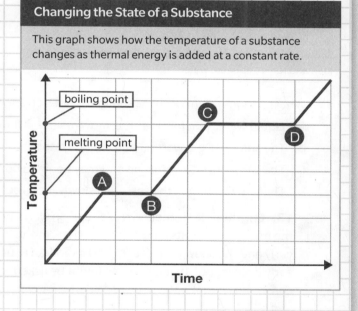

Changing the State of a Substance

This graph shows how the temperature of a substance changes as thermal energy is added at a constant rate.

 EVIDENCE NOTEBOOK

  11. How might melting point and a change in the kinetic energy of particles help to explain why a piece of metal could melt in someone's hand? Record your evidence.

Classify and Explain a Change of State

Snow is made up of frozen water in the form of ice. As the temperature increases, the snow begins to melt and run off as liquid water.

12. What changes might occur as sunlight shines on snow? Select all that apply.

   A. Liquid water that forms as the snow melts will flow downhill.

   B. The snow will get warmer and change into a large chunk of ice.

   C. The snow quickly warms up and may begin to boil.

   D. The temperature of the snow will slowly increase.

13. **Engineer It** Some towns depend on water from snow that falls high up in the mountains, melts, and flows down the mountain. Some years, spring comes early and the snow begins to melt earlier than usual. What is one problem of early water runoff that engineers might be asked to solve? What criteria and constraints might need to be considered for concerns such as materials, space, and cost?

_____

_____

_____

_____

_____

_____

_____

_____

_____

Modeling the Removal of Thermal Energy from a Substance

Energy Loss and Change of State

You now know that when enough energy is added to a substance, it can change state. But what happens when a substance loses energy? Think about what happens when you put water in a freezer. The temperature of the liquid water is warmer than the temperature inside the freezer. As a result, energy from the water is lost to the air inside the freezer and the water particles slow down. When enough energy is lost, the attractive forces between the water particles hold them in a regular pattern, and the particles can only vibrate. The liquid water changes to solid ice.

Explore Online

In the winter, ice forms on this lake. The ice starts to form on the water closest to shore.

Over the course of the winter, the lake continues to freeze. Eventually, most of the lake is covered in ice.

14. The photos show the process of a lake freezing in the winter. Why does the lake water change to ice in the winter? Include the gain or loss of energy in your explanation.

Change of State: Gas to Liquid

A gas changes state and becomes a liquid when the gas particles lose enough thermal energy. The process of a gas changing state to a liquid is called *condensation*. A common example of condensation is when liquid water droplets form on the outside of a glass of ice water. Water vapor from the air condenses and becomes liquid water on the cold surface of the glass of ice water.

Change of State: Liquid to Solid

The process in which a liquid changes to a solid is called *freezing*. Many people think that freezing means liquid water turning into ice, but freezing is the term used to describe any change from a liquid state to a solid state.

Think again about water placed in a freezer. The liquid water freezes to become solid ice. The temperature at which water freezes is its *freezing point*. The freezing point of a substance is the same as its melting point. In other words, a liquid substance that has a freezing point of 20 °C will not only freeze at 20 °C, but if the substance were a solid, it would also begin to melt at 20 °C.

15. Write freezing or condensation to label each photo.

a dripping faucet on a cold day

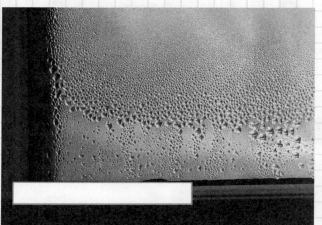

a window on a cold day

your breath in cold air

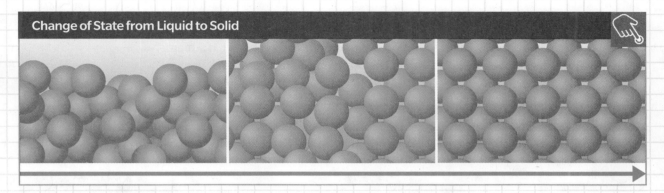

Change of State from Liquid to Solid

16. The process being modeled is condensation / freezing .

As the particles slow down / speed up, particle attraction forces hold them in a regular pattern.

This causes the particles to lock into the fixed arrangement of a liquid / solid .

The change in particle motion happens because of a(n) increase / decrease in the particles' kinetic energy.

Energy Loss and Particle Motion Decreases

As the temperature of a substance decreases, the motion of its particles also changes and these changes affect the properties of the substance. The particles in a gas have a high amount of energy and move very fast. As thermal energy decreases, particle motion slows, allowing the attractive forces between particles to pull the particles closer together. The gas will become a liquid. If temperatures continue to decrease, the attraction between particles eventually overcomes the energy of their motion. The particles are then locked into the fixed arrangement of a solid.

 17. Language SmArts | Draw In the space below or on a piece of paper, finish the drawing to show what happens to the particles in a substance when a gas becomes a liquid. Add a caption to describe what happens to the particles' motion and energy during this change of state.

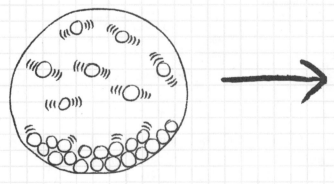

Gas particles are far apart and moving quickly above the surface of the liquid because gas particles have enough energy to overcome particle attraction.

© Houghton Mifflin Harcourt Publishing Company

Analyze Changes of State

Lava is liquid rock that comes out of a volcano. Lava sometimes comes out in streams, called lava flows, that travel slowly downhill. The temperature of lava when it first erupts can vary between 700 °C–1,200 °C. As the lava flows, it slowly cools.

Lava Flowing Into the Ocean

As lava flows downhill, it sometimes reaches a body of water, such as the ocean. These two photos show what happens as the lava spills into the water.

time

18. What changes of state do you see happening in the photos?

_____

_____

_____

_____

_____

_____

19. What evidence do you see in the photos to support your answer?

_____

_____

_____

_____

_____

20. When thermal energy is removed from a substance, the substance may condense or freeze. But when something loses energy, that energy is not "lost." The energy is transferred to something else. When the lava loses thermal energy as it cools, where is the energy going? Select all that apply.

A. The thermal energy is transferred from the lava to the air.

B. The thermal energy is transferred from the lava to the ground.

C. The thermal energy is transferred from the lava to the water.

D. The thermal energy is held within the solid rock that forms.

Evaluating How Pressure Can Affect Changes of State

Pressure

As gas particles move freely, they collide with surfaces around them. The gas particles have kinetic energy, and their collisions with surfaces produce a force. These collisions produce a force spread out over an area, known as **pressure**.

In the morning, this bike rider gets ready to go for a long bike ride. As part of getting ready, she checks the tire pressure.

The bike rider finishes her ride in the afternoon. She checks the tire pressure again.

21. The tire pressure changed between morning and afternoon. In the afternoon, the tire pressure was less / greater than the tire pressure in the morning. This change in pressure is caused by a warmer / cooler temperature of the air in the tires compared to morning. As the temperature increases, the kinetic energy of the gas particles increases / decreases .

Elevation and Air Pressure

You might not think about the pressure that air puts on your body, but it is always present. Gas particles in the atmosphere exert pressure on everything, including you.

The diagram shows that as you move toward a higher elevation, there are not as many air particles to collide with a surface. As a result, at higher elevations, the air pressure is lower. Air at lower elevations contains a greater number of air particles in a given volume, resulting in a greater number of particle collisions with the ground and other surfaces. Therefore, lower elevations have greater air pressure.

The air at lower elevations contains more particles in a given volume than air at higher elevations.

Pressure and Changes of State

Even if the kinetic energy of particles does not change, a change of state can occur when there is a change in pressure. The relationship between a change in pressure and a change of state is especially noticeable for the changes that occur between the liquid and gas states.

If you increase the pressure on a substance, its particles are brought closer to each other. When this happens to a gas, attractive forces may be strong enough to hold the particles close together, and the gas can condense into a liquid.

When the pressure on a substance is decreased, particles can move farther apart from each other. Fewer collisions occur, putting less force on the particles. With less force acting on the particles, it takes less energy for a liquid to change into a gas. With less air pressure on the surface of a liquid, particles can move from the liquid state to the gas state with less energy than that change would require at a higher pressure.

Boiling Point of Water at Different Elevations			
Location	Elevation (meters above sea level)	Pressure (in atmospheres)	Boiling point of water (°C)
San Francisco, CA	sea level	1.0	100.0
Denver, CO	1,609	0.82	95.0
Quito, Ecuador	2,850	0.71	90.0
Mount Everest	8,848	0.31	76.5

22. **Discuss** Water boils at 100 °C in San Francisco, which is at sea level. But as you can see in the table, the boiling point of water varies at other locations. Consider this scenario: You are at sea level and you have some liquid water at 80 °C. What would happen to the water if it was suddenly transported to an elevation of 8,848 meters above sea level? Work with a group to explain what would happen and why. Include the relationship of pressure, energy, and changes of state in your explanation.

Determine the Effect of Pressure on a Change of State

23. Soft-boiled eggs are cooked by placing the eggs in boiling water. In Denver, it takes about 4 minutes to make a soft-boiled egg whereas at sea level, it takes about 3 minutes and 11 seconds to make a soft-boiled egg. Why does it take more time to soft-boil an egg in Denver than at sea level?

_____

_____

_____

_____

_____

_____

_____

_____

© Houghton Mifflin Harcourt Publishing Company

Continue Your Exploration

Name: _____ **Date:** _____

Check out the path below or go online to choose one of the other paths shown.

| Careers in Science | • **Freezing Point Depression** • **Hands-On Labs**  • **Propose Your Own Path** | Go online to choose one of these other paths. |

Forensics

A scientist who analyzes evidence and presents data in a court of law is called a forensic scientist. Forensic scientists apply scientific knowledge and procedures to criminal investigations. They may analyze clues from crime scenes or accident scenes. Forensic scientists are able to help solve crimes using scientific analysis.

Evidence is collected at a crime scene. Just looking at an item may not tell an investigator much. However, an expert in a crime lab can learn more from a detailed analysis of the evidence.

1. Which of the following processes would a forensic scientist use? Select all that apply.

   A. analyzing fragments to determine what they are made of

   B. analyzing paint flecks to determine the color and chemical makeup

   C. determining the identity of a person based on a shoe print

   D. identifying a substance that was found on a fiber

   E. determining whether liquids found are the same or different

Continue Your Exploration

Analyzing the Evidence

Gas chromatography (GC) is a method used to identify certain chemicals. A tiny bit of a sample is dissolved in a liquid called the solvent and the liquid is then injected into a chamber where the sample is heated until it becomes a gas. The gas travels through a long, thin tube. The different chemicals that make up the sample travel at different rates because of their different properties. A sensor detects when a chemical passes and records the time. The scientist can identify each chemical by the amount of time it takes to pass through the gas chromatograph.

Scientists can use GC to make sure that the chemical composition of a product is correct, to identify pollutants, or to identify unknown substances in a crime scene sample.

2. Which statement best describes the process that happens in the heated sample chamber of a gas chromatograph?

   A. The sample melts and becomes a gas.

   B. The sample boils and becomes a gas.

   C. The sample condenses and becomes a gas.

When using gas chromatography to identify an unknown sample, a scientist first prepares a standard that contains known chemicals. The standard is analyzed to see how long it takes those chemicals to go through the gas chromatograph. By comparing the results for the unknown sample with a standard of known chemicals, the identity of the unknown sample can be determined.

A forensic scientist has been asked to examine a fiber from the scene of a fire. Gas chromatography was used to identify an oil, which is composed of a mixture of different chemicals, found on the fiber. The analysis of the sample is shown in the chromatogram. From the results, the scientist determined that the sample was linseed oil. Linseed oil is commonly used as paint thinner and is very flammable.

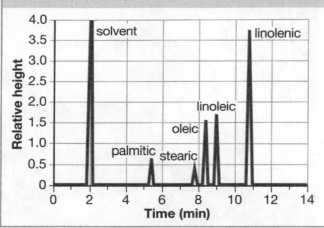

Chromatogram of the Evidence Sample

The different peaks are used to identify the solvent, substances in the sample, and their amounts.

3. How might knowing that the material on the fiber was paint thinner help an investigator solve a crime?

4. **Collaborate** Work with a partner to put together a brief presentation for the class about how forensic scientists use chemical analysis to help solve crimes. Use some kind of technology in your presentation to support your idea, such as presentation software, a video link, or digital photos.

Can You Explain It?

Name: _____   **Date:** _____

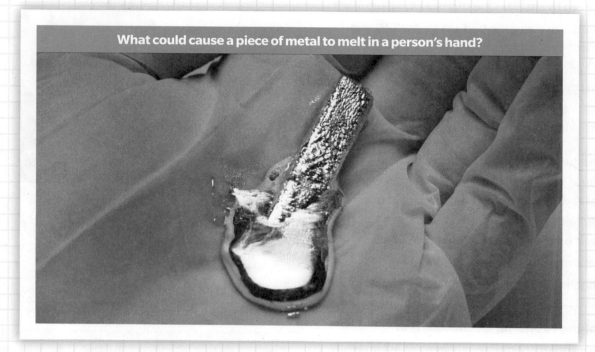

What could cause a piece of metal to melt in a person's hand?

EVIDENCE NOTEBOOK

Refer to the notes in your Evidence Notebook to help you construct an explanation for what could cause a piece of metal to melt in someone's hand.

1. State your claim. Make sure your claim fully explains how the gallium could melt in a person's hand.

2. Summarize the evidence you have gathered to support your claim and explain your reasoning.

Checkpoints

Answer the following questions to check your understanding of the lesson.

Use the photo to answer Questions 3–4.

3. Sweating is one way the body cools itself. Which statement best explains this cooling process?

    A. Water condenses on the skin, adding thermal energy to the body.

    B. Water from the body evaporates from the skin, removing thermal energy from the body.

4. Which situation models a process similar to sweating? Select all that apply.

    A. water droplets forming on the outside of a glass of ice water

    B. a wet bandana around the neck of a hiker

    C. wet clothes hanging on a clothes line

    D. a hot, moist towel placed on sore muscles to soothe them

Use the photo to answer Questions 5–6.

5. Which weather conditions would most likely create the fog as shown in the photo?

    A. rapidly cooling air that is low in water vapor

    B. rapidly cooling air that is high in water vapor

    C. rapidly warming air that is low in water vapor

    D. rapidly warming air that is high in water vapor

6. Clouds and fog form under similar conditions. Air pressure at higher altitudes affects the formation of clouds. As air rises, the reduced pressure allows the air to expand and cool until water vapor *evaporates / freezes / condenses* into water droplets that form the clouds.

7. As snow slowly melts in the sunshine, what is happening to the particles of water that make up the snow? Select all that apply.

    A. Particles are gaining energy.

    B. Particle motion is decreasing.

    C. Particle motion is increasing.

Interactive Review

Complete this section to review the main concepts of the lesson.

A change of state is the change of a substance from one physical state to another, such as from a liquid to a solid.

A. Explain whether the identity of a substance changes during a change of state. Give an example.

A change of state can occur when thermal energy is added to a substance.

B. Describe the change in motion and kinetic energy of the particles as thermal energy is added to a liquid. Which change of state might happen?

A change of state can occur when thermal energy is removed from a substance.

C. Describe the change in motion and kinetic energy of the particles as thermal energy is removed from a liquid. Which change of state might happen?

Changes in pressure can affect changes of state.

D. Explain why liquid particles at a high pressure would need more energy to change to a gas than liquid particles at a low pressure.

Organisms and Nonliving Things Are Made of Atoms

Penguins, grass, water, and all other matter are all made up of different types of particles.

© Houghton Mifflin Harcourt Publishing Company • Image Credits: ©Andrew Peacock/Lonely Planet Images/Getty Images

Explore First

Building Objects Use crafting materials to make two objects. Use the same materials in both of your objects, but try and make the two objects as different as possible. What are some of the ways that you were able to make your two objects different?

CAN YOU EXPLAIN IT?

Why can objects made of the same materials have different properties?

Propane is a natural gas that is used as a fuel. It is often burned to cook food or heat water. Despite being an invisible gas, propane is composed of many of the same types of matter as humans. Propane is composed of hydrogen and carbon, which also account for nearly 30% of the matter in the human body.

1. What are some of the major differences between humans and propane?

2. Both humans and propane are mostly composed of the same types of matter. Why might humans and propane have different properties?

 EVIDENCE NOTEBOOK As you explore the lesson, gather evidence to help explain how objects made of the same materials can have different properties.

Analyzing Particles of Matter

Think about the materials that you see every day. Some materials can be separated physically into their parts. For instance, you can filter sand out of water or melt rocks in order to separate metals from the rock.

Some substances cannot be physically separated into parts because all the particles have the same properties. Physically separating pure water will just give you two volumes of water. Many of these substances can only be separated into components by chemically changing the substance.

Sugar particles can be physically separated out of sugar cane.

3. Do you think that every substance can be separated physically or chemically into other substances? Explain your answer.

Elements

Even though water cannot be physically separated, running electricity through water causes a chemical change that breaks the water down into oxygen and hydrogen. Chemical changes such as this can break down many pure substances into their components, but there are some pure substances that cannot be separated physically or chemically. An **element** is a substance that cannot be separated into simpler substances by chemical changes. Elements are the building blocks of all other substances. Both oxygen and hydrogen are elements. Currently, 118 elements are known and each element has a one, two, or three letter symbol associated with it. For instance, carbon is represented by the symbol C. Most objects that you see are made up of combinations of these elements. For example, a humans and propane gas both contain large amounts of oxygen, hydrogen, and carbon. On the other hand, a diamond is made of pure carbon.

Properties of Elements

Each element has a unique set of physical and chemical properties. Oxygen is very different from copper. Carbon is very different from either oxygen or copper. Some elements may have similar colors or similar densities, or they may react in similar ways, but no two elements have the exact same set of properties. Copper and silver can both conduct electricity. They are also both malleable and can be used to make jewelry, but they have different colors and densities.

 EVIDENCE NOTEBOOK

4. All matter is composed of atoms of various elements. What are the elements that make up both humans and propane? Record your evidence.

5. An element cannot be broken down into other substances by chemical or physical means. But you can still split a sample of an element into smaller pieces. For example, a piece of aluminum foil can be cut in half and then in half again, and all of the pieces will still be aluminum. What do you think would eventually happen if you could continue dividing that piece of aluminum foil?

Types of Particles

All matter is made up of particles. However, as you have seen when modeling matter, not all particles behave in the same way. There are two main types of particles: atoms and molecules. Atoms are the building blocks of matter. Every piece of matter that you interact with is composed of atoms. Sometimes atoms can be connected together to form extended structures of atoms, such as crystals or metals.

Molecules are another type of particle that composes matter. Molecules are composed of atoms that are bonded together to form a new particle. These bonded atoms behave as a single particle that has its own unique set of properties.

Water particles are actually molecules. These molecules are made up of oxygen and hydrogen atoms.

© Houghton Mifflin Harcourt Publishing Company

Atoms

Although an element cannot be broken down into other substances, a sample of the element can be divided into smaller pieces. An **atom** is the smallest unit of an element that has the chemical identity of that element. Atoms of the same elements have the same chemical properties and behave similarly. Iron atoms found on a meteorite will behave the same way as iron atoms pulled up from the bottom of the ocean.

Each element has its own chemical and physical properties due to the properties of its atoms. Every object that you see is made up of a huge number of atoms. Atoms are so tiny that they cannot be seen with an optical microscope. Even the most advanced microscopes can barely detect individual atoms.

This image shows individual atoms on the surface of a piece of silicon. The image was made using data from a scanning tunneling microscope.

Do the Math
Model the Scale of an Atom

Atoms are very tiny objects. It is difficult to even imagine how small they are, so people use models to describe atoms. The largest atoms measure less than one nanometer in diameter. A nanometer is one one-billionth of a meter. If matter were expanded so that an atom could barely be seen, your body would be big enough to reach from Philadelphia, Pennsylvania, to Miami, Florida.

One of the tiny grains of iron shown has a mass of about 0.9 mg, or 9×10^{-4} grams.

6. Each iron atom has a mass of about 9×10^{-23} grams. Even a small grain of iron has an incredible number of atoms in it—about 1×10^{18} atoms in one grain. Which of these is most similar to the number of atoms in a grain of iron?

   A. the number of people in a large stadium; about 1×10^{5}

   B. the number of people on Earth; about 1×10^{10}

   C. the number of meters between Earth and the star Vega; about 2.4×10^{17}

7. This stadium can hold 100,000, or 1×10^{5}, people. The number of atoms in a grain of iron is about 1×10^{18}. Would you need 1×10^{10} or 1×10^{13} stadiums to hold the same number of people as the number of atoms in a grain of iron? Explain your answer.

Molecules

A **molecule** is two or more atoms held together by chemical bonds. A *chemical bond* is the attractive force that holds atoms together. For example, an oxygen molecule contains two oxygen atoms connected by a chemical bond. Molecules are particles of matter. They can range in size from two atoms to thousands of atoms. The wide variety of matter that you see is a result of the ways different atoms can combine. Because there are so many molecules, there are names for many of them. Three oxygen atoms form a molecule known as ozone. All ozone molecules have the same properties.

Compounds

In some molecules, such as an oxygen molecule, all the atoms are the same type of atom. This type of molecule makes up certain elements. Elements are pure substances made entirely of the same type of atom.

Other molecules are made up of two or more different types of atoms. These molecules make up a type of matter called a compound. A **compound** is a substance made up of two or more different types of atoms joined by chemical bonds.

Compounds can be broken down into simpler substances and those substances always form in a fixed ratio. For example, water always has two hydrogen atoms for every one oxygen atom. Each particle of water is a molecule because it is made up of two or more atoms held together by bonds. Water is also a compound because the water particle is made up of more than one type of atom, specifically hydrogen and oxygen.

8. Circle the molecules that are also compounds.

A	B	C
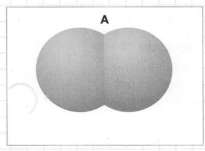	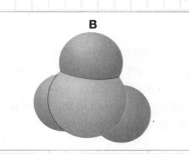	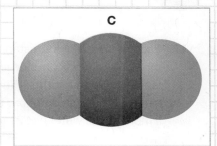

9. Which statements are true about molecules and compounds? Select all that apply.

  A. Molecules are made of one atom and compounds are made of two or more atoms.

  B. Some molecules are also compounds.

  C. Molecules are always composed of two or more elements.

  D. Compounds are always composed of two or more elements.

 EVIDENCE NOTEBOOK

  10. What are some ways that the same types of atoms could be present in two different samples when the two samples have different properties? Record your evidence.

11. **Draw** A sodium atom joined with a chlorine atom forms the compound sodium chloride. Sodium chloride has properties that are different from the properties of sodium or chlorine alone. In a similar way, a compound word is the joining together of two different words. The word *dog* joined with the word *house* forms the compound word *doghouse*. The word *doghouse* has a different meaning compared to the meanings of the words *dog* or *house* alone.

Write two more compound words that are formed by joining two words and then draw a picture to show the meaning of your new compound words.

sodium atom   +   chlorine atom   =   sodium chloride

dog   +   house   =   doghouse

Word 1	Word 2	Compound Word	Drawing

Do the Math
Identify Ratios

12. Each molecule of a substance is exactly the same. The atoms that make up the molecule always combine in a fixed ratio. A ratio tells how much of one thing there is compared to another. When describing molecules, a ratio tells how much of one element there is compared to another element in the same molecule. For example, a molecule of water has 2 hydrogen atoms for every 1 oxygen atom. The ratio of hydrogen atoms to oxygen atoms is 2 to 1. Other ways to write the ratio are 2:1 and $\frac{2}{1}$.

For the statements below, write the correct ratio for the molecules described.

○ sulfur
● oxygen
● nitrogen

A. For every molecule of sulfur dioxide, the ratio of sulfur atoms to oxygen atoms is 1:_____.

B. In a molecule of nitrogen dioxide, the ratio of nitrogen atoms to oxygen atoms is _____: 2.

C. For every molecule of nitrous oxide, the ratio of nitrogen atoms to oxygen atoms is: $\frac{\quad}{1}$.

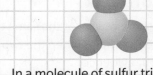

D. In a molecule of sulfur trioxide, the ratio of sulfur atoms to oxygen atoms is _____:_____.

Pure Substances

When understanding the properties of elements and compounds, it is useful to look at how they behave as pure substances. A **pure substance** is a sample of matter that has specific chemical and physical properties, such as appearance, melting point, and reactivity. A pure substance will always be made of the same matter. A sample of atoms or molecules of one element is a pure substance. A sample of molecules of a compound is a pure substance. The particles in pure substances can be atoms or molecules as long as the matter is consistent throughout the entire substance. The properties of an element or compound can be measured when you have a pure sample.

13. The particle structure of three pure substances are modeled below. Observe the arrangement of the atoms. Record your observations in the table.

Pure substance	Particle structure	Observations
chlorine	Cl Cl	
hydrogen	H H	
hydrogen chloride	H Cl	

Compare Models of Elements and Compounds

The diagrams show models of three different pure substances: water, table salt, and tin metal.

water

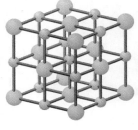
table salt

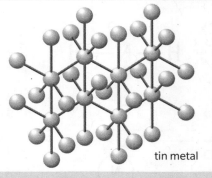
tin metal

14. Water, table salt, and tin are all pure substances. Which of these pure substances are compounds? Explain your reasoning.

_____

_____

_____

Modeling Molecules

Molecules are extremely small. A water molecule, for instance, is about 3×10^{-10} m (0.0000000003 m) in diameter, which is very much smaller than the period at the end of this sentence. The structure of matter at the atomic and molecular levels is too small to observe directly. So what do scientists do when they want to study these structures? They develop and use models of atoms and molecules. Scientists use models to help them understand the real world and how it works. Models can help people learn about and visualize things they cannot see directly.

15. There are many different types of models. The diagrams to the right show some different ways to model molecules. How are the models alike? How are they different?

Examples of Molecular Models

These diagrams show three different molecules modeled in different ways.

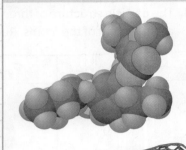

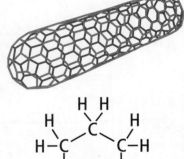

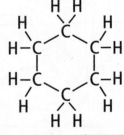

16. Molecules are atoms held together by attractive forces. Which of these diagrams could be a way to model a simple molecule of three hydrogen atoms joined to a nitrogen atom? Select all that apply.

A

$$H-\underset{\underset{\displaystyle H}{|}}{N}-H$$

B

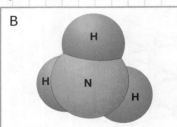

C

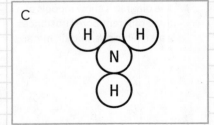

D

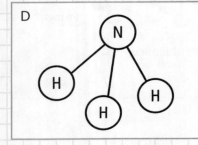

E

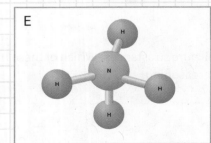

F

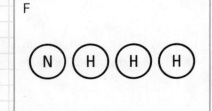

© Houghton Mifflin Harcourt Publishing Company

Models of Simple Molecules

There are many different ways to model molecules. A model of the simplest molecule would show just two atoms joined together. The atoms could be the same, such as in hydrogen, which has two hydrogen atoms. Or the atoms could be different, such as in a molecule of carbon monoxide, which is made up of one carbon atom and one oxygen atom. Other models could show three or more atoms.

Molecules are groups of atoms joined together by chemical bonds. In some models, you may see the chemical bonds represented by lines or sticks. But a chemical bond is not a physical thing. It is the attractive force that holds atoms together. Some models do not show anything at all to represent chemical bonds. They may instead show two atoms—perhaps modeled by two spheres—that touch each other.

Two Types of Molecular Models

| a molecule of water | a molecule of methane | a molecule of acetic acid |

17. The diagrams show two different ways that water, methane, and acetic acid can be modeled. Look closely at each type of model. Explain what each type of model shows best.

Hands-On Lab
Model Molecules

Observe two compounds that are made of only carbon, hydrogen, and oxygen atoms. Plan and carry out an investigation to explore how models of each molecule can explain why the compounds have different properties.

MATERIALS
- acetic acid
- clay
- isopropyl alcohol
- toothpicks

Procedure

STEP 1 Look at the samples of acetic acid and isopropyl alcohol. What properties can you observe? Record your observations in the table below.

STEP 2 On a separate piece of paper, make a plan to build a model of each molecule. Use the molecular structures from the table to help you. Think about how you can use the materials provided by your teacher to build the models. What can you make with the clay to represent part of the models? What can the toothpicks represent? Write the steps of your plan.

STEP 3 Carry out your plan for building the models. Then draw what you built in the table.

Compound Name	Molecule Structure	Observations	Draw Your Model
Acetic Acid			
Isopropyl Alcohol			

© Houghton Mifflin Harcourt Publishing Company

Analysis

STEP 4 How are the structures of acetic acid and isopropyl alcohol similar? How are they different?

STEP 5 Why do you think acetic acid and isopropyl alcohol have different properties? Use the models you developed to help you explain.

Models of Complex Molecules

A simple molecule may contain a few atoms bonded together. A complex molecule may contain thousands of atoms. The atoms in complex molecules often form a repeating pattern. A repeating unit can be formed by a single type of atom or two or more different types of atoms. Most of the molecules that make up living things are complex molecules based around carbon. Complex molecules like these are possible because carbon atoms are able to form very stable bonds with each other.

Some plastics, such as the PVC plastic in these chairs, contain thousands of carbon, hydrogen, and chlorine atoms joined together in long chains.

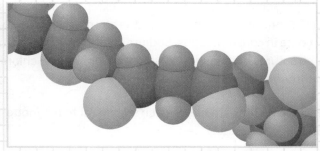

This model shows how a molecule of the plastic polyvinyl chloride (PVC) is made up of repeating units of carbon, hydrogen, and chlorine atoms.

18. This model is another way to show the structure of a molecule of PVC. Circle the unit that repeats.

$$
\begin{array}{cccccc}
H & H & H & H & H & H \\
| & | & | & | & | & | \\
-C- & C- & C- & C- & C- & C- \\
| & | & | & | & | & | \\
H & Cl & H & Cl & H & Cl
\end{array}
$$

19. Observe the diamond photo and its molecular structure diagram. Describe the repeating unit in the structure.

The Structure of the Diamond Substance

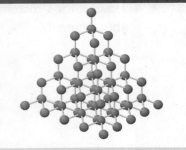

You may be familiar with diamonds as a precious gemstone. Diamonds are also one of the hardest natural materials on Earth. Diamond can be used to cut through other very hard materials, such as rock.

Diamond is a pure carbon substance. There is a repeating structure in a diamond, even though the atoms are all the same.

Extended Structures

Some solid elements and compounds are not composed of particles that are single atoms or individual molecules. Instead, they are made of extended structures. Extended structures are made up of repeating subunits of atoms. These subunits do not form individual particles in the same way that molecules do. Some extended structures, such as those in diamonds, are also crystals. *Crystals* are extended structures with a repeating structure of atoms. These structures define many of a crystal's properties.

Some elements occur as extended structures made of one type of atom. For example, aluminum has an extended structure. Aluminum atoms form a repeating subunit that makes the substance consistent throughout.

Some compounds also have extended structures made up of more than one type of atom. Similar to molecules, the atoms that make up these extended structures also come in constant ratios. Sodium chloride, or table salt, is a compound that has extended structures. A repeating structure of sodium and chlorine atoms makes it consistent throughout the substance.

20. Draw lines to match each statement to the model it describes.

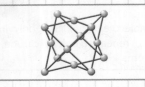

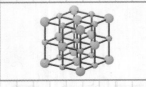

Table sugar is a molecule made up of carbon, hydrogen, and oxygen atoms arranged as two rings joined together.

Silver metal is an extended structure made up of atoms of silver arranged in a regular pattern.

Table salt is an extended structure made up of sodium and chlorine atoms arranged in a repeating pattern.

Language SmArts
Evaluate Molecule Models

Deoxyribonucleic acid (DNA) is a molecule that contains genetic information. DNA is found in all living things. DNA is a *macromolecule,* or large molecule, that is made up of many smaller molecules.

The diagram shows two models to help you analyze the structure of DNA.

- The model on the left looks something like a curved ladder. The blue "ribbon" represents a sugar-phosphate backbone of smaller molecules that forms the structure of the DNA. Each of the four colored "bars" represents a different type of smaller molecule. This model shows how the smaller molecules are connected within the DNA macromolecule.

- The model on the right also shows the overall spiral structure of DNA, but it shows the individual atoms rather than showing types of molecules.

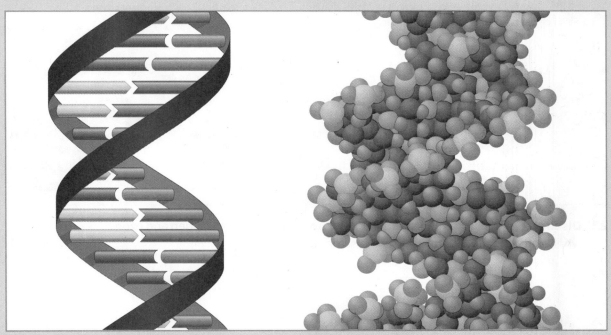

Both models show a section of DNA. The models use color to distinguish the various parts of the structure of DNA, but they show the DNA differently. The model on the left shows how smaller molecules within the DNA macromolecule are connected. The model on the right shows individual atoms.

---

21. If you are interested in finding patterns in the way the smaller molecules bond to make up DNA, which model would be most helpful?

The model on the left / right shows the atoms that make up the smaller molecules. It shows the detailed shape of the entire section of DNA, but molecules are not clearly seen. The model on the left / right shows how smaller molecules within the DNA are bonded to each other. It shows the order and relative position of the smaller molecules and the general shape of the DNA.

The model on the left / right is best for finding patterns in the way the smaller molecules bond.

Relating the Identity and Structure of Matter to Its Properties

Many of the physical and chemical properties that you observe come from the particles that make up the matter around you. The vast majority of the matter you interact with is composed of molecules or extended structures. The makeup and structure of those molecules and extended structures affect their properties. These properties impact how ecosystems and humans interact with substances. Atoms of the same elements can form molecules necessary for life as well as molecules that are toxic to living things.

Molecular Structure of Oxygen and Ozone

Both oxygen gas and ozone are made up of only oxygen atoms—but they are completely different substances. Both occur in the atmosphere and are important for life on Earth. Humans and animals need to breathe oxygen gas to live. Ozone absorbs ultraviolet radiation. Its presence in the atmosphere acts as a protective layer so less of this damaging radiation reaches Earth's surface. Ozone can also be used to sterilize drinking water.

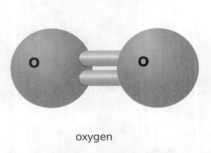

oxygen

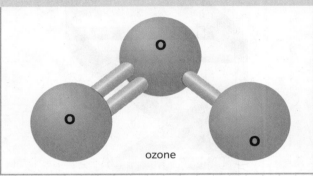

ozone

22. Discuss What might explain differences in properties between oxygen and ozone when both substances are made of the same type of atoms?

Differences in Composition

The type and number of the atoms that make up a molecule or extended structure affect the properties of that matter. For instance, when even a single atom is different between molecules, they may behave very differently. A single oxygen atom is known as monoxide, a toxic gas that is poisonous to humans. Two oxygen atoms bonded together form an oxygen molecule, which humans need to survive. Three oxygen atoms bonded together form ozone, a gas that absorbs ultraviolet radiation in the atmosphere. The particles that make up a sample of matter greatly affect the properties of that matter.

EVIDENCE NOTEBOOK

23. How might differences in the combinations of atoms change the properties of carbon and hydrogen? Record your evidence.

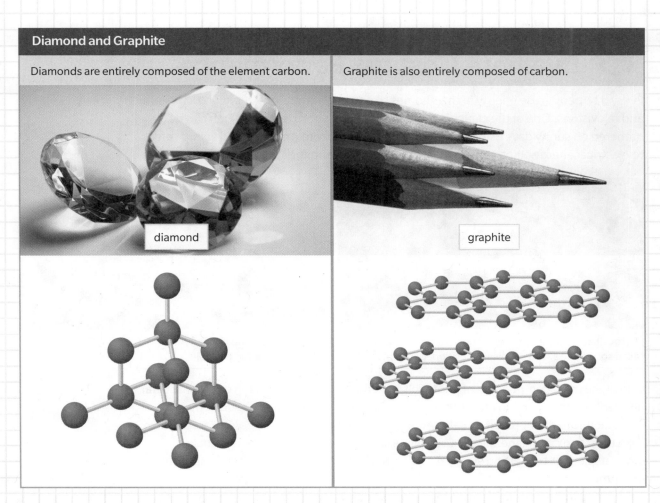

Diamond and Graphite

Diamonds are entirely composed of the element carbon.

diamond

Graphite is also entirely composed of carbon.

graphite

24. Diamond and graphite are both pure carbon. They are both pure substances made of carbon atoms, but the atoms are arranged in different ways. Diamonds are one of the hardest substances on Earth. Graphite is very soft and will easily break apart. What is it about the structure of graphite that might explain its properties?

A. The layered structure of graphite causes the bonds between atoms to strengthen.

B. Graphite is soft because its structure causes the individual atoms to bend.

C. The layered structure of graphite allows the layers to slide past each other.

D. Graphite breaks apart easily because its atoms are dark in color.

Differences in Structure

The way that atoms connect to one another affects the properties of matter. This is easy to observe in some extended structures. Diamonds and the graphite in your pencil are both entirely composed of carbon. Graphite is one of the softest materials and diamonds are one of the hardest. In graphite, the carbon atoms are loosely connected into sheets, leading to the flaky nature of graphite. In diamonds, extreme temperatures and pressure force the carbon atoms to bond in a rigid, ordered structure that gives a diamond its incredible hardness.

Molecules can also have different structures, even when they are made of atoms of the same elements. Propadiene and propyne are composed of the same combination of atoms, but have different structures. They have different melting and boiling points.

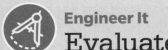

Engineer It

Evaluate Cost vs. Performance

Every day, people use energy in their homes to power electrical devices such as heaters and televisions. One of the cleanest sources of energy is solar energy, which can be gathered on sunny days using photovoltaic cells. *Photo* refers to light, and *voltaic* refers to electrical energy. Photovoltaic cells directly convert sunlight to electrical energy.

Photovoltaic cells are carefully manufactured in a factory. Then they are formed into larger frames called solar panels. The panels are positioned to capture as much direct sunlight as possible.

One of the main components of photovoltaic cells is silicon. Pure silicon exists in several different forms, including amorphous and crystalline. Both forms are used in the manufacturing of photovoltaic cells. Amorphous silicon has a less ordered, less uniform structure than crystalline silicon. Crystalline silicon's ordered arrangement makes it more efficient at converting sunlight to electrical energy, but it is also more expensive to use. Amorphous silicon, while less efficient, is less expensive to use, and can be thinner, lighter, and more flexible than the crystalline silicon.

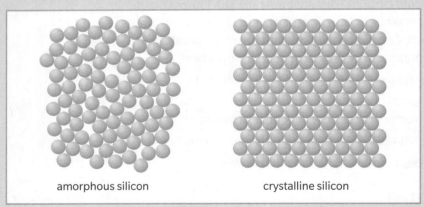

amorphous silicon   crystalline silicon

25. Assess the pros and cons of using crystalline silicon and amorphous silicon to manufacture photovoltaic cells. Which material would be used if the main criterion was keeping the cost of materials as low as possible? Which material would be used if the main criterion was getting the best performance from the material? Explain your reasoning.

_____

_____

_____

_____

© Houghton Mifflin Harcourt Publishing Company • Image Credits: (tl) ©Norm Betts/Bloomberg/Getty Images; (tr) ©Smileus/Shutterstock

Continue Your Exploration

Name: _____   Date: _____

Check out the path below or go online to choose one of the other paths shown.

People in Science

- **Molecules and Your Sense of Smell**
- **Hands-On Labs** 🖐
- **Propose Your Own Path**

Go online to choose one of these other paths.

Joseph Proust, Chemist

In the 18th century and early 19th century, French chemist Joseph Proust worked and taught in France and Spain. He is best known for his work on what is called the law of definite proportions. This law states that a pure chemical compound always contains the same elements in exactly the same proportions by mass. Although many scientists assumed this to be true, it was Proust who first gathered evidence to support it.

Suppose you have a sample of sodium chloride, or table salt. You determine that the sample consists of 39% by mass of the element sodium and 61% by mass of the element chlorine, a ratio of 39 sodium to 61 chlorine. This ratio is true not only for this sample of sodium chloride, but for all samples of sodium chloride. No matter where this pure substance is found, this ratio holds true.

The Law of Definite Proportions

As shown in the top row, 10.00 g of lead reacts with 1.55 g of sulfur to produce 11.55 g of lead sulfide. If you only add more sulfur (middle row) or only add more lead (bottom row), you will still end up with exactly 11.55 g of lead sulfide with the added substance left over. The compound always contains the same elements in exactly the same proportion.

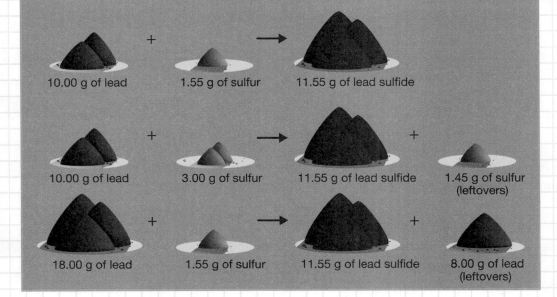

10.00 g of lead + 1.55 g of sulfur → 11.55 g of lead sulfide

10.00 g of lead + 3.00 g of sulfur → 11.55 g of lead sulfide + 1.45 g of sulfur (leftovers)

18.00 g of lead + 1.55 g of sulfur → 11.55 g of lead sulfide + 8.00 g of lead (leftovers)

Continue Your Exploration

1. Why is Proust's law of definite proportions important? Why is it important to know the ratios in which elements combine to make different substances?

Copper Carbonate

Through investigation, Proust showed that copper carbonate always has 5.3 parts copper to 4 parts oxygen to 1 part carbon. In other words, the ratio of copper to oxygen to carbon is 5.3 : 4 : 1. The picture shows that in a 103 g sample of copper carbonate, there are 53 g of copper, 40 g of oxygen, and 10 g of carbon.

| 103 g of copper carbonate | → | 53 g of copper | + | 40 g of oxygen | + | 10 g of carbon |

2. In a sample of copper carbonate, how much copper and oxygen would there be for 5 g of carbon? Use the ratio of copper to oxygen to carbon.

3. A sample of copper carbonate was found to contain 15.9 g of copper. How many grams of copper carbonate were in the sample? Use the ratio of copper to oxygen to carbon.

4. **Collaborate** Work with a partner. An oxygen atom is 16 times more massive than a hydrogen atom. A carbon atom is 12 times more massive than a hydrogen atom. Determine the mass ratios of two of the following pure substances:

   • Water is made up of 2 hydrogen atoms and 1 oxygen atom.

   • Hydrogen peroxide is made up of 2 hydrogen atoms and 2 oxygen atoms

   • Methane is made up of 1 carbon atom and 4 hydrogen atoms.

Can You Explain It?

Name: _____ **Date:** _____

Why can objects made of the same materials have different properties?

 EVIDENCE NOTEBOOK

Refer to the notes in your Evidence Notebook to help you construct an explanation for how the objects made of the same materials can have different properties.

1. State your claim. Make sure your claim fully explains how humans and propane can be made of many of the same materials.

2. Summarize the evidence you have gathered to support your claim and explain your reasoning.

Checkpoints

Answer the following questions to check your understanding of the lesson.

3. You have a sample of a substance that you cannot physically separate into components. You also cannot chemically separate that substance into components. Which of the following are true about your sample? Choose all that apply.

   A. The sample is made up of one type of atom.

   B. The sample is made up of multiple elements.

   C. The sample is made up of a single element.

   D. The sample is made up of several types of atoms.

Use the diagram to answer Questions 4–5.

4. Which of the following can be observed from the model of water? Select all that apply.

   A. Water is a molecule.

   B. Water is a compound.

   C. Water is made up of three types of atoms.

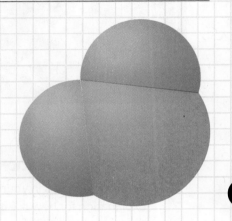

5. Another way to model water is with letters and lines like this: H–O–H. What is one way that these two models are different?

   A. They show different types and numbers of atoms.

   B. The atoms are connected in a different order.

   C. The chemical bonds are represented differently.

   D. One model clearly shows a repeating pattern.

Use the models to answer Question 6.

6. Based on the models of these structures, white phosphorus is a(n)

   simple molecule / extended structure.

   Red phosphorus is a(n)

   simple molecule / extended structure.

   Both are examples of a(n) *compound / element.*

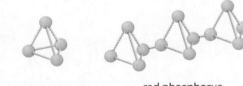

white phosphorus   red phosphorus

7. The structure of carbon tetrachloride, CCl_4, is similar to the structure of carbon tetrabromide, CBr_4. Both molecules have four atoms connected to a central carbon atom. Does that mean the two substances have the same properties?

   A. Yes, because molecules with similar structures must have the same properties.

   B. Yes, because the carbon atom determines the properties of both substances.

   C. No, because the types of atoms in a molecule and its structure both influence the properties of a substance.

Interactive Review

Complete this section to review the main concepts of the lesson.

Atoms make up all matter. Some matter is made of individual atoms, and some matter is made of atoms arranged in molecules.

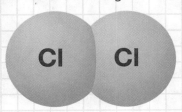

A. How are atoms, molecules, compounds, and pure substances related?

Models can be used to study simple molecules, complex molecules, and extended structures.

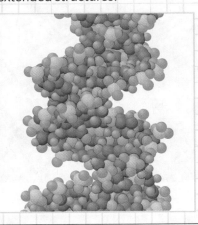

B. What do models of molecules and extended structures show?

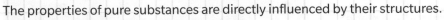

The properties of pure substances are directly influenced by their structures.

C. What is the relationship between the structure of a substance and the properties of a substance? Explain.

Choose one of the activities to explore how this unit connects to other topics.

☐ People in Science

Dorothy Hodgkin, Chemist Dorothy Hodgkin was born in 1910 and first became interested in chemistry at age ten. She eventually attended Somerville College of Oxford University where she researched X-ray crystallography. She continued her research at Cambridge, where she earned her PhD. Hodgkin was a pioneer of crystallography and studied the structure of biomolecules. She identified the three-dimensional structures of many molecules, including insulin in 1969. Hodgkin was awarded the Nobel Prize in Chemistry in 1964 for her work.

Research how three-dimensional models of molecules were developed and Dorothy Hodgkin's influence on the field.

☐ Technology Connection

Silicon Valley Silicon Valley is the region in the San Francisco Bay Area where a large number of tech companies are based and many technological innovations are developed. Its name comes from the fact that the element silicon is a key component of computer chips.

Research how silicon is obtained and why its physical properties make it useful for the computer industry. Create a presentation highlighting silicon's properties and give examples of how it is used in electronic devices.

☐ Art Connection

Working with Wax Not all "paintings" are made with paints. Some artists practice hot wax painting, also known as encaustic painting. This technique gives paintings unique characteristics quite different from traditional oil or latex paintings. It was often used for Coptic Egyptian mummy portraits.

Research encaustic painting. Describe the materials used and how artists utilize a change of state to create their artwork. Prepare a visual display and verbal presentation that describes the technique of encaustic painting. Provide several example images to share in your presentation.

An encaustic painting on the mummy of Marco Antinous.

Name: _____ **Date:** _____

Complete this review to check your understanding of the unit.

Use the diagram to answer Questions 1 and 2.

1. Air _is / is not_ a pure substance because it is made up of _a single / more than one_ type of matter.

2. Which of the following components of air is a compound?

   A. carbon dioxide

   B. oxygen

   C. nitrogen

   D. argon

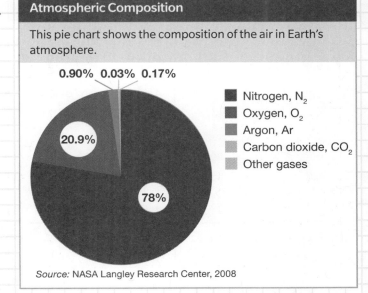

Atmospheric Composition

This pie chart shows the composition of the air in Earth's atmosphere.

0.90% 0.03% 0.17%

20.9%

78%

■ Nitrogen, N_2
■ Oxygen, O_2
■ Argon, Ar
■ Carbon dioxide, CO_2
■ Other gases

Source: NASA Langley Research Center, 2008

3. A molecule of carbon dioxide is made up of a carbon atom and two oxygen atoms. Which of the following models represents carbon dioxide?

   A.    **B.**    **C.**    **D.**

These are images of wet paper towels placed on a bag of room temperature water and a bag of hot water. Use the images to answer Questions 4 and 5.

4. The water molecules that are warmed by the hot water are moving _faster / slower_ than the water molecules on the room temperature water bag.

5. From which paper towel do you expect the water to evaporate first?

   A. the room temperature paper towel, because the molecules are moving slower

   B. the heated paper towel, because the molecules are moving faster

   C. water will evaporate from both paper towels at the same time because higher temperatures do not affect the water molecules

   D. water will not evaporate from either paper towel

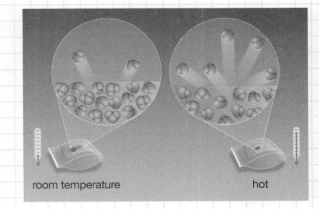

room temperature   hot

6. Complete the table by providing at least one example of how each category of matter relates to each big concept.

Matter	Scale	Structure	Everyday examples
atom	the smallest unit of an element that has the chemical identity of that element		
molecule			
compound			
extended structures			

Name: **Date:**

Use the images of sodium and silver to answer Questions 7–10.

Pure sodium, Na, and pure silver, Ag, appear similar when they are in their solid forms. When sodium is added to water, an explosive reaction occurs. However, no reaction occurs when pure silver is placed in water.

sodium

sodium in water

silver

silver in water

7. Describe the physical properties of sodium and silver.

8. Describe the chemical properties of sodium and silver. Why is silver often used to make eating utensils?

9. Sodium and silver are both pure elements. If the sodium atoms were bonded to other atoms to form a compound, would you expect that compound to behave the same as sodium? Explain your answer.

10. Compare sodium and silver before and after they are placed in water. Has a new substance been produced in each case?

Use the graph to answer Questions 11–14.

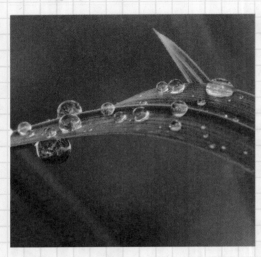

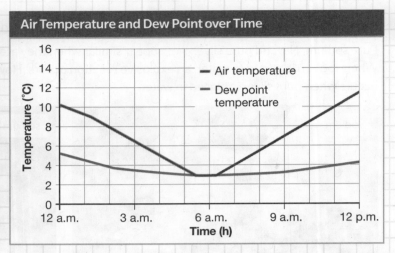

Air Temperature and Dew Point over Time

11. Dew forms when the air temperature
is low enough for water in the air to condense on outdoor surfaces. At what time
would you expect to see dew, according to the graph? Explain your answer.

12. What would you expect to happen if the temperature dropped to below freezing
after 6:00 a.m.? Explain your answer.

13. In terms of thermal and kinetic energy, describe how water vapor forms when dew
evaporates.

14. In terms of thermal and kinetic energy, describe how water droplets form on a blade
of grass.

Name: _____   Date: _____

Molecular Clues!

Scientists use their knowledge of matter's structure and properties to develop new technologies and processes. Gel electrophoresis is a method used to study proteins and other large molecules. It enables scientists to separate these complex molecules based on their sizes and can be used in many different scientific fields, including forensics and medicine.

Research gel electrophoresis. Describe the technique and how it works, provide examples of when it is used, and design a model to demonstrate this useful technology. Then prepare a presentation that highlights your findings.

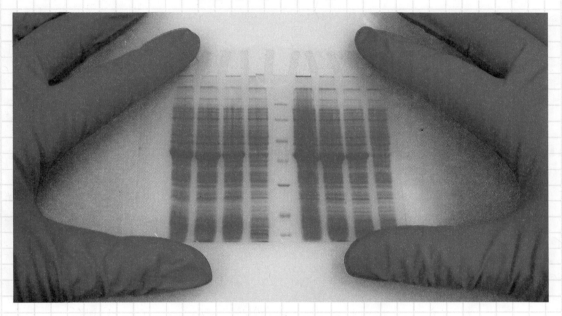

The steps below will help guide you to develop and carry out your plan.

1. **Conduct Research** Research examples of situations in which gel electrophoresis is used and the types of molecules that scientists separate using this technique.

2. **Ask a Question** How do scientists take advantage of differences between the properties of substances to make this technique work?

3. **Construct an Explanation** Based on your research, write a report that explains how gel electrophoresis works and how a scientist can interpret the results in an electrophoresis gel.

4. **Develop a Model** Create your own physical model representing how electrophoresis is used to separate substances.

5. **Communicate** Present your findings to the class, and share your model of gel electrophoresis.

✓ **Self-Check**

	I conducted research on how gel electrophoresis is used and examples of its application.
	I explained how gel electrophoresis separates molecules based on differences in their properties and how scientists can interpret the results.
	I developed a model to show how electrophoresis works.
	I communicated my results by presenting my findings to the class and sharing my model.

© Houghton Mifflin Harcourt Publishing Company

Chemical Processes

How do matter and energy change in chemical processes?

Unit Project		134
Lesson 1	Matter Changes Identity in Chemical Reactions	136
Lesson 2	Chemical Equations Model Chemical Reactions	154
Lesson 3	Engineer It: Using Thermal Energy in a Device	174
Lesson 4	Synthetic Materials Are Made from Natural Resources	194
Unit Review		219
Unit Performance Task		223

This is a crystal of progesterone, an important hormone in the human body. It can be synthetically produced from plant materials using a series of chemical reactions known as the Marker degradation.

You Solve It How Can You Design a Heat Pack? Design the chemical system for a heat pack by testing different amounts of chemical components to see which combination best meets the design criteria.

Go online and complete the You Solve It to explore ways to solve a real-world problem

Design a Chemical Cold Pack

Cold packs are used to reduce swelling after an injury.

A. Look at the photo. On a separate sheet of paper, write down as many different questions as you can about the photo.

B. Discuss With your class or a partner, share your questions. Record any additional questions generated in your discussion. Then choose the most important questions from the list that are related to designing a chemical cold pack. Write them below.

C. Based on your experience using cold packs in the past, what are some ways that you think you could improve cold packs?

D. Use the information above to help design a cold pack.

Discuss the next steps for your Unit Project with your teacher and go online to download the Unit Project Worksheet.

Language Development

Use the lessons in this unit to complete the network and expand your understanding of these key concepts.

	Similar term
	Phrase
	Cognate
	Example
	Definition

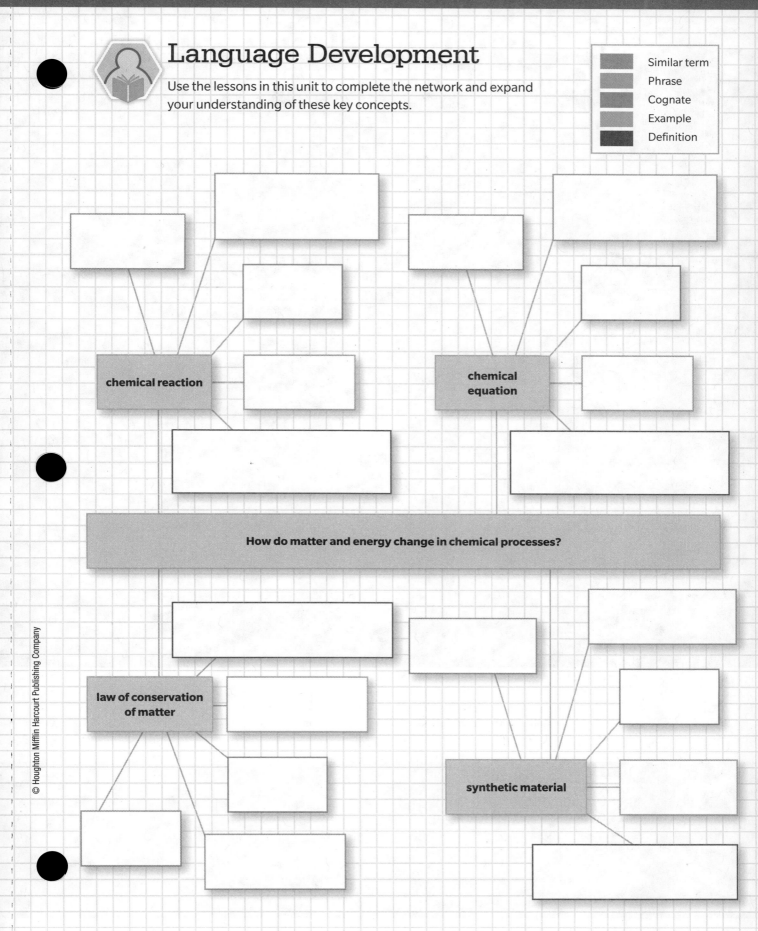

chemical reaction

chemical equation

How do matter and energy change in chemical processes?

law of conservation of matter

synthetic material

Matter Changes Identity in Chemical Reactions

© Houghton Mifflin Harcourt Publishing Company ○ Image Credits: ©Noman/Tomosang/ Getty Images

Fireflies, also called lightning bugs, are small insects that generate their own light using chemical reactions.

Explore First

Reorganizing Materials Build a structure out of building blocks. Make a sketch of your structure and then trade structures with a partner. Disassemble your partner's structure and build one or two new structures using the same blocks. Make a sketch of your new structures. How are the original structure and the new structures different?

Go online to view the digital version of the Hands-On Lab for this lesson and to download additional lab resources.

CAN YOU EXPLAIN IT?

What happens to the matter when sulfuric acid is added to powdered sugar?

These photos shows concentrated sulfuric acid mixing with powdered sugar.

Explore Online

1. What do you observe when sulfuric acid is added to the powdered sugar?

2. Is the black substance that grows out of the beaker the same as the white sugar? Explain your answer.

 EVIDENCE NOTEBOOK As you explore the lesson, gather evidence to help explain what happens to matter when the sulfuric acid is added to the sugar.

Analyzing Natural Systems

You can look at the universe as a collection of systems. A system can be tiny, such as a cell, or it can be huge, such as a solar system. A system can also be an event or phenomenon. When you look at a system, you can identify the different pieces and how they interact with one another. You can also identify the inputs, which are things entering the system, and the outputs, which are things leaving the system. By identifying the inputs and outputs, you can track how different parts of the system behave. For example, you can track matter and energy by modeling their movements in a system. You can identify how matter and energy change or how the parts of the system interact.

A volcanic eruption can be treated as a system. Some of the inputs include thermal energy and magma from below Earth's surface. The outputs include ash and lava.

3. **Discuss** What are five possible inputs and outputs of Earth as a system?

Matter and Energy

While Earth as a system has inputs and outputs, matter and energy cycle through many smaller systems on Earth. For instance, water evaporates out of lakes and rivers. In the atmosphere, the water then condenses and forms clouds. Eventually, that same water can become rain and return to Earth's surface. Energy also moves through systems. Grass takes in energy from the sun to grow. Cows eat grass in order to get that energy. Millions of processes occur every second, and these processes cycle atoms and molecules through Earth's systems.

4. Describe two examples of how matter moves through a cycle on Earth.

5. Classify the following items as either inputs or outputs of a forest.

Inputs	Outputs

word bank
- sunlight
- nutrients
- wood
- oxygen

Trees use nutrients from the ground and air as well as energy from the sun to grow. They produce oxygen and wood.

Changes in Matter and Energy

When matter and energy cycle through Earth's systems, they are often transformed. When you burn a piece of wood, you are not destroying matter or making energy. You are transforming both. The matter that makes up the wood becomes ash, smoke, and gases. The chemical energy that was stored in the wood is transformed into thermal energy and light. Matter and energy are conserved. When an object changes, the matter and energy that were associated with it are redistributed.

While different molecules are formed when something undergoes a chemical change, atoms are not created or destroyed. For instance, oxygen atoms are used by organisms and are bonded to carbon atoms to make carbon dioxide. Plants then use carbon dioxide during photosynthesis and separate the molecule back into carbon and oxygen. Oxygen atoms can be involved in many chemical changes, but they never disappear.

Model a System

6. **Draw** Treat your classroom as a system. Draw a diagram showing the inputs, outputs, and internal components of the system.

Using Properties to Identify Substances

Properties of Matter

If someone offers you a choice of two fruits—a banana or an orange—you can make your choice based on which kind of fruit you like better. But how do you know which fruit is which? You know that a banana is long and yellow, and an orange is round and orange. You may know how each tastes. In a similar way, you can identify most substances by identifying their properties.

7. **Discuss** Iron pyrite is commonly called "fool's gold" because it looks like real gold, but it is not valuable. Both fool's gold and real gold may be found in the same area, but they have different properties. Why would it be important for a miner to know about the properties of real gold and fool's gold?

Which substance is real gold?

These two substances look similar. The one on the left is gold, but the other is a mineral called iron pyrite. One property that miners use to identify gold is density. Gold has a much higher density than iron pyrite.

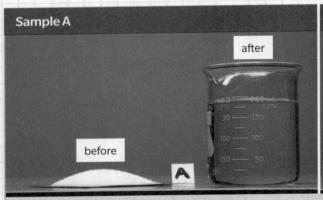

Sample A

after

before

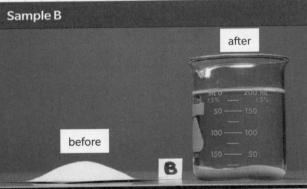

Sample B

after

before

Two unknown samples, Sample A and Sample B, are shown before and after they are stirred into a beaker of water.

8. Are Sample A and Sample B in the photos the same substance? Explain.

Physical Properties

All substances have properties that can be used to identify the substance. Each substance has a unique combination of properties. The more properties of a substance you can determine, the more likely you are to correctly identify that substance.

The physical properties of a substance are those that can be observed or measured without changing the substance's identity. Physical properties include density, melting point, boiling point, color, texture, odor, solubility, malleability, and conductivity. There are many more physical properties that can be measured.

Every substance has a set of physical properties that are used to describe the substance. Scientists use physical properties to describe and to help identify substances. The two unknown samples in the previous photos are different substances; one substance dissolved in water and the other substance did not dissolve in water.

Chemical Properties

Another type of property, a chemical property, can be determined by observing whether or not a substance can change into another substance under a given set of conditions.

9. The two nails in the photos are shown before and after being left outside in the rain. Are the two nails made of the same substance? Explain.

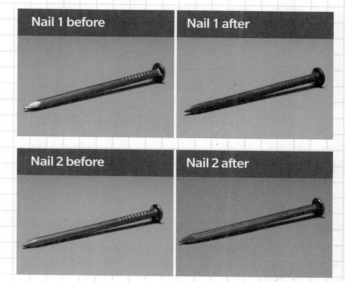

All substances have chemical properties. Chemical properties describe ways a substance can change to form different substances. Some examples of chemical properties are flammability and reactivity. When a substance changes to form a new substance, the atoms in the original substance are arranged in different ways. In the new substance, the original atoms form new molecules or arrangements of atoms. As a result, the new substance has its own unique set of properties that differ from the original substance.

When the two nails that looked alike were left outside, only one changed in a way that indicated that a new substance had formed. Nail 1 rusted, while nail 2 did not. The rust is made of particles that are different from the particles in nail 1. The particles that make up nail 2 did not change into a new substance. Therefore, the two nails left outside are not made of the same substance.

EVIDENCE NOTEBOOK

10. How might the properties of a substance help you explain what happened when sulfuric acid was mixed with powdered sugar? Record your evidence.

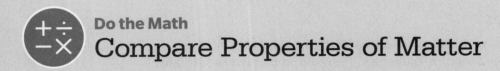

Compare Properties of Matter

Different substances may have some similar properties, but not all of their properties will be the same. You may need evidence about several different properties to determine whether two substances are identical.

11. Use the information in the table to calculate the density of each sample, and enter it in the table. Then compare the properties of these two samples.

	Sample A	Sample B
Color	colorless	colorless
Odor	odorless	odorless
Boiling Point	100 °C	100 °C
Freezing Point	0 °C	75 °C
Mass	5.5 g	10.4 g
Volume	5.5 mL	7.0 mL
Density = $\frac{mass}{volume}$	_____ $\frac{g}{mL}$	_____ $\frac{g}{mL}$

12. Using the data in the table for color, odor, and boiling point, circle the correct words to complete each statement.

The colors of Sample A and Sample B are ~~the same~~ / different.

The odors of Sample A and Sample B are ~~the same~~ / different.

The boiling points of Sample A and Sample B are ~~the same~~ / different.

13. Now use the data in the table for freezing point and density. Circle the correct words to complete each statement.

The freezing points of Sample A and Sample B are the same / different.

The densities of Sample A and Sample B are the same / different.

14. Based on all the data from the table, are these two samples the same substance? Explain why it is important to look at several properties before drawing a conclusion. Cite evidence to verify your claim.

Comparing Physical Changes and Chemical Reactions

Changes to substances take place all around you every day. Changes such as water freezing or metal being hammered into a thin sheet do not alter the identity of the substance. Changes such as milk spoiling or silver tarnishing do change the identity of the substance.

15. Discuss Explain in your own words what changes you see taking place in the photo.

Physical Changes

When a physical change takes place, the identity of a substance remains the same after the physical change. The particles that make up the substance are the same before and after the physical change. When you bend a paper clip, it is still a paper clip made of all the same particles. Physical changes only change the appearance of the substance.

Ice is solid water. When ice melts, it becomes liquid water. If liquid water boils, it becomes water vapor, a gas. Whether the water is a solid, liquid, or gas, it is the same substance. There is no change to the identity of the water molecules. Physical changes do not change water into a new substance.

This wood is being cut with a saw.

16. The photo shows wood undergoing a physical change. Compare the cut wood to the original piece of wood. Write the same or different to complete each sentence.

After cutting, the size and shape of the wood are _____. The smaller pieces of wood are _____ substance as the original, larger piece of wood. The smaller pieces of wood are made of _____ particles as the original, larger piece of wood. The identities of wood and sawdust are _____.

17. Why doesn't a change in a physical property change the identity of the substance? Explain in terms of the particles of a substance and give a new example.

Chemical Changes

When substances are mixed together, a chemical change may or may not take place. When a chemical change does take place, the original substance changes into a different substance with different properties.

Mixing Baking Soda and Vinegar

A student measures baking soda into a balloon, attaches the balloon to the top of a flask containing vinegar, and empties the baking soda into the flask.

Explore Online

18. Observe what happens in the flask as the baking soda is added to the vinegar. Why do you think the balloon inflates?

19. What happens when the baking soda and vinegar are mixed? Circle the correct words to complete the explanation.

When these two substances are mixed, a gas / liquid forms.

The baking soda and vinegar react with each other and
change state / form a new substance.

A chemical reaction changes the identity of a substance. A **chemical reaction** is the process in which atoms are rearranged to produce different substances. The original substance or substances in a chemical reaction are called **reactants**. The substance or substances that form in a chemical reaction are called **products**. During a chemical reaction, the atoms that make up the reactants regroup into different particles to form the products. The particles that make up the products can be atoms, molecules, or subunits of extended structures.

In a chemical reaction, all the atoms present in the reactants will also be present in the product. Chemical reactions generally follow defined patterns each and every time they occur. Under the same conditions, the same reactants will always form the same products in a chemical reaction.

20. Write chemical reaction or physical change to label each photo.

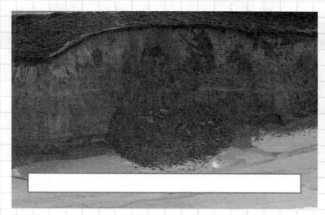

chemical reaction

Analyze a Change in Matter

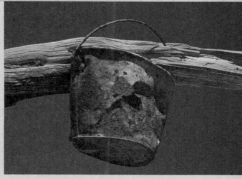

21. Look at the photo. Which changes have happened to the bucket? Circle all that apply.

A. A chemical reaction has formed a new substance.

B. The metal has reacted with air to form rust.

C. The metal has changed to a different state.

D. The color has changed to a dark, reddish color.

22. How do you think the chemical reaction has affected how the bucket can be used?

_____

_____

_____

_____

 23. Engineer It | Collaborate You have been asked to design a pipe system to deliver water. What criteria might you need to consider when choosing materials to use? Work together with a partner to develop a list. Choose one or two items from your list to incorporate into a short presentation for the class.

_____

_____

Analyzing Substances Before and After a Change

In a chemical reaction, the atoms of the reactants are rearranged to form new products. The products are different from the reactants, and they have different properties. A change in properties is evidence of a chemical reaction.

Signs of a Possible Chemical Reaction

You cannot always see new substances form in a chemical reaction. But there are some signs that you can observe to indicate that a chemical reaction may have taken place.

24. Each photo shows an indication that a chemical reaction may have taken place. Write the letter to label each photo.

A. Energy is released.
B. A solid forms.
C. The color changes.
D. A gas appears.
E. The odor changes.

 C

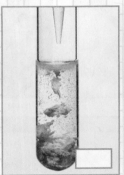

Some observations that are signs of a chemical reaction include a change in color, a change in odor, the appearance of a gas, the release of energy as light or heat, and the formation of a precipitate. A precipitate is a solid that is produced as a result of a chemical reaction in a liquid.

Most of these changes could also happen in ways that are not the result of a chemical reaction. The appearance of bubbles can indicate formation of a new gas, but bubbles also form when water boils. The only way to know for sure whether a chemical reaction has taken place is to perform more testing.

Evidence of a Chemical Reaction

To determine whether a chemical reaction has taken place, you can test the properties of the substances both before the change and after the change. The products of a chemical reaction are different substances from the reactants and will have different properties. These different properties can help identify the products.

 EVIDENCE NOTEBOOK

25. How might knowing the signs of a chemical reaction help you explain what happened when sulfuric acid was mixed with powdered sugar? How does this relate to the rearrangement of atoms that occurs in a chemical reaction? Record your evidence.

Hands-On Lab
Observe Substances Before and After a Change

Mix substances together, and then determine whether a chemical reaction has taken place.

Procedure and Analysis

STEP 1 In bag 1, add 1 level spoonful of baking soda and 1 level spoonful of powdered sugar. Record observations in the table.

STEP 2 In bag 2, add 1 level spoonful of baking soda and 1 level spoonful of road salt. Record observations in the table.

STEP 3 Add 10 mL of water to each of the small containers.

STEP 4 Carefully place a container of water into each bag. Do not spill the water. Zip each bag closed with little air in it.

STEP 5 Tip the container over in bag 1. Observe what happens and record observations in the table. Repeat for bag 2.

MATERIALS

- bags, sealable plastic, gallon size (2), labeled *bag 1* and *bag 2*
- baking soda (sodium bicarbonate)
- calcium chloride
- film canisters or small containers (2)
- graduated cylinder
- spoons, plastic (3)
- sugar, powdered

	Observations
Bag 1: baking soda + powdered sugar	
Bag 2: baking soda + road salt	
Bag 1: baking soda + powdered sugar + water	
Bag 2: baking soda + road salt + water	

STEP 6 Do you think a chemical reaction occurred in the bag with baking soda, powdered sugar, and water? What about the bag with baking soda, road salt, and water? Give evidence to support your answers.

26. Which observations could be evidence of a chemical reaction? Circle all that apply.

    A. A substance dissolved.

    B. A precipitate formed.

    C. A substance changed state.

    D. A gas was produced.

27. Draw lines to match each list of observations with the conclusion that it indicates.

• a gas was produced • the color changed

• the sample melted • the sample dissolved in water

• bubbles formed • the temperature climbed

does not indicate a chemical reaction

may indicate a chemical reaction

definite evidence of a chemical reaction

Observations such as the formation of a precipitate, the production of light or heat, or a change in color suggest that a chemical reaction has taken place. However, these signs do not always mean a chemical reaction took place. Definite evidence for a chemical reaction requires proof that at least one new substance is present after the change. The presence of a new substance is determined by comparing the physical properties and chemical properties of the substances before and after the change.

Analyze Physical Changes and Chemical Reactions

28. Circle the correct terms to complete each sentence.

    A. The burning of the candle wick shows a
    chemical reaction / physical change .

    B. The melting of the wax shows a
    chemical reaction / *physical change* .

    C. The *change of state* / *generation of light and heat*
    indicates a chemical reaction may be occurring.

29. Language SmArts Create a labeled diagram using your own pictures and words to show and explain the processes that are going on as a candle burns. Note any physical changes or chemical reactions that may be taking place. Make sure to illustrate and describe any sign that supports a claim of a chemical reaction.

Continue Your Exploration

Name: _____   Date: _____

Check out the path below or go online to choose one of the other paths shown.

Chemistry and Engineering: Airbags

- **Chemical Reactions Are Essential for Life**
- **Hands-On Labs** ✋
- **Propose Your Own Path**

Go online to choose one of these other paths.

Using Chemical Reactions in a Product

Chemical reactions take place all around us. One chemical reaction you hope you never need is the one that takes place in the airbags of cars. During certain accidents, airbags inflate very quickly and cushion the people in a car to protect them from serious injury. An airbag inflates because a chemical reaction happens quickly after a crash sensor is activated. The chemical reaction produces a large volume of gas that fills the airbag. Airbags are not meant to replace safety belts. They are additional safety features.

Explore Online

The chemical reaction that inflates an airbag happens very quickly. The time it takes for the airbag to fully inflate is less than a second!

Continue Your Exploration

Inside an airbag is a chemical called sodium azide, which is made up of sodium and nitrogen atoms. When the crash sensor is triggered, thermal energy is sent to the sodium azide. This energy causes the sodium azide to undergo an explosive chemical reaction. The sodium azide molecules break apart and produce a large volume of nitrogen gas. This causes the airbag to inflate rapidly.

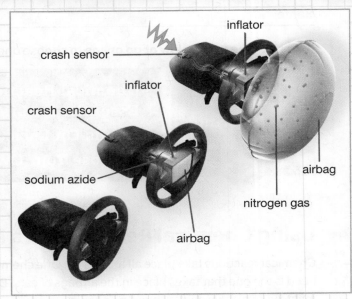

1. Which best describes how the chemical reaction that produces nitrogen gas inflates the airbag?

   A. The sodium azide quickly breaks apart.

   B. The sodium azide suddenly melts.

   C. The sodium azide rapidly forms a precipitate.

2. What indicates that a chemical reaction has taken place? Explain why the indicator would be a sign of a chemical reaction and not a sign of a physical change.

3. Chemical reactions are part of many different products. Which are important considerations about a particular chemical reaction when it is used as part of the product design? Circle all that apply.

   A. the properties of product formed

   B. the properties of the reactants

   C. the cost of the reactants

   D. the safety of the chemical reaction

4. **Collaborate** Together with a partner, choose one of the topics below to discuss. Present your ideas to the class.

   • What criteria are important for an airbag? What would need to be tested?

   • Can airbags be reused? Is it important to be able to reuse airbags? Why or why not?

   • Think about the problem for which the airbag was designed. Can you think of a different solution? Make a drawing or diagram to illustrate your idea.

   • What safety issues would need to be considered when designing airbags?

   • What environmental issues would need to be considered when designing airbags?

Can You Explain It?

Name: **Date:**

What happens to the matter when sulfuric acid is added to powdered sugar?

EVIDENCE NOTEBOOK

Refer to the notes in your Evidence Notebook to help you construct an explanation for what you observed when sulfuric acid was added to powdered sugar.

1. State your claim. Make sure your claim fully explains what happens when these two substances are mixed.

2. Summarize the evidence you have gathered to support your claim and explain your reasoning.

Checkpoints

Answer the following questions to check your understanding of the lesson.

3. Students were given a solid Sample A and made these observations. Write physical property or chemical property to indicate what kind of property is being tested.

    Sample A melted when heated to 52 °C. _____

    Sample A floated when dropped into water. _____

    Sample A burned when held in a flame. _____

4. A science class did an experiment in which two substances were mixed. After 15 minutes, everything looked the same, but the students noticed an odor coming from the experiment. What does this likely indicate?

    A. A liquid was formed.

    B. A temperature change occurred.

    C. A chemical reaction occurred.

    D. A physical change occurred.

Use the photo to answer Question 5.

5. Which of the following is the best evidence that a chemical change has taken place?

    A. The apple is smaller in size after cutting.

    B. The apple is turning brown.

    C. The apple has changed shape.

Use the photo to answer Questions 6 and 7.

6. Two metal samples are each placed in a beaker containing the same solution. What evidence indicates that a chemical reaction is taking place in one of the beakers? Circle all that apply.

    A. A gas is being given off.

    B. There is a change in color.

    C. The solution is clear and colorless.

    D. Bubbles are forming.

7. Based on what you observe in the beakers, which of the following statements is true?

    A. Chemical reactions can always be seen.

    B. The two samples of metal are different substances.

    C. Chemical reactions are unpredictable.

    D. New substances are formed in each beaker.

Interactive Review

Complete this section to review the main concepts of the lesson.

Using a systems approach to examining phenomena allows matter and energy to be tracked through chemical changes and through Earth's systems.

A. Describe how analyzing the inputs and outputs of a system can help you to determine what occurred in the system.

Physical properties and chemical properties are used to identify a substance.

B. Explain the difference between a physical property and a chemical property and give at least one example of each.

Physical changes do not form new substances but chemical reactions do.

C. Explain the changes that happen in a chemical reaction in terms of atoms.

The products of a chemical reaction have different properties than the reactants.

D. How can you gather evidence to determine whether a chemical reaction has taken place?

Chemical Equations Model Chemical Reactions

When copper sulfate reacts with ammonia, a solid precipitate forms and the solution color changes to deep blue.

Explore First

Writing Formulas Gather ten small items. Divide them into at least two groups. Describe the items in each group using symbols or numbers, but not words. Trade items and written descriptions of the groups with a partner to see if you can replicate one another's groups. How well were you able to communicate your groups to one another?

Go online to view the digital version of the Hands-On Lab for this lesson and to download additional lab resources.

CAN YOU EXPLAIN IT?

How does this chemical equation explain what happens when copper reacts with silver nitrate?

$$Cu + 2AgNO_3 \rightarrow Cu(NO_3)_2 + 2Ag$$

When a copper wire is placed in a solution of silver nitrate, copper nitrate and silver metal form.

Explore Online

1. Based on the photos, what do you think happens when copper reacts with silver nitrate?

2. What do you think the letters, numbers, and arrow represent in the chemical equation?

 EVIDENCE NOTEBOOK As you explore the lesson, gather evidence to help you account for the matter that is rearranged in a chemical reaction.

Using Chemical Formulas

Students connected blocks together in three different combinations. They labeled each group with a code to describe how it was built.

Each code represents the group of blocks above it.

R₂   BR₂   YR₄

3. Explain how the code describes each group of blocks in the images above.

Chemical Formulas

You and everything around you, including air, water, your desk, and your clothes, are made of chemical substances. These substances are made of the atoms of chemical elements combined with one another in different ways.

Think about the code used to show the combinations of blocks. How could a similar code be used to represent a chemical substance? Each element has a one-, two-, or three-letter chemical symbol associated with it. A combination of chemical symbols and numbers that is used to represent a single unit of a substance is known as a **chemical formula**. For many substances, this single unit is a molecule. A molecule is a specific group of atoms held together by chemical bonds. In other substances, the single unit is part of a larger, repeating pattern of atoms. The chemical formula shows the exact atoms in each molecule or unit.

In any pure substance containing atoms of different elements, the atoms are always present in the same ratio. In other words, a chemical formula shows the relative numbers of atoms of each kind in a chemical compound.

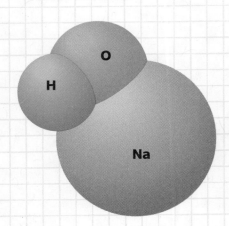

Sodium hydroxide (NaOH) is made up of a sodium atom (Na), an oxygen atom (O), and a hydrogen atom (H).

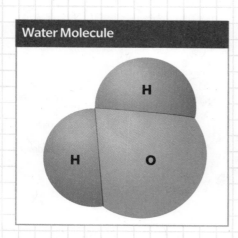

Water Molecule

H

H   O

4. The chemical formula for water is H_2O. Explain how this chemical formula describes the model of a water molecule shown in this diagram.

A chemical formula uses chemical symbols of the elements that make up the substance. A *subscript,* a number below and to the right of the symbol, shows how many atoms of that element there are. If there is no subscript, then one atom of that element is present.

5. Write the chemical formula to identify each model shown.

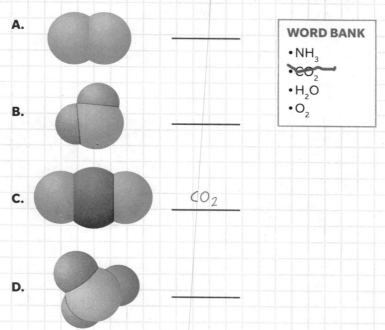

A. _____

B. _____

C. __CO$_2$__

D. _____

WORD BANK
- NH$_3$
- ~~CO$_2$~~
- H$_2$O
- O$_2$

Chemical Formula of Sulfuric Acid

A molecule of sulfuric acid is made up of 2 hydrogen atoms, 1 sulfur atom, and 4 oxygen atoms.

symbol H_2SO_4 subscript

Sometimes a formula includes a group of symbols in parentheses. Symbols in parentheses represent atoms that are held together as a group within the compound. Subscripts outside the parentheses show the number of groups there are in the compound. For example, the chemical formula $Al_2(SO_4)_3$ describes a compound that contains 2 aluminum atoms, 3 sulfur atoms, and 12 oxygen atoms.

6. How many atoms of each element are in the compound described by this chemical formula?

$$(CH_3)_2N$$

Each molecule of the compound has ___2___ atom(s) of carbon (C), _____ atom(s) of hydrogen (H), and _____ atom(s) of nitrogen (N).

7. The chemical formula below describes the model shown in the diagram, but a subscript is missing. Write the subscript. Then write numbers to show how many atoms of each element are in the formula.

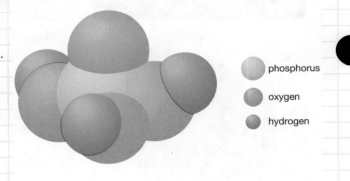

phosphorus

oxygen

hydrogen

H₃PO ☐

The chemical formula shows there is (are):

_____ atom(s) of hydrogen

_____ atom(s) of phosphorus

_____ atom(s) of oxygen

Analyze the Chemical Formulas of Minerals

8. Minerals are natural substances that form as a result of processes in the rock cycle. Most minerals consist of repeating units of atoms or groups of atoms. The chemical formula given for each mineral describes its composition. Write numbers in the blanks below each photo to show the number of atoms of each element that make up a unit of the mineral.

hematite: Fe_2O_3

halite: NaCl

pyrite: FeS_2

A. __2__ iron (Fe),
__3__ oxygen (O)

B. _____ sodium (Na),
_____ chlorine (Cl)

C. _____ iron (Fe),
_____ sulfur (S)

diamond: C

grossular: $Ca_3Al_2(SiO_4)_3$

malachite: $Cu_2CO_3(OH)_2$

D. _____ carbon (C)

E. _____ calcium (Ca),
_____ aluminum (Al),
_____ silicon (Si),
_____ oxygen (O)

F. _____ copper (Cu),
_____ carbon (C),
_____ oxygen (O),
_____ hydrogen (H)

Analyzing Chemical Equations

During a chemical reaction, new substances form. Atoms grouped together in molecules or chemical units in the reactants rearrange and form different molecules or units in the products. The products of the chemical reaction have properties that are different from the reactants, because the molecules that make up the products are different from those in the reactants.

The changes in these robots model the kinds of changes that happen in a chemical reaction.

9. Explain what is happening in the image. How are the changes in the robots like a chemical reaction?

10. **Draw** Make your own drawing to model reactants rearranging and forming new products.

Chemical Equations

Chemical formulas model chemical substances. A **chemical equation** uses chemical formulas to model what happens in a chemical reaction. It shows how the reactants change and form the products of the reaction. The way a chemical equation is written is similar to that of a mathematical equation.

On the left side of a chemical equation, one or more chemical formulas are shown, separated by addition signs. Those formulas are followed by an arrow pointing to the right. This arrow indicates the direction of the reaction. Then one or more different chemical formulas are shown on the right side of the equation. The formulas for the reactants are to the left of the arrow, and the formulas for the products are to the right.

11. Look at the chemical equation below. There is a number in the chemical equation that is not a subscript. What do you think the number 2 on the right side of the chemical equation represents?

$$H_2 + Cl_2 \rightarrow 2HCl$$

In a chemical equation, a *coefficient* is a number placed in front of a chemical formula to show how many molecules of the substance are represented in the chemical equation. In the reaction shown above, the coefficient of HCl is 2, because two molecules of hydrogen chloride are formed in the reaction for every one molecule of H_2 and Cl_2.

The Electrolysis of Water

When an electric current passes through water, the water breaks down into hydrogen and oxygen. The stable products of this reaction are molecules of hydrogen gas and oxygen gas, which are both composed of two of each atom. To model this reaction correctly, the chemical equation shows hydrogen and oxygen as the gas molecules H_2 and O_2. The coefficients of the water and of the hydrogen gas are 2. Only one molecule of oxygen is produced, so no coefficient appears in front of the chemical formula for the oxygen gas.

$$2H_2O \longrightarrow 2H_2 + O_2$$

A Chemical Equation

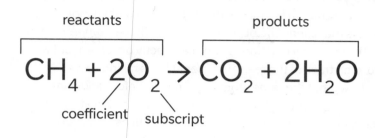

reactants   products

$$CH_4 + 2O_2 \rightarrow CO_2 + 2H_2O$$

coefficient   subscript

12. Circle the correct word to make each sentence true.

    A. A chemical *equation / formula* shows both the reactants and the products of a chemical reaction.

    B. The same number of *atoms / substances* are present on both sides of a chemical equation.

    C. The arrow in a chemical equation points to the *products / reactants* .

Use a Model to Write a Chemical Equation

13. Write formulas in the boxes to show the chemical equation for this model of a chemical reaction.

~~Na₂S~~	H_2S
2NaCl	2HCl

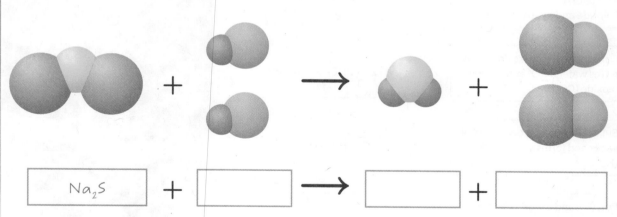

Na_2S + ☐ → ☐ + ☐

Cl   H

Na   S

Chemical Equations and Chemical Reactions

During a chemical reaction, the reactants change into different substances, which are called the products. A chemical equation is a model that represents that change. Models help people learn about things that cannot be observed directly. The rearrangement of atoms that is happening in the chemical reaction cannot be directly observed, but the chemical equation helps to keep track of the rearrangement that is taking place.

A chemical equation shows that the same atoms are present before and after a reaction. Each side of the equation contains the same number and types of atoms. For example, think about the chemical equation that describes how glucose, a type of sugar, is broken down by cells to release energy:

$$C_6H_{12}O_6 + 6O_2 \rightarrow 6CO_2 + 6H_2O$$

This chemical equation models a chemical reaction. The chemical bonds between carbon, hydrogen, and oxygen and between oxygen atoms are broken. New chemical bonds form between carbon and oxygen and between hydrogen and oxygen.

The substances on one side of the arrow are different from the substances on the other side of the arrow. Atoms have recombined into new molecules, which are modeled by the chemical formulas.

The equation shows what happens to the reactants under a certain set of conditions. If an experiment is carried out under the same conditions that were used to determine the equation, the same reactants will always form the same products.

 14. Language SmArts Draw a line to match each description of a chemical reaction with the equation that models it.

Zinc (Zn) and hydrochloric acid (HCl) react and form zinc chloride and hydrogen gas.	$4Fe + 3O_2 \rightarrow 2Fe_2O_3$
Carbonic acid breaks down and forms water (H_2O) and carbon dioxide (CO_2).	$Zn + 2HCl \rightarrow ZnCl_2 + H_2$
Sulfur trioxide reacts with water vapor and forms sulfuric acid (H_2SO_4).	$SO_3 + H_2O \rightarrow H_2SO_4$
Iron (Fe) and oxygen gas react and form iron oxide (rust).	$H_2CO_3 \rightarrow H_2O + CO_2$

When zinc metal is added to hydrochloric acid, a chemical reaction produces hydrogen gas.

Hands-On Lab
Observe a Chemical Reaction

Plan and carry out an investigation to observe what happens when acetic acid and baking soda are mixed. Acetic acid is a liquid ingredient in vinegar, that gives vinegar its distinctive odor and taste.

Procedure and Analysis

STEP 1 Measure an amount of baking soda between 5–10 grams into the bag. Record the amount in the table.

STEP 2 Measure 30 mL of vinegar using the graduated cylinder. Pour the vinegar into the cup.

STEP 3 Place the bag into the pan. Place the cup of vinegar upright into the bag. Be careful not to spill the vinegar. Get as much air out of the bag as possible, and zip the bag closed.

STEP 4 Tip the cup over in the bag. Observe what happens, and record your observations in the table.

Vinegar/Baking Soda Experiment		
Baking soda (g)	Vinegar (mL)	Observations
	30	

STEP 5 The chemical equation for the reaction that you observed is:

sodium bicarbonate + acetic acid → sodium acetate + water + carbon dioxide
    (solid)   (liquid)   (solution)   (liquid)   (gas)

$$NaHCO_3 \;+\; C_2H_4O_2 \;\rightarrow\; NaC_2H_3O_2 \;+\; H_2O \;+\; CO_2$$

How can you use the chemical equation to explain what you observed when you added vinegar (acetic acid) to baking soda (sodium bicarbonate)? Explain what happens to the atoms of the different elements involved in the reaction.

MATERIALS
- bag, sealable plastic, sandwich-size
- baking soda
- cup, 3-ounce, paper or plastic
- graduated cylinder, 50 mL
- pan or tray
- scale
- spoon, plastic
- vinegar

15. How does a chemical equation help to keep track of what happens in a chemical reaction? Record your evidence.

Identify a Chemical Equation

A solution of hydrogen peroxide can be used to kill germs on a small cut. Over time, the peroxide becomes less effective.

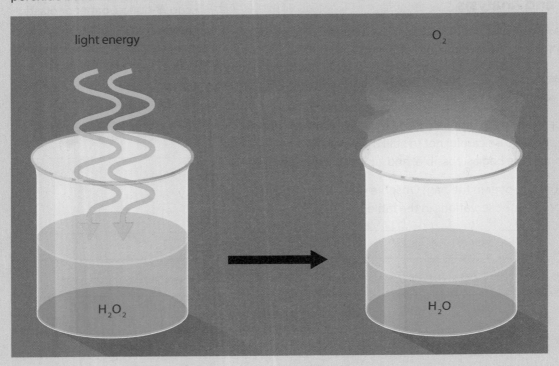

light energy

O_2

H_2O_2

H_2O

16. The image shows that hydrogen peroxide (H_2O_2) changes to oxygen gas and water. What chemical equation models this reaction?

A. $H_2O_2 \rightarrow H_2O$

B. $2H_2O_2 \rightarrow O_2 + 2H_2O$

C. $O_2 + 2H_2O \rightarrow 2H_2O_2$

17. Engineer It A packaging engineer is designing a container to hold hydrogen peroxide. The engineer knows that light speeds up the chemical reaction that changes hydrogen peroxide into oxygen and water. How might the engineer use that information when designing the container?

_____

_____

_____

_____

_____

_____

Modeling Chemical Reactions

Any change that produces a new substance, or substances, is a chemical reaction. Chemical reactions occur around you all of the time. Some reactions, such as a log burning in a campfire, occur quickly and are easy to observe. Some reactions, such as the reactions that cause a green banana to ripen over several days, are much slower. Other reactions are harder to observe, such as the formation of ozone in the atmosphere.

18. In some chemical reactions, such as photosynthesis, several different compounds take part in the reaction. How do you think that the atoms present at the end of this kind of reaction compare to the atoms present at the beginning of the reaction? Explain.

In the green parts of trees, the chemical reaction photosynthesis uses energy from the sun to convert carbon dioxide and water into sugar and oxygen.

The Law of Conservation of Matter

Chemical reactions do not always produce a visible product. For example, one product of photosynthesis, oxygen, cannot be observed by looking at a leaf. Scientists have measured the amount of carbon dioxide and water that react during photosynthesis. When they compared the mass of reactants and the mass of oxygen and plant material produced, they confirmed that the reactants and the products have the same mass.

The **law of conservation of matter** states that matter cannot be created or destroyed in ordinary chemical or physical changes. During any ordinary chemical or physical change, the total mass of the substances involved in the change is the same before and after the change. Matter is conserved during chemical reactions because atoms are conserved. The new substances formed during a chemical reaction are made up of exactly the same atoms as the atoms of substances that reacted. Because the same atoms are present before and after the reaction, the mass of the reactants is the same as the mass of the products.

19. How do you think a chemical equation shows that matter is being conserved?

Balanced Chemical Equations Model the Conservation of Matter

Because a chemical equation is a model of a chemical reaction, the equation must show that the number of atoms does not change during the reaction. A chemical equation is *balanced* when it has the same number of each type of atom on both sides of the equation.

The fact that chemical equations have the same number and types of atoms on both sides of the equation demonstrates the law of conservation of matter.

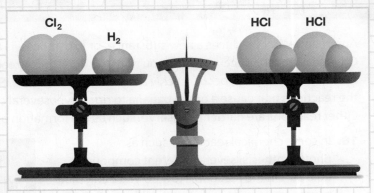

When H_2 and Cl_2 react and form 2HCl, the same number and types of atoms are in the reactants and in the products. The two sides balance.

Balanced Chemical Equations

Hydrogen and chlorine can combine and form hydrogen chloride, as shown in the diagram and modeled by this chemical equation:

$$H_2 + Cl_2 \rightarrow 2HCl$$

20. If the reactants contain one chlorine molecule, do you know how many chlorine atoms will be in the product? Include conservation of matter in your explanation.

21. How do you think subscripts and coefficients help to tell whether a chemical equation is balanced?

You can determine whether a chemical equation is balanced by comparing the number of atoms of each element on both sides of the arrow. Every element must have the same number of atoms in the reactants and in the products for the equation to be balanced. As you count atoms in a chemical formula, remember that the subscript following a symbol tells you the number of atoms of that element present in one molecule or unit of a substance. If a coefficient is in front of a chemical formula, multiply the number of atoms of each element in that formula by the coefficient. For example, if an equation includes the term $2H_2O$, then 4 hydrogen atoms and 2 oxygen atoms are present.

The Conservation of Matter

A chemical equation is a model of what happens during a chemical reaction. It shows what reactants are changed and what products form. Because every chemical reaction follows the law of conservation of matter, the chemical equation must also demonstrate that law.

When a chemical equation is balanced, all matter on one side of the equation is also shown on the other side of the equation. The equation correctly models the chemical reaction by showing that matter is conserved.

Model a Balanced Chemical Equation

22. As methane burns, it reacts with oxygen and forms carbon dioxide and water. The balanced chemical equation below models this chemical reaction. Examine each molecule represented in the chemical equation. Write the numbers of each type of atom in the reactants and products. Compare the numbers when you are finished.

$$CH_4 \ + \ 2O_2 \ \longrightarrow \ CO_2 \ + \ 2H_2O$$

Reactant side

Product side

_____ C atom(s)   _____ C atom(s)

_____ H atom(s)   _____ H atom(s)

_____ O atom(s)   _____ O atom(s)

23. Act Work with a group to demonstrate the law of conservation of matter by acting out this chemical equation:

$$CH_4 + 2O_2 \rightarrow CO_2 + 2H_2O$$

 EVIDENCE NOTEBOOK

24. How do balanced chemical equations help to account for everything that happens in a chemical reaction? Record your evidence.

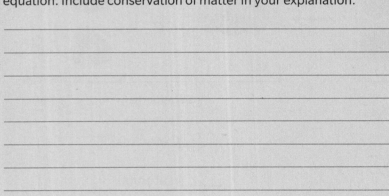

25. **Do the Math** Compare the number of atoms of each element on both sides of each chemical equation. Write *balanced* or *not balanced* to describe each equation.

A. $C_2H_6 + 5O_2 \rightarrow 2CO_2 + 3H_2O$ _____

B. $3CO + Fe_2O_3 \rightarrow 2Fe + 3CO_2$ _____

C. $H_2SO_4 + 2NaOH \rightarrow Na_2SO_4 + 2H_2O$ _____

D. $2AgNO_3 + CaCl_2 \rightarrow 2AgCl + Ca(NO_3)_2$ _____

Evaluate a Chemical Equation

The photo shows that when a clear, colorless solution of lead nitrate is added to a clear, colorless solution of sodium iodide, a yellow solid, lead iodide, forms.

lead nitrate	+	**sodium iodide**	→	**lead iodide**	+	**sodium nitrate**
(solution)		**(solution)**		**(solid)**		**(solution)**
Pb(NO$_3$)$_2$	**+**	**NaI**	**→**	**PbI$_2$**	**+**	**NaNO$_3$**

26. Explain how the equation shown is not currently a balanced equation. Include conservation of matter in your explanation.

_____

_____

_____

_____

_____

_____

_____

_____

27. A student proposed that the balanced chemical equation for this reaction is:

$$Pb(NO_3)_2 + 2NaI \rightarrow PbI_2 + 2NaNO_3$$

Determine whether this is a correctly balanced equation and give evidence for your conclusion.

_____

_____

_____

_____

_____

_____

_____

_____

_____

Continue Your Exploration

Name: _____ Date: _____

Check out the path below or go online to choose one of the other paths shown.

Balancing
a Chemical
Equation

- **People in Science**
- **Chemistry in the Kitchen**
- **Hands-On Labs** 👋
- **Propose Your Own Path**

Go online to choose one of these other paths.

If you know the reactants and the products of a chemical reaction, you can write a balanced chemical equation. You can model balancing a chemical reaction by using parts of an object that combine to form a complete object.

As in a balanced chemical equation, all of the parts on the left are shown in the bike on the right.

1. To build a bicycle, you need to start with the number of each part needed for the finished bicycle. A word description for constructing a bicycle could be written as:

frame + wheels + seat + pedals → bicycle

With a partner, write a "balanced equation" for a bicycle. Use F, W, S, and P as symbols for the "reactants." Use subscripts and coefficients to balance the bicycle equation. Include the formula for the finished bicycle.

Continue Your Exploration

To balance a chemical equation, change the coefficients to balance each type of atom. Subscripts are part of the chemical formula and cannot be changed.

$$C + O_2 \longrightarrow CO$$

C = 1   O = 2   C = 1   O = 1

Count the atoms in the reactants and in the product. There are more oxygen atoms in the reactants than in the product. There are two oxygen atoms in the reactants, so you need two oxygen atoms in the product.

$$2C + O_2 \longrightarrow 2CO$$

C = 2   O = 2   C = 2   O = 2

In order to have two oxygen atoms in the product, place a coefficient 2 in front of CO. Now the oxygen atoms balance, but the carbon atoms do not. Placing the coefficient 2 in front of the C reactant balances the equation.

2. Count the atoms of each element in the reactants and product in the unbalanced chemical equation. Write the numbers in the blanks below the model.

$$H_2 + O_2 \longrightarrow H_2O$$

H = _____ O = _____ → H = _____ O = _____

3. To balance the number of each type of atom, place coefficients in front of the appropriate chemical formulas. Then sketch the products and reactants, showing the correct number of molecules of each. Write the number of hydrogen and oxygen atoms in the reactants and products for the balanced reaction.

_____ H_2 + _____ O_2 → _____ H_2O

→

H = _____ O = _____ → H = _____ O = _____

4. **Collaborate** Work with a partner. Choose one of the unbalanced chemical equations shown. Find the coefficients needed to balance the equation and model the balanced equation by sketching the products and reactants. Present your sketch to the class and explain how it shows the balanced chemical equation.

$Al + O_2 \rightarrow Al_2O_3$	$Na + H_2O \rightarrow NaOH + H_2$

Can You Explain It?

Name: _____

Date: _____

How does this chemical equation explain what happens when copper reacts with silver nitrate?

$$Cu + 2AgNO_3 \rightarrow Cu(NO_3)_2 + 2Ag$$

Explore Online

EVIDENCE NOTEBOOK

Refer to the notes in your Evidence Notebook to help you construct an explanation for the solid that forms when a copper wire is placed in a silver nitrate solution.

1. State your claim. Make sure your claim fully describes how the chemical equation explains what happens when copper reacts with silver nitrate.

2. Summarize the evidence you have gathered to support your claim and explain your reasoning.

Checkpoints

Answer the following questions to check your understanding of the lesson.

Use the model to answer Question 3.

3. This model shows a single unit of a compound containing several elements. What is the chemical formula for the substance?

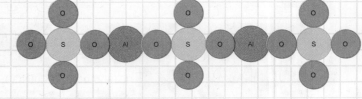

 A. Al_2SO_4

 B. $Al_2(SO_3)_4$

 C. $Al_2(SO_4)_3$

 D. $(AlO)_2(SO_4)_3$

Use the photo to answer Questions 4–5.

4. Zinc and hydrochloric acid are combined in a test tube. What can you conclude about the chemical reaction taking place? Circle all that apply.

 A. The mass of the products is exactly the same as the mass of the reactants.

 B. At least one new product formed is a gas.

 C. Molecules are changing into different molecules.

 D. Atoms are changing into different atoms.

5. The photo shows the reaction between zinc and hydrochloric acid that forms zinc chloride and hydrogen gas. Which of these is a correctly balanced equation that models the reaction?

 A. $Zn + HCl \rightarrow ZnCl_2 + H_2$

 B. $Zn + 2HCl \rightarrow ZnCl_2 + 2H_2$

 C. $Zn + 2HCl \rightarrow ZnCl_2 + H_2$

 D. $Zn + 4HCl \rightarrow ZnCl_2 + 2H_2$

---

6. What is shown by this balanced chemical equation? Select all that apply.

$$H_2 + Cl_2 \rightarrow 2HCl$$

 A. The atoms in the original substances regroup and form a different substance.

 B. The product is a new substance made up of different atoms than the reactants.

 C. The total number of atoms changes in the reaction.

 D. The same atoms are present before and after the reaction.

 E. Matter is conserved.

7. How many oxygen (O) atoms are involved in this chemical reaction?

$$2Fe(OH)_3 \rightarrow Fe_2O_3 + 3H_2O$$

 A. 2

 B. 3

 C. 6

 D. 12

Interactive Review

Complete this section to review the main concepts of the lesson.

A chemical formula is a model of a molecule or unit of a substance.

A. What information about a molecule can you determine from its chemical formula?

A chemical equation models what happens in a chemical reaction. It shows how the substances that are reacting change and form the products of the reaction.

B. Explain how a chemical equation shows that the reactants change and form the products.

The law of conservation of matter states that matter is not created or destroyed in ordinary chemical or physical changes.

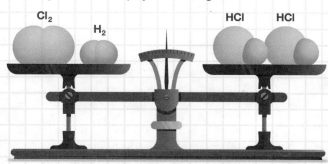

C. How does a balanced chemical equation show that a chemical reaction obeys the law of conservation of matter?

Using Thermal Energy in a Device

As the chemical reactions of the bonfire proceed, the air around the fire becomes hot.

Explore First

Measuring Changes in Energy Measure the temperature of a small glass of water. Place several ice cubes into the glass of water and measure the temperature again after several minutes. Is the ice absorbing or releasing energy? Mix some of the powdered laundry detergent into a small amount of water and measure the temperature. Is this chemical process absorbing or releasing energy?

CAN YOU EXPLAIN IT?

How can a device warm food without using fire or electricity?

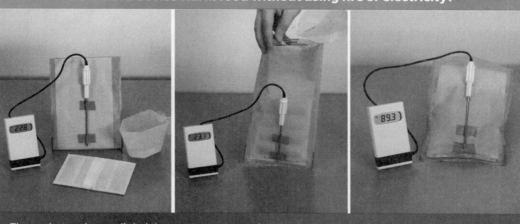

These photos show a digital thermometer measuring the temperature of a flameless heater. Flameless heaters produce energy for cooking without flames or electricity. This heater contains a mixture of iron and magnesium. Once water is added to the heater, the heater begins to warm quickly. A bag of food can be warmed by putting it inside the heater.

Explore Online

1. Observe the photos. What could be occurring inside the device to release thermal energy for cooking?

 EVIDENCE NOTEBOOK As you explore the lesson, gather evidence to help explain how a device could warm food without using fire or electricity.

Exploring Systems and Energy Flow

When you shoot a basketball, kinetic energy from your hand is transferred to the ball. Thermal energy can also be transferred between objects. Think about what happens when you touch a warm pan. How do you know that the pan is warm? Thermal energy from the pan is transferred to your hand. You experience this energy transfer as a feeling of warmth.

2. The hot metal in the photo cools quickly and soon stops glowing. What happens to the energy as the metal parts cool?

During the production of steel goods, the metal becomes so hot that it glows. After each piece of metal is removed from the furnace, it begins to cool and to glow less brightly.

Energy Flow in Systems

A system is a set of interacting parts. Systems can include matter, energy, and information. By grouping a set of related parts or events into a system, scientists and engineers can study how matter and energy behave.

A system can have inputs (things that enter the system) and outputs (things that leave the system). Inputs and outputs can be matter, energy, or information. New matter or energy cannot be created or destroyed. Instead, matter and energy can only be transformed into new forms or move in or out of the system. To accurately model a system, you must understand the inputs and outputs of that system. You also have to understand the flow of matter, energy, and information through the system.

For example, an automobile engine uses energy to make a car move. The inputs of the system include gasoline and air. When gasoline and air enter the engine system, they react with one another. The chemical energy released by the gasoline-air reaction is converted into thermal energy and then kinetic energy by the engine. The kinetic energy is an output of the engine system and is used to move the car. By tracing the flow of energy, you can understand how the system functions.

3. Use the temperatures of the water, the metal object, and the air to explain the flow of thermal energy in this system. What do the arrows show?

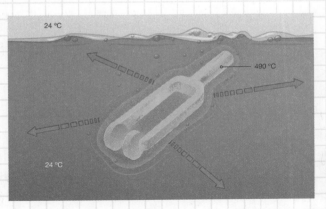

24 °C

490 °C

24 °C

4. Why do the contents of the ice chest in the photo stay cold even though the air around the chest is warm?

  A. Thermal energy flows from the ice to the drink containers.

  B. Thermal energy flows from the drink containers to the ice chest.

  C. The ice chest accelerates the flow of thermal energy to the environment.

  D. The ice chest slows the flow of thermal energy from the environment to the ice and drinks.

The ice chest and its contents can be studied as a system.

Types of Energy Transfer

All matter is made up of tiny particles that are in constant motion. The particles of matter that make up an object move faster when the object is warm than when the object is cold. When thermal energy flows from one object to another, it always flows from the warmer object to the cooler object. As a result, the motion of the particles in the two objects changes. The thermal energy being transferred is known as **heat**. While heat will always move from a warmer object to a colder object, the way this energy is transferred is not always the same. Thermal energy can be transferred between objects through conduction, convection, or radiation.

Conduction, Convection, and Radiation

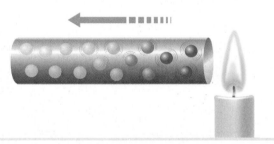

Conduction Thermal energy is transferred between particles through conduction. In this example, the candle is warming one end of the metal bar. The particles in the metal bar start to move faster as they gain more thermal energy. As the particles move faster, they bump into each other and transfer thermal energy through the metal rod.

Convection Thermal energy is transferred throughout liquids and gases through convection. In this example, the candle is heating the box. As air in the box warms, the air particles begin to move faster, and the air becomes less dense. The colder, denser air sinks and pushes up the warmer air. This movement transfers thermal energy through liquids and gases.

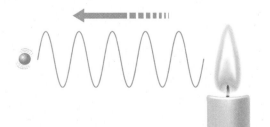

Radiation Radiation is the transfer of energy through electromagnetic waves. In this example, the candle produces infrared radiation. This radiation travels through air. As the radiation is absorbed by particles, it is converted into thermal energy. Radiation can also travel through empty space, which is how thermal energy is transferred from the sun to Earth.

5. The airless vacuum of space is extremely cold, but objects in space do not cool nearly as fast as you might expect. Which statement most likely explains this?

A. Objects in space are already cold, so they do not transfer thermal energy.

B. There is no matter in space to transfer thermal energy to by conduction or convection.

C. Convection carries thermal energy from the sun to objects in space and keeps them warm.

D. Radiation does not occur in space because of the lack of air.

Specially designed suits protect astronauts from the cold and airless space around them.

Model Energy Movement

If you want to understand a device that uses energy, it is important to know how energy will move through the device and any system that the device could be part of. You can map energy flows with arrows to visualize how energy flows through any system.

6. Show how thermal energy would flow through this system. Draw arrows to show the direction of thermal energy flow.

EVIDENCE NOTEBOOK

7. How would the energy flow in a device that warms food without using a flame or electricity? Record your evidence.

© Houghton Mifflin Harcourt Publishing Company • Image Credits: (t) ©NASA

Analyzing Energy in Chemical Processes

Thermal energy is not the only form of energy. Many systems produce thermal energy when a different form of energy is transformed into thermal energy. For example, pavement can feel hot in the summer, because it absorbs energy from the sun's radiation. Other forms of energy that can be changed into thermal energy include chemical, kinetic, and electrical energy.

Explore
Online

Energy Changes in a Hand Warmer

When a small tab in this hand warmer is bent, the sodium acetate inside the hand warmer starts to form crystals. As the crystals form, the sodium acetate releases thermal energy.

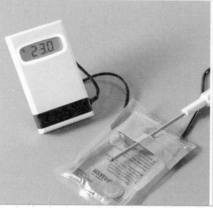

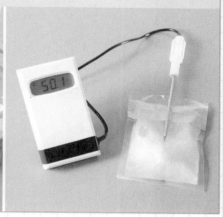

8. Which type of energy is likely changed into thermal energy in this hand warmer?

A. electromagnetic energy

B. electrical energy

C. chemical energy

D. gravitational potential energy

Energy and Chemical Processes

One way that energy can be transformed is through chemical processes. Chemical processes include chemical reactions in which the identity of matter changes, and physical changes such as a change of state or the dissolution of a solid in a liquid. Chemical processes can transform the energy stored in chemical bonds or in the arrangement of molecules into thermal energy.

Most chemical processes involve a change in energy. Some processes, such as melting ice cubes, absorb thermal energy. Other processes, like the burning of paper, release thermal energy. The change in thermal energy will depend on the change in the energy stored in the chemical bonds or molecular structures. If a large amount of a solid melts, the amount of thermal energy absorbed will be larger than if a small amount of the solid melts.

The temperature of the steel wool increased from 20.6 °C to 26.5 °C when the iron in the steel wool rusted. Vinegar was used to accelerate this normally slow reaction.

Explore Online

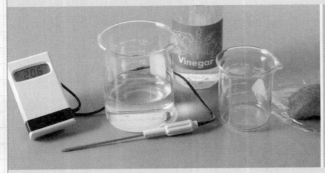

The temperature of this solution dropped from −0.8 °C to −8.0 °C when the rock salt was dissolved in the water.

9. Draw a line connecting the chemical processes shown in the photos to the change in thermal energy that occurs during the process.

| iron rusting | absorbs thermal energy |

| salt dissolving in water | releases thermal energy |

Rates of Energy Transformation

Chemical processes do not all transform energy at the same rate. The rate of energy transformation depends on the type of chemical process. A fire releases thermal energy very quickly. Inside a muscle, a similar chemical reaction releases the energy that the muscle needs to move. This process transforms chemical energy into thermal energy at a slower rate than a fire does. The rate of energy transformation also depends on how quickly a chemical process occurs. A candle burning quickly will release energy faster than a candle that is barely burning. The muscles of a hamster running on a wheel will release energy faster than those of a sleeping hamster. Both the chemical process and the rate of the chemical process affect how quickly energy is transformed in a given situation.

EVIDENCE NOTEBOOK

10. How might the rates of energy transformation affect how the flameless heater is able to warm objects? Record your evidence.

Do the Math
Analyze Thermal Energy

Two things must be considered when you use a chemical process to release thermal energy. One factor is the amount of chemical energy that a process can transform into thermal energy. This can be measured as the number of joules of energy produced by one unit of reactant. The second factor to consider is how quickly the process releases energy. This rate is the number of units of reactants that react per second.

This table shows the amount of energy released when one unit of each substance combines with oxygen in a combustion reaction. Combustion reactions usually involve a fire or explosion.

Reactant	kJ/unit Released in combustion
hydrogen	286
ethanol	1,371
propane	2,219

11. Which reactant releases the most energy when a single unit is combusted?

12. In each sentence, choose the number that represents the correct answer.

A. Under certain conditions, 6 units of hydrogen will burn in 1 second. This process releases energy at a rate of 286 / 572 / 1,716 kJ per second.

B. Under the same conditions, 1 unit of ethanol will burn in 1 second. This process releases energy at a rate of 686 / 1,371 / 8,226 kJ per second.

C. Under these conditions, hydrogen / ethanol will release more energy in 1 second.

13. Which of the following factors affect how quickly burning hydrogen, ethanol, and propane will release energy? Choose all that apply.

A. whether the reactant burned

B. the number of reactants in the chemical process

C. the time when the chemical process takes place

D. the amount of reactant burned per second

Factors That Affect Reaction Rates

In order to use a chemical process to control the flow of thermal energy, you must understand how the process works. Knowing the type of process and how to control the rate at which it takes place allows you to adjust the rate of the process. There are many factors that control the rates of chemical processes. The diagrams show some important factors that can be used to control the rates of chemical reactions.

Chemical Reaction Rate Variables

 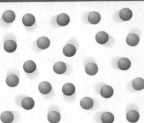 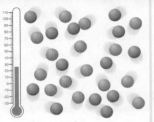 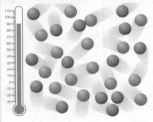

Concentration Increasing the concentration of reactants can cause a reaction to occur faster. This happens because increasing the concentration means that the reactants come into contact more often.

Temperature Increasing temperature can cause the reaction to occur faster. When particles have more energy, they move faster. The faster particles are moving, the more often they will come into contact with each other.

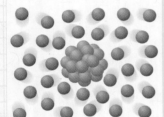  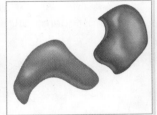 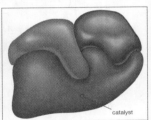

catalyst

Surface Area Increasing the surface area of a solid reactant increases the reaction rate because the increased surface area allows more particles of the other reactants to collide with the particles of the solid.

Catalysts Catalysts are materials that increase the rate of a chemical reaction by bringing together reactants. The catalyst itself is not used up or changed very much.

Chemical reactions are only one type of chemical process. The rates of other chemical processes, such as dissolution or state changes, can be affected by some of these same factors. For instance, temperature can affect how quickly a solid dissolves in a liquid. The surface area of a solid can affect how quickly the solid changes state to a liquid. Not all chemical processes will be affected in the same way by these factors and some chemical processes may be affected by other factors as well. For instance, a catalyst may not have much effect on how quickly a liquid boils, but elevation of the liquid above sea level will.

14. Which statement correctly explains how increasing the reaction rate affects the thermal energy of a chemical reaction?

   A. It increases the total amount of energy absorbed or released.

   B. It decreases the total amount of energy absorbed or released.

   C. It increases the rate at which energy is transformed, but not the amount of energy of the reaction.

   D. It increases the total amount of energy transformed, but not the rate at which energy is transformed.

Analyze a Chemical Process

Ammonium chloride is a white crystalline compound. When crystals of ammonium chloride are mixed with water, they dissolve to form a solution. As the crystals dissolve, the solution absorbs thermal energy. The temperature of the solution will decrease. The temperature of the solution can decrease enough to cause water on the outside of the container to freeze.

15. Draw Make a sketch that shows how thermal and chemical energy interact in the system made up of water and ammonium chloride.

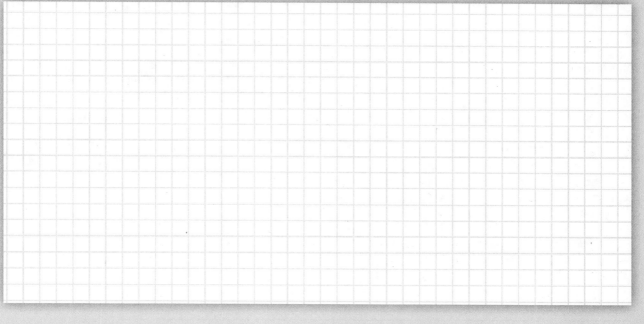

16. Describe the flow of energy shown in your sketch of the water and ammonium chloride system.

_____

_____

_____

_____

_____

_____

_____

Designing a Cold Pack

When you twist an ankle or sprain your wrist, an ice pack can help reduce the swelling and pain from the injury. If you are hiking in the wilderness or playing on a ball field, ice might not be easy to find. In that case, how could you treat your hurt ankle? A chemical cold pack might be just what you need. You can carry the cold pack with you. You do not need a cooler or ice to store it. When you do need a cold pack, you just start the chemical process inside the sealed package. Within a few seconds, the pack will begin to cool.

To keep swelling down, treat a sprained ankle as soon as possible.

17. Which of the following would be included in the criteria for a chemical cold pack that you could take along on a hike? Choose all that apply.

    A. small and easy to carry

    B. becomes cold quickly when activated

    C. flexible enough to form around injured area

    D. packaging that transfers thermal energy well

Hands-On Lab
Choose a Chemical Process

Test different chemical processes that might be used in a chemical cold pack. Then calculate the temperature changes that occur. Make observations about how each chemical process might behave in a cold pack.

To design a chemical cold pack, determine what characteristics a process should have in order to be a solution to your engineering problem. Think about the criteria and constraints of the problem as you test each process. The cold pack must get cold as a result of a chemical process. The process must occur rapidly so that the cold pack is available when needed.

Procedure

STEP 1 Choose a pair of liquid and solid components from Table 1 at the bottom of the page. Measure 100 mL of the liquid component into a beaker. Measure the temperature of the liquid. Record your measurement in Table 2 on the next page.

STEP 2 Add 10 grams of the solid component to the beaker. Stir the mixture. Record any changes that you observe in Table 1.

STEP 3 After 2 minutes, measure the temperature of the liquid. Record your measurement in Table 2.

STEP 4 Repeat Steps 1–3 with each of the other combinations of materials. Note any observations that might affect the usefulness of each combination.

MATERIALS
- ammonium chloride
- baking soda
- balance
- beakers, 500 mL, (4)
- calcium chloride
- graduated cylinders, 100 mL (2)
- paper towels
- steel wool, fine
- stirrers
- thermometer
- vinegar
- water

Table 1		
Liquid component	Solid component	Observations
vinegar	steel wool	
vinegar	baking soda	
water	calcium chloride	
water	ammonium chloride	

Analysis

STEP 5 Calculate the temperature change that takes place during each chemical process by subtracting the initial temperature from the final temperature. Record your answers in Table 2.

Table 2				
Liquid component	Solid component	Starting temperature (°C)	Ending temperature (°C)	Temperature change (°C)
vinegar	steel wool			
vinegar	baking soda			
water	calcium chloride			
water	ammonium chloride			

STEP 6 Which chemical processes absorbed thermal energy? Select all that apply.

    A. vinegar/steel wool

    B. vinegar/baking soda

    C. water/calcium chloride

    D. water/ammonium chloride

STEP 7 Which process would you choose to use for your instant cold pack? What adjustments to the chemical process, if any, would you make? Include an explanation of the flow of energy in your answer and cite evidence from your observations to justify your reasoning.

© Houghton Mifflin Harcourt Publishing Company

How to Design a Container

After you determine the best chemical process to use for the cold pack, you will design the cold pack itself. For the cold pack to be useful, it must be ready to become cold when you need it. However, the components of the chemical process cannot mix too soon because the process cannot be repeated. You must design a way to keep the two components apart until it is time to use the cold pack. Your design should be one package that is able to keep the two components separate, so that they do not accidentally mix. Your design should also have a way to mix the two components easily, so that you can use the cold pack when you need it.

18. What criteria would apply to the packaging or container in order to make the product useful? Select all that apply.

    A. flexible

    B. brightly colored

    C. keeps components separate during storage

    D. allows easy mixing when needed

19. Draw Make a sketch of a possible design for the device.

20. Explain your sketch and how the components would be separated in your device. How could they be combined easily when needed?

21. Draw Make a sketch of the outside of your device. You may design a name and logo for your device if you like.

Choose a Material

When you choose materials for your device, you must consider how those materials could affect the function of the entire system. The device must be durable and able to form to an injured body part. It should also transfer thermal energy well. The table lists several different materials that you can consider. It shows the thermal conductivity value, which is the rate at which thermal energy passes through a material. Thermal conductivity is higher for materials that transfer thermal energy faster. Other factors may be as important, or even more important, than thermal conductivity.

Material	Thermal conductivity	Characteristics
Aluminum foil	205.00	Flexible, tears easily
Glass	1.05	Rigid, strong, hard, breakable
Polythene	0.33	Flexible, strong, soft
Polystyrene	0.03	Rigid, easily punctured
Rubber	0.13	Flexible, very strong, soft

22. Which material would best meet the criteria and constraints of the cold pack? Would using multiple materials improve your design? Explain your reasoning.

_____

_____

_____

_____

_____

© Houghton Mifflin Harcourt Publishing Company

Continue Your Exploration

Name: _____   Date: _____

Check out the path below or go online to choose one of the other paths shown.

| People in Science | • **Researching Chemical Processes**
 • **Hands-On Labs** 🖐
 • **Propose Your Own Path** | *Go online to choose one of these other paths.* |

Fritz Haber and Carl Bosch, Chemists

Ammonia is an important chemical in many industries and in fertilizer. The Haber-Bosch process was developed to address the need for a renewable source of ammonia. Fritz Haber, a German research chemist, developed the initial process. Haber's process reliably produced ammonia from nitrogen and hydrogen. Carl Bosch, a German industrial chemist, later engineered high-pressure equipment that could mass produce ammonia using Haber's initial process. Both men received Nobel Prizes for their work.

This process was the first industrial chemical process to use high pressure in chemical production. It combines nitrogen with hydrogen under very high pressures and temperatures. An iron catalyst allows the reaction to be carried out at a lower temperature, a still very high 400 °C to 650 °C, than would otherwise be possible.

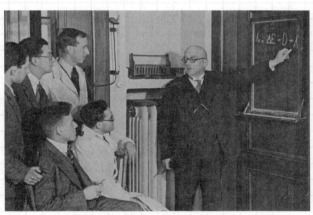

Fritz Haber was a chemical researcher and professor who developed the chemical reaction still used to make ammonia.

Carl Bosch used the engineering design process to develop equipment to produce ammonia on a large scale.

1. How does the Haber-Bosch process demonstrate the connection between science and engineering?

Continue Your Exploration

A Haber-Bosch reactor uses catalysts and a series of pipes to combine nitrogen and hydrogen under high pressure.

2. Haber's original lab reaction worked on a very small scale. Once Bosch began to scale it up, it was apparent that the reaction produced large amounts of thermal energy. Which statement best explains why this might be a problem?

   A. Higher temperature increases the reaction rate.

   B. Too much thermal energy could damage equipment.

   C. Chemical processes work better when there is less thermal energy.

   D. Catalysts are never useful when the temperature is high.

3. High temperatures can damage equipment. Which of the following are ways to keep a Haber-Bosch reactor from getting too hot? Choose all that apply.

   A. Insulate the outside of the reaction vessel.

   B. Perform the reaction in a system that transfers thermal energy well.

   C. Surround the reaction vessel with flowing water that absorbs thermal energy.

   D. Remove some catalysts from the reaction.

4. **Collaborate** As a team, research ways that chemical industries control thermal energy involved in manufacturing processes. Prepare a report or presentation to describe one method. Use a poster, models, or diagrams to assist your report or presentation.

© Houghton Mifflin Harcourt Publishing Company • Image Credits: ©SZ Photo / Scherl/ Sueddeutsche Zeitung Photo/Alamy

Can You Explain It?

Name: _____   Date: _____

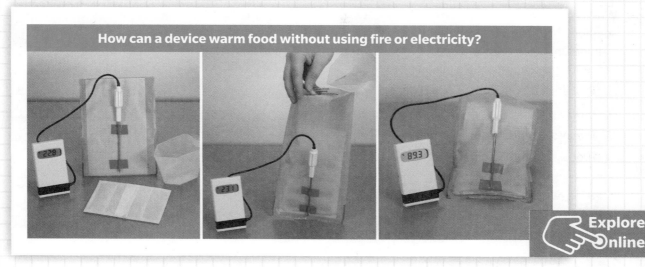

How can a device warm food without using fire or electricity?

 EVIDENCE NOTEBOOK

Refer to the notes in your Evidence Notebook to help you construct an explanation for how thermal energy could be released and transferred in order to warm food in a flameless cooking device.

1. State your claim. Make sure your claim fully explains how a device can warm food without using fire or electricity.

2. Summarize the evidence you have gathered to support your claim and explain your reasoning.

Checkpoints

Answer the following questions to check your understanding of the lesson.
Use the table to answer Question 3.

3. When ammonium chloride is mixed into water to form a solution, the solution absorbs thermal energy. Which process might represent 3 g of ammonium chloride mixed into a certain amount of water, and which process might represent 6 g mixed into the same amount of water?

    A. Process E represents 3 g and Process F represents 6 g.

    B. Process F represents 3 g and Process E represents 6 g.

    C. Process G represents 3 g and Process H represents 6 g.

    D. Process H represents 3 g and Process G represents 6 g.

Process	Temperature change (°C)
E	3.0
F	5.0
G	−4.0
H	−7.0

4. A high-quality sleeping bag will keep you warm even during a winter camping trip high in the mountains. How do you stay warm when the air around you is very cold?

    A. The sleeping bag produces thermal energy that keeps you warm.

    B. The sleeping bag transfers thermal energy from the air to your body.

    C. The sleeping bag slows the transfer of thermal energy produced by your body into the air.

    D. The sleeping bag increases the production of thermal energy by your body.

5. Samples of baking soda and vinegar at room temperature are mixed together. The resulting solution has a lower temperature than the original temperature of the vinegar. Which statement correctly describes how the system could be modified so that thermal energy is absorbed faster?

    A. Decrease the amount of baking soda used.

    B. Increase the concentrations of the chemicals used.

    C. Increase the size of the container used.

    D. Decrease the temperature of the environment so more energy flows away from the solution.

Use the photos to answer Question 6.

6. Which statement correctly describes what is occurring in the photos? Choose all that apply.

    A. The hand warmer is absorbing thermal energy.

    B. The hand warmer is releasing thermal energy.

    C. The hand warmer's temperature increased.

    D. The liquid in the hand warmer underwent a chemical process.

Interactive Review

Complete this page to review the main concepts of the lesson.

Systems can be used to model the flow of energy between objects.

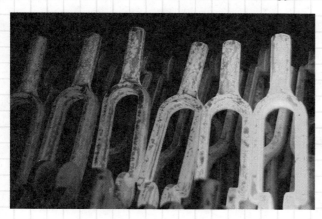

A. Why is it useful to model systems that use energy?

Chemical processes can release or absorb thermal energy.

B. Explain how different factors affect how thermal energy is absorbed or released by a chemical process.

A chemical process can be used in a device designed to release or absorb thermal energy.

C. Describe the process that you would go through when deciding on a chemical reaction to use in a device.

Synthetic Materials Are Made from Natural Resources

The material that makes up these fabrics is ideal for clothing. Fabric can be made with natural or synthetic materials.

Explore First

Categorizing Substances Find at least five different objects in the room and identify what substances they are made of. Categorize each of these objects as being made of either a natural or synthetic substance. Identify where the natural substances came from. How might the synthetic materials have been made?

Go online to view the digital version of the Hands-On Lab for this lesson and to download additional lab resources.

CAN YOU EXPLAIN IT?

How can a plastic kayak be made from oil?

crude oil

The synthetic material that makes up this kayak cannot be harvested or mined. It is made from crude oil, which is found naturally on Earth. Scientists and engineers have developed different types of plastics with different properties. Some synthetic materials make great kayaks, and others make beautiful fabrics.

1. How do the properties of the oil and of the plastic of the kayak differ? What makes the plastic a good choice for kayak material?

2. How do you think oil could be made into a plastic kayak?

 EVIDENCE NOTEBOOK As you explore this lesson, gather evidence to help explain how oil can be made into a plastic kayak.

Analyzing Natural Resources

If you go on a picnic in the park, you are surrounded by nature. Trees, grass, birds, rocks, and water are all parts of nature. The fruit in your picnic basket comes from nature. In fact, many of the materials around you every day come from nature, including materials found inside your classroom. A desk is made by people, but the wood of the desk comes from trees. The metal comes from rocks. The fabric of your cotton clothing is made from cotton plants. Even chalk originally came from nature.

The materials and objects at this picnic are obtained from different sources.

3. What materials do you see in the photo? Which of those materials come from nature?

Natural Resources

Trees are a natural resource. A **natural resource** is a substance, material, object, or source of energy that is found in nature and that is useful or valuable to humans. Humans use natural resources as sources of food and fuel. They may also use them to make other substances or materials. Some resources are used in many ways. Trees are used to produce lumber and paper, and wood from trees is sometimes used as fuel for heating people's homes.

Natural resources may be living things or nonliving things. Plants and animals provide food and materials, such as cotton, wool, and leather. Rocks and ores provide building materials, such as granite and iron. Sources of energy, such as coal, petroleum, natural gas, and sunlight, are also natural resources.

4. Choose an object near you. Explain whether the materials that make up the object are natural resources.

© Houghton Mifflin Harcourt Publishing Company • Image Credits: ©ChesiireCat/iStockPhoto.com

Animals and plants provide food, materials, and fuel. Cows give us meat, milk, and materials for leather. Corn gives us food and materials to make fuel and starch.

Metals come from ores that are mined. Copper is separated from other materials in this ore by chemical reactions and physical processes.

5. Describe how you use two living and two nonliving natural resources every day.

Properties of Natural Resources

Natural resources have physical and chemical properties that make them useful. Some natural resources are used primarily for their physical properties. Copper is a good conductor of electricity and is used to make wire. Granite, a type of rock, is hard and dense. It is used in buildings. Natural resources are even used for their color. Many dyes are made from plants. For example, indigo, a blue dye that gives jeans their color, is made from the indigo plant.

Some natural resources are mainly used for their chemical properties. Fuels such as petroleum, coal, and natural gas are highly flammable. They are used as fuels. Other resources, such as metals, are not flammable. They can be used to build stoves and cookware.

Plant materials, such as grass and the grains stored in these silos, are made of many substances, including cellulose. Cellulose makes plants useful in the manufacturing of paper, fabric, and building materials.

Chemical Makeup of Natural Resources

Natural resources have many different chemical makeups. Most elements occur naturally—from aluminum to gold to uranium. However, very few elements are found in their pure form. Instead, they are combined in different ways in the compounds found in nature. Graphite is a form of pure carbon found in nature. Carbon also combines with other elements, such as oxygen and hydrogen, to make up the huge variety of substances in living things.

Most natural resources are mixtures of substances. Rocks are mixtures of different compounds. Petroleum is a mixture of carbon-based compounds. Plants and animals are made up of many substances. Cellulose is one of the many substances found in plants. It is the main substance in cotton fabric, and it makes wood strong.

Graphite is found naturally. It is soft and feels greasy. It is used to make pencil lead and lubricants.

Natural Resources for Different Uses

The way people use natural resources has changed as technologies and needs have changed. Ancient civilizations made tools from copper, because pure copper was found in nature. They eventually learned to mix copper with other metals to make the harder material, bronze. Today, copper is used to make electrical wire and computer parts.

The resources used to meet needs have also changed. People have used trees for energy and building materials for a long time. Once engines were invented, the use of fossil fuels for energy increased. Wood is still used in building materials, but steel has made taller buildings possible.

A hickory tree is made up of many substances that give it certain physical and chemical properties.

energy

Hickory wood is flammable. When it burns, energy is released.

materials

Hickory wood is strong and hard. It is used for floors because it does not dent or scratch easily.

6. Write some of the chemical and physical properties and uses of each natural resource shown in the photos below.

Natural resource	Properties	Uses
granite		
natural gas		
wool		

Do the Math
Analyze Natural Resource Use

A single natural resource may be used in different ways. Trees are used as building materials, to make paper, for fuel, and for other applications. The way wood is used depends on the type of wood, the size of the tree, and the quality of the wood. Saw mills inspect the properties of the logs before deciding how to process them. On average, saw mills use about 25% of the wood for lumber and other building materials, 25% for paper, 35% for fuel, and 15% for other uses. The percentages may vary from mill to mill depending on the logs that they accept and the way they process the wood.

After being cut down, trees are sent to mills where they are cut and processed into lumber products.

7. A saw mill produces about 28 m³ of dried lumber each day. About 70% of the lumber is cut into boards for use in construction, 25% is used to make thin sheets of wood used in plywood, and 5% is ground into pulp and used for paper products. Fill in the table below with the cubic meters of wood that are turned into each type of material each day.

Lumber produced	70% boards	25% plywood	5% paper
28 m³			

8. It takes about 38 m³ of boards and plywood to build an average-size, single-family home. About how many days will it take for the saw mill to produce enough lumber to build a neighborhood of 100 average-size homes? Show how you found your answer.

Evaluating the Effects of Using Resources

Imagine that you and a friend take a long bike ride. You fill your water bottles and start out on your ride. The day is hot, and you both drink all of your water quickly. You can drink as much water as you want when you get home. But right now your water supply is gone.

9. **Discuss** Think about everything you use in a day, such as water. What are some things that affect how quickly you are able to replace the materials you used?

This bike rider has used up his supply of water to drink.

The Availability of Natural Resources

The more a resource is used, the sooner it will be used up, unless it can be replaced. As people use a resource, its supply decreases. The ability to replace a resource depends on how much of it can be found, grown, mined, or processed. When some resources are used up, no more is available. Other resources are easily replaced. Resources can be categorized by how quickly they can be replaced.

10. Look at the list below. Think about how each resource grows or forms. Determine whether it could be replaced within a human lifetime (quickly) or whether it would take many human lifetimes (slowly).
Write quickly or slowly to describe how fast each resource can be replaced.

A. trees _____
B. cotton ___quickly___
C. petroleum _____
D. fish _____
E. soil _____
F. coal _____

Crop resources, such as the cotton shown here, can be replaced quickly. Quickly may mean a time period as short as a growing season or as long as a human lifetime.

11. The following conditions occurred in a town one summer. Which could negatively affect the replacement rate of the town's water resources? Circle all that apply.

  A. The town put a limit on how often people could water their lawns.

  B. More rain fell than normal.

  C. Temperatures were higher than normal.

  D. Twice as many tourists visited the town than normal.

Nonrenewable Resources

A **nonrenewable resource** is a natural resource that cannot be replaced as quickly as it is used. Rocks and minerals form beneath Earth's surface over millions of years. Coal, petroleum, natural gas, and uranium do not form as quickly as they are used. People cannot control or speed up the geologic processes that form rocks, minerals, or fossil fuels. Therefore, these resources are almost always nonrenewable.

Cassiterite, the main ore of tin, forms in veins of rock.

Renewable Resources

A **renewable resource** is a natural resource that can be replaced at the same rate it is used, or faster. Hydroelectric energy, wind energy, solar energy, and biomass are renewable energy resources. One type of renewable resource is an *inexhaustible* resource. These resources cannot be used up by human activity. Wind and solar energy are inexhaustible renewable resources because the supply of these resources is not affected by human use.

Another type of renewable resource is a *potentially renewable resource.* Air, water, fish, animals, and plants can be renewable material resources, but they must be managed so they do not run out. If they are used too quickly, they may not be able to be replaced. For example, passenger pigeons, such as the one in the photo, were hunted to extinction. Today in some places, there are conservation limits on hunting and fishing. These limits are designed to allow the populations of those species of animals to be maintained. Water can also be a renewable resource, but it must be managed so that it is not polluted or used more quickly than it can be replaced. Water, biomass, and animals are examples of renewable resources that could be used up if not managed.

The passenger pigeon was once the most common bird in North America, numbering 3–5 billion pigeons. Mass hunting led to extinction within 300 years. In 1914, the last passenger pigeon died in the Cincinnati Zoo.

12. Resources that come from living things can be considered either nonrenewable or renewable. Crude oil and corn both were originally living things, but oil is considered nonrenewable while corn is considered renewable. Why is there a difference in how we treat these resources?

© Houghton Mifflin Harcourt Publishing Company • Image Credits: (t) ©repOrter/iStock/Getty Images Plus/Getty Images; (b) ©Science Source

The Cycling of Matter and Energy

Matter and energy naturally cycle through Earth's systems. Living organisms will consume other organisms and move matter and energy through an ecosystem. Nonliving resources move through their own cycles, such as water's evaporating, condensing into clouds, and then raining back to the ground. The time that each of these cycles and processes take affects the availability of different natural resources. For instance, some types of bamboo can grow a foot or more a day. The giant panda, which eats bamboo, can live for over twenty years in the wild. Earth has some cycles that can last seconds and others that last thousands or millions of years.

Natural resources cycle through Earth's systems at varying rates.

Humans can dramatically affect different cycles on Earth. Due to our technology and the number of people on Earth, humans can have wide-ranging impacts on the planet. A farm can disturb how nutrients cycle through an ecosystem. A city dramatically affects the ecosystems and water cycles around it. Humans are able to affect Earth's systems in ways no other organisms can through activities like shipping, mining, and driving cars.

Do the Math
Compare Rates of Renewal

Pine trees are harvested as building material after growing for about 40 years. About 14 acres of pine are needed to build a 1,000 ft² house. About 2 acres of bamboo are needed for the same size house. A bamboo stand regrows and is ready for harvesting in about 5 years.

Complete the equation. Then solve it.

13. About how many times as many acres of pine are needed to produce the same amount of building material as using bamboo?

$x =$ _____ ÷ _____

$x =$ _____

About _____ times as many acres of pine are needed to produce the same amount of building material as using bamboo.

14. About how many harvests of bamboo can be collected during the time it takes to fully grow one pine tree?

$y =$ _____ ÷ _____

$y =$ _____

About _____ harvests of bamboo can be collected in the same time it takes to fully grow one pine tree.

Bamboo is a fast-growing alternative to wood. It can be used as a building and flooring material.

Consequences of Using Natural Resources

A *consequence* is a result that follows naturally from the actions of a person or group. Consequences may be good or bad. They can occur immediately or over a long time. For example: You choose to ignore the alarm clock one morning. You get more sleep, but you arrive late to school and get detention. These are immediate consequences of your decision to sleep later than usual.

15. **Discuss** Imagine that you earn ten dollars for babysitting. You decide to go to the movies with your friends, and spend all of your money on the ticket. What is a positive consequence of this decision? What is a negative consequence of this decision?

The extraction of resources can negatively affect other resources. Offshore drilling for oil can pollute marine environments, which are resources for food and medicine.

Human use of resources results in consequences for people and the environment. Imagine a paper factory near a forest and a river. The paper is made using trees from the forest and water from the river. Paper is an important product, but the processes used to make it pollute the river, the forest, and the air. Also, using river water and trees can degrade and destroy habitats. These negative effects can be reduced by using less paper, recycling paper, using less-polluting processes in the factory, and by replanting trees.

Positive and Negative Consequences

Human use of resources has positive and negative effects on people and on the environment. For example, nuclear power plants provide energy and do not pollute the air. But they produce radioactive wastes that must be handled and stored safely for thousands of years or more.

Management of resources can help reduce negative consequences. For example, clear-cutting is a way of harvesting trees in which every tree in an area is cut down and removed. It destroys forests and increases soil erosion. But selective cutting and replanting allow trees to be used while still conserving forest resources. New energy technologies, such as those that use solar or wind power, reduce human use of nonrenewable fossil fuels.

Resources can be protected. For example, The Pacific Remote Islands Marine National Monument is an area that is protected from practices such as offshore drilling.

Consequences of Resource Use

Wind is an energy resource that does not pollute the environment. It also reduces dependence on fossil fuels.

Road construction cuts through a natural ecosystem. This can interrupt migration patterns and cause animals to cross dangerous roads.

Because resource use can have both positive and negative consequences, choices have to be made about how to use them. A *tradeoff* is a situation that involves giving something up in return for gaining something else. For example, crude oil can be processed into gasoline. The tradeoff is that we gain gasoline so that people can travel, but we lose air quality because the processing and the burning of the gasoline sends pollutants into the air.

16. Give an example of how using soil, trees, or air might result in a tradeoff.

Short-Term and Long-Term Consequences

Human use of resources has both short- and long-term effects on people and on the environment. A short-term effect would last a human lifetime or less. A long-term effect would last longer than a human lifetime. Burning fossil fuels introduces pollutants to the air, including greenhouse gases and chemicals that cause acid rain and affect human health. In the short-term, these pollutants affect air quality and may affect people with asthma and other respiratory conditions. In the long-term, acid rain may cause damage to structures and environments. Greenhouse gases cause a warming of Earth's atmosphere that can last for centuries.

Wetlands are areas with standing water that covers the soil. Wetlands filter pollutants from water before they reach rivers and streams. Many wetlands have been drained or filled in so that crops can be grown or structures can be built. Short-term consequences of wetland loss include increased erosion and chemical pollution of rivers. Fish populations also decrease because wetlands are fish nurseries. Long-term consequences of wetland loss include habitat loss, extinction of organisms, and increased vulnerability of the area to severe weather and climate events.

Examples of Short-Term and Long-Term Consequences

Oil spills from deep-sea drilling can have short-term, negative consequences for wildlife. For example, oil from an oil spill coated this bird's feathers, preventing it from flying. Rescuers washed the bird with dish soap to remove the oil.

Mountaintop removal mining has long-term, negative consequences for the environment. For example, explosives are used to remove rock and soil above this coal deposit. This practice destroys habitats and leaves behind pollutants.

17. Write _S_ to label the event as a *short-term* effect or write _L_ to label the event as a *long-term* effect.

_____ A large, fast-flowing river is cloudy and muddy for a few days after 1000 kilograms of soil are spilled by a barge.

_____ People who live near an oil refinery are advised to avoid outdoor activity for a week after a smokestack filter malfunctions and releases toxic chemicals.

_____ A nuclear energy accident results in a permanent evacuation of a 40-kilometer radius because of radioactive contamination.

_____ An oil spill in the ocean coats penguins' feathers with oil until volunteers can clean them up.

Engineer It

Identify the Effects of an Engineering Solution

An engineering team has developed an idea for a drinking straw that filters out parasites from polluted water.

18. Identify at least one way this engineered solution might affect the health of people in a positive way or a negative way. Explain.

_____

_____

_____

_____

19. Identify at least one way this engineered solution might affect the health of the environment in a positive way or a negative way. Explain.

_____

_____

_____

Investigating Synthetic Materials

Some of the materials that make up many objects around you are not natural materials. If you look around the room, you will see a lot of plastic—in chairs, the parts of pens, eyeglasses, shoes, and even some fabrics. You will not find plastic occurring naturally in the environment. Instead, plastic must be made using chemical reactions.

Many materials that are not plastic are also not natural materials. The bicycle frame in the photo might look like painted metal, but it is much stronger and lighter than metal. Plastic and carbon fibers are mixed together to make a new material. In this case, the new material is made by a physical process and has properties of both plastic and carbon fibers.

A bicycle is made of many kinds of materials. Some are natural materials, and others are made by chemical or physical processes that form a new material.

20. **Discuss** On a separate sheet of paper, make a list of the parts of the bicycle in the photo and the materials that they might be made of. Sort your list into materials that might be natural resources and those that might not be natural resources. With a partner, compare and discuss your lists. Revise your list as you come to an agreement about the types of materials used in the bike. Share your final list with the class.

Synthetic Materials

Many parts of a bicycle are synthetic materials rather than natural materials. **Synthetic materials** are human-made materials that are produced using natural or synthetic materials. Plastics are one type of synthetic material. There are many types of plastic, from the soft plastic that makes up a water bottle to the harder plastic that is used to make eyeglass lenses. Glass and ceramics are also synthetic materials. You will not find clear window glass in nature. Many foods, medicines, and personal care products are synthetic materials or contain synthetic materials. Some fuels, such as biodiesel and ethanol, are synthetic materials as well.

21. Which of the following items are most likely made from synthetic materials: a drinking glass, orange juice, a dinner plate, a paper bag, an insulated lunch bag? Explain your reasoning.

Synthetic materials, such as this nylon, can be made in a lab.

© Houghton Mifflin Harcourt Publishing Company • Image Credits: (t) ©BillionPhotos.com/Fotolia; (b) ©Charles D. Winters/Science Source

Formation of Synthetic Materials

Most synthetic materials are formed through chemical reactions. The reactants may be natural or synthetic substances. The diagram shows the reaction that forms polyethylene, a solid used to make plastic bottles. The reactant is ethylene, a gas made from crude oil. The ethylene molecules join together to form polyethylene, the product. Polyethylene is one of the most common plastics used to make bags. Reactants change into new products in all chemical reactions. Bonds between the atoms break and new bonds form. As a result, the atoms are rearranged to make one or more new products.

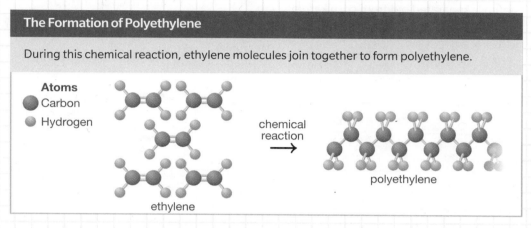

The Formation of Polyethylene

During this chemical reaction, ethylene molecules join together to form polyethylene.

Atoms
- Carbon
- Hydrogen

chemical reaction →

ethylene

polyethylene

22. Act With a group, model how ethylene molecules react to form polyethylene.

Properties of Synthetic Materials

The properties of a pure substance depend on the identity and the arrangement of the atoms that make up the substance. Therefore, the products of a reaction have different chemical and physical properties than the reactants have. Ethylene and polyethylene have different properties because their atoms are arranged differently.

Some synthetic materials, such as composites, are made by mixing together materials to form a new material. Mixing is a physical change. The materials that make up the composite keep their original properties, but the composite material also has new properties. Concrete, plywood, and fiberglass are composites.

23. How do the properties of polyethylene compare to the properties of ethylene?

24. Why do synthetic materials have different properties than the materials used to make them?

EVIDENCE NOTEBOOK

25. How might the substances in oil change into the substances that make up the plastic of a kayak? Record your evidence.

Hands-On Lab
Make a Synthetic Material

Use a chemical reaction to make a ball out of a synthetic material.

    Your reactants are glue, water, borax, and cornstarch. Glue is a synthetic material. Water, borax, and cornstarch are natural materials. Borax is mined from rocks, and cornstarch is separated out from corn kernels.

MATERIALS
- borax, $1\frac{1}{2}$ tsp
- cornstarch, 1 tbsp
- craft stick
- cups (2)
- food coloring (optional)
- glue, 1 tbsp, white
- water, 2 tbsp, warm

Procedure

STEP 1 In the table, describe the properties of each starting material.

Materials	Properties
borax	
cornstarch	
water	
white glue	

STEP 2 Make a borax solution by adding $1\frac{1}{2}$ tsp borax to 2 tbsp warm water in a cup. Stir until the borax disappears.

STEP 3 Add 1 tbsp glue to the second cup. If you are using food coloring, add about 3 drops.

STEP 4 To the glue, add $\frac{1}{2}$ tsp of the borax solution and 1 tbsp of cornstarch.

STEP 5 Wait 10 seconds, and then stir the contents of the cup until you cannot stir anymore.

STEP 6 Roll the mixture in your hands until it forms a smooth ball. Explore the properties of the new material.

Analysis

STEP 7 How do the properties of the synthetic material you made compare to the properties of the starting materials?

STEP 8 What caused the properties to change?

How Synthetic Materials Are Used

Synthetic materials have a wide variety of chemical and physical properties. Some are very strong and hard, while others are soft and flexible. Some have low reactivity and others undergo very specific chemical reactions. The synthetic material used to make a bouncy ball is soft and it bounces. The carbon fiber reinforced bike frame is strong and light. A medicine reacts in the body in a certain way. The properties of each of these synthetic materials make them well-suited for the ways that they are used.

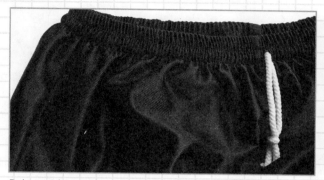

Polyester is a synthetic material that is used to make clothes. It is lightweight and does not shrink when washed and dried.

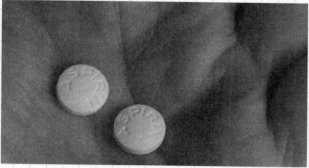

Aspirin is a synthetic material that is used as medicine. It reacts in the body to relieve pain.

26. Nylon is a synthetic material that can be made into string. Mountain climbers use ropes that are made of nylon string that is woven together and braided. What properties of the nylon rope are important for the mountain climbers who use it?

Relate the Properties and Uses of a Synthetic Material

Fiberglass is a composite material made of glass fibers mixed in plastic. The mixture of the glass fibers and plastic makes a strong, lightweight material that can be molded into many shapes. Fiberglass does not conduct electricity well.

27. List two ways that fiberglass could be used. Explain how the properties of fiberglass would be important for each use.

Fiberglass is a composite synthetic material.

_____

_____

_____

_____

_____

Analyzing the Design of Synthetic Materials

Take a glance around the room and you will see many types of synthetic materials. Why are there so many kinds of synthetic materials? Scientists and engineers design them to meet specific needs. The polyester used in clothes needs to be able to be drawn into soft threads. The glass in a window needs to let in light. Engineers have even designed glass, such as the glass in the photo, that does not break as easily as other glass.

This glass might shatter when an object hits it, but it does not break apart. This glass can help reduce damage when it is used for windows in places where there are hurricanes.

28. What are two uses of glass? How do the requirements of these two uses differ?

Types of Synthetic Materials

All synthetic materials are made by chemical and physical processes, instead of being extracted from a natural resource. Plastic is one type of synthetic material. The starting materials for most plastics come from oil, which is a natural resource.

Plastics are polymers. **Polymers** are long molecules that are made up of five or more repeating units. Recall the reaction of ethylene to form polyethylene. Polyethylene is a polymer that is made of repeating ethylene units.

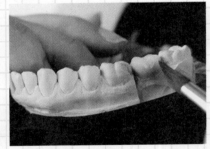

A strong composite made of a polymer and glass is used in tooth-colored fillings and crowns.

29. Nonstick cooking pans are easy to clean, because they are coated with a polymer. What properties of the polymer meet the specific needs of this application?

Composites are synthetic materials that are made from a mixture of two or more materials. Polymers are used to make some composites, such as fiberglass. Dental fillings and tooth-shaped caps that cover teeth, called crowns, can be made using composite material made from a polymer and glass. This material is strong and the same color as teeth.

 EVIDENCE NOTEBOOK

30. How could a chemical reaction change oil into a new material with different properties? What properties of the plastic are important for a kayak? Record your evidence.

Medicine

Most medicines are synthetic materials that are designed to have specific chemical properties. Medicines are used to treat specific conditions, such as diabetes, pain, and allergies. Many people with diabetes take insulin. While some substances, such as insulin, are found naturally in the body or environment, it is often easier and more economical to synthesize the substance. Genetically modified bacteria produce most of the insulin that is used as medicine today.

Materials for Products

Synthetic materials are used in many products, including paints, building materials, clothing, and electronics. Different materials are made by using different combinations of starting substances, which may be natural or synthetic materials. Plastics can have a variety of properties for different uses—from thin plastic films used for sandwich bags to hard plastic used for car bumpers. Materials such as concrete and plywood are used in construction. Some synthetic materials even glow to light up computer screens.

Synthetic materials are designed for use in some electronic screens to provide properties such as resolution and brightness.

31. Engineer It Synthetic materials such as organic light-emitting diodes, called *OLEDs*, are used to make some computer and television screens. These materials glow when an electric current is applied to them. OLEDs that glow different colors are combined to make screens. What are some of the criteria to consider when designing a computer or phone screen? What properties of OLED materials would engineers try to produce when they make the materials?

Foods

Synthetic materials are added to many foods today to help them last longer or add color and flavor. Preservatives, such as citric acid, make food last longer by slowing chemical reactions or the growth of mold and bacteria. Some synthetic materials in food are found in nature. Citric acid and banana flavoring are found in fruits or seeds. However, citric acid and banana flavoring are also made from other materials.

Fuels

Some fuels are synthetic materials that are made from natural materials. Ethanol is added to gasoline. Ethanol is made from materials in plants, such as corn and wood. Algae can also be used to make fuel. Algae produce oils that can be turned into biodiesel. The algae may also be genetically modified to produce more oil than they normally would.

Algae make oils that can be turned into biodiesel, which is a fuel that is used in some vehicles.

32. The plant and algae resources used to make biofuels can be regrown after they are used. How does this make biofuels different from fossil fuels?

Determine Sources and Uses of Synthetic Materials

Vanilla is a common flavor in many foods, including ice cream, cookies, and cereal. It is also used as a scent in candles. It is found naturally in vanilla beans, but most vanilla flavoring that is added to food is the synthetic substance vanillin. Synthetic vanillin is chemically the same as the main substance that gives vanilla beans their vanilla flavor and scent. How and why is synthetic vanillin made?

You can find information about how synthetic vanillin, or almost any synthetic material, is made and how it is used. However, some of that information may not be reliable. When you are looking for information about chemical reactions, primary sources such as scientific journals with research articles are reliable sources of information. But, they may not be easy to understand. Secondary sources like university websites, chemical societies, and science magazines are good places to look. They try to present accurate information, even if they did not gather it. Company websites may be reliable sources for certain types of information. The companies are experts on how they make materials and the properties of those materials. However, the companies have biases because they make money from the material. Websites for organizations that promote certain points of view are also likely to present biased information.

Possible sources of information
a nationally accredited college research department
an independently funded science organization
a government website
a national research lab
a company that makes the material
an organization that supports a natural diet
a society of professional materials scientists or chemists
an organization that promotes the use of food additives
a popular science magazine

33. Which of the sources listed above would be the most reliable sources of information about synthetic vanillin? Would some sources be reliable for certain types of information, but not others?

_____

_____

_____

_____

_____

34. Research how synthetic vanillin is made. What are the sources of the starting materials? Are there advantages or disadvantages to using synthetic vanillin? Should people choose foods with natural vanilla over synthetic vanillin? On a sheet of paper, write a marketing pitch for synthetic vanillin for a consumer audience.

Continue Your Exploration

Name: _____   **Date:** _____

Check out the path below or go online to choose one of the other paths shown.

Careers in Engineering

- Biomimicry
- Hands-On Labs ✋
- Propose Your Own Path

Go online to choose one of these other paths.

Biomass Engineer

Biomass is organic matter that can be processed to make fuel. Biomass engineers apply engineering practices to process biomass into biofuel. Some biomass engineers focus on ensuring that the source of the biomass remains a renewable resource.

Biomass engineers and biologists work together in teams. These teams develop and test cost-efficient ways to make biofuels. They conduct research and use technology to find ways to turn plant waste into biofuel sources. They come up with environmentally safe ways to get rid of or use biomass waste. Biomass engineers also help design machines that use biofuel. Biomass engineers need at least a bachelor's degree in engineering or a related science field.

This biomass engineer investigates the quality of biofuel made from algae, a type of organism that grows in many parts of the world.

Making Biofuel

Using biomass for fuel began when humans first built fires with wood. Wood is still the largest biomass energy resource worldwide.

Many types of biomass can be used to produce biofuel. For example, used vegetable oils and animal fats can be turned into biodiesel fuel to run a school bus. Any plant matter—such as wood shavings, grass, leaves, algae, wheat straw, and corncobs—can be turned into biofuel. Some common biofuel sources include soybeans, corn, and waste products from wood production. In the future, biomass engineers hope to find new ways to make fuel, plastics, chemicals, and other products from plant matter.

Farmers used to harvest soybeans only for food. Now they harvest the soybeans and the rest of the plant matter too. Stalks, stems, and leaves are used to produce biofuel.

Continue Your Exploration

Use the circle graph to answer Questions 1–2.

1. What can you conclude from the information shown in the graph?

   A. Used cooking oil is used more than canola oil to produce biofuels in the United States.

   B. People in the United States use twice as much animal fat for biofuel as they do soybean oil.

   C. More corn oil is used for biofuel in the United States than was used in the past.

   D. More people in the United States would use corn oil if there were no canola oil.

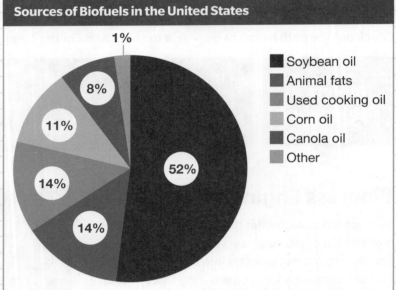

Sources of Biofuels in the United States

- Soybean oil
- Animal fats
- Used cooking oil
- Corn oil
- Canola oil
- Other

1%, 8%, 11%, 14%, 14%, 52%

Source: U.S. Energy Information Administration, Monthly Biodiesel Production Report with data for December 2015, February 2016

2. A biomass engineering team is developing a new way to power lawnmowers by using biofuel. What might influence their decision about which oil to use? Circle all that apply.

   A. Soybean oil is the most common source of biofuels in United States.

   B. A new opportunity for using used cooking oil might encourage people to recycle.

   C. Canola oil is one of the least common sources of biofuels in the United States.

   D. Engineers would not want to use a type of biofuel that is already in use.

3. Which of these is a positive consequence of using biomass as an energy resource?

   A. No burning is required.

   B. More new machines are designed.

   C. It is potentially renewable.

   D. No waste is produced.

4. **Collaborate** Biofuel can be made from wood, grass clippings, leaves, crops, or crop waste. Methane can be collected from rotting garbage and community landfills to produce biofuel. Ethanol can be made from fruit or other crops, such as corn. These energy resources can be used to do the same work as fossil fuels.

   Together with a partner, come up with an idea to power a household item with a biofuel. Draw and label a diagram to show your idea. Present your diagram to the class, along with any new or different ideas you and your partner had about promoting biomass energy.

Can You Explain It?

Name: _____   Date: _____

How can a plastic kayak be made from oil?

crude oil

EVIDENCE NOTEBOOK

Refer to the notes in your Evidence Notebook to help you construct an explanation for how a plastic kayak can be made from crude oil.

1. State your claim. Make sure your claim fully explains how a plastic kayak can be made from oil.

2. Summarize the evidence you have gathered to support your claim and explain your reasoning.

Checkpoints

Answer the following questions to check your understanding of the lesson.

Use the photo to answer Questions 3–4.

3. What properties are needed in the material used to make these items? Select all that apply.

    A. It breaks easily.

    B. It stretches.

    C. It is strong.

    D. It holds in air.

4. Some balloons are made of latex, which can be made from substances that come from crude oil. These substances undergo chemical reactions to form latex. The latex of the balloons is a natural material / synthetic material.

Use the photo to answer Questions 5–6.

5. In order to use a field for sports, the field needs grass. However, sports often quickly destroy grass. A solution to this problem can be achieved with synthetic materials. Why might a synthetic material be the best choice for the solution?

    A. Synthetic materials can be designed to fit a certain need.

    B. Synthetic materials are easier to make than obtaining natural materials.

    C. The use of natural materials has a negative impact on the environment.

6. What properties of plastic make it useful for fake grass? Select all that apply.

    A. It can be colored green.

    B. It is durable.

    C. It can be made into thin strips.

    D. It breaks down in the sun.

7. Are plants and animals potentially renewable natural resources?

    A. Yes, because some plants and animals are resources that can be replaced at the same rate they are used, if managed well.

    B. No, because it is not possible for humans to use plant and animal resources at a faster rate than they can be replaced.

    C. No, because plants and animals are inexhaustible resources.

    D. Yes, because we use plant resources at the same rate as we use animal resources.

© Houghton Mifflin Harcourt Publishing Company • Image Credits: (t) ©anand purohit/ Moment/Getty Images; (b) ©Mike Graffigna/Alamy

Interactive Review

Complete this section to review the main concepts of the lesson.

Natural resources are found in nature and are used by humans.

A. What properties of a natural resource make it useful to humans as a material or energy source?

Natural resources can be classified as renewable or nonrenewable.

B. What is the difference between a renewable resource and a nonrenewable resource?

Synthetic materials are made by people using chemical reactions or by mixing together materials.

C. Explain why chemical reactions are used to form synthetic materials.

Engineers design synthetic materials to meet specific needs.

D. Why are synthetic materials sometimes used when designing a way to improve existing materials?

Choose one of the activities to explore how this unit connects to other topics.

☐ People in Engineering Connection

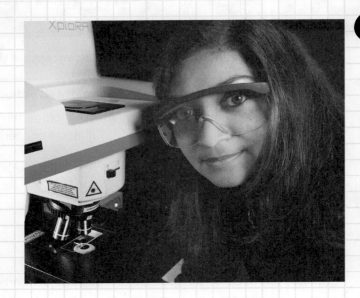

Mahmooda Sultana, Engineer Dr. Mahmooda Sultana has a PhD in chemical engineering and is a researcher at NASA. She develops sensors using nanocrystal semiconductors and graphene, a one atom thick material made of carbon. The sensors made from nanocrystal semiconductors are designed to detect the chemical make-up of substances and the graphene-based sensors are designed to detect oxygen concentrations.

Research ways that the chemical make-up of a substance can be measured. Develop a presentation that discusses one way that chemicals can be measured and the importance of these measurements.

☐ Health Connection

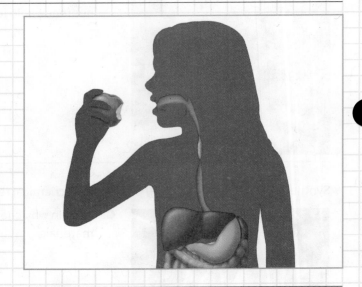

The Chemistry of Digestion When you eat food, it is physically changed into small pieces through chewing. Carbohydrates, proteins, and fats are then chemically changed by reactions with enzymes and are absorbed into the bloodstream. Carbohydrates are converted to glucose, proteins become amino acids, and fats become glycerol and fatty acids.

Research the main category of your favorite food: carbohydrates, proteins, or fats. Then investigate how long it takes for that food to be chemically converted in your body and how your body uses the digested products. Create a short presentation on your findings.

☐ Environmental Science Connection

Acid Rain Burning fossil fuels produces sulfur dioxide and nitrogen oxides. These oxides react with water and oxygen in the atmosphere, producing sulfuric acid and nitric acid. Acid rain results when these products are carried to the ground with precipitation. Acid rain is harmful when it gets into soil and waterways because it can damage structures and organisms.

Research a specific animal or plant, and describe how it is affected by chemical reactions from acid rain. Create a pamphlet, including visuals, to showcase your findings.

This statue has been damaged by acid rain.

Name: _____   Date: _____

Complete this review to check your understanding of the unit.

Use the photos to answer Questions 1–2.

1. The image of the fried eggs is / is not an example of a chemical reaction. The image of the whisked eggs is / is not an example of a chemical reaction.

2. Which of the following statements are true about the reaction rates of cooked eggs? Circle all that apply.

   A. Increasing the temperature causes the reaction to occur more slowly.

   B. Increasing the temperature causes the reaction to occur more quickly.

   C. Increasing the temperature causes the eggs' particles to have more energy and move faster.

   D. Increasing the temperature causes the eggs' particles to lose energy and move more slowly.

3. What are some possible benefits of using a synthetic material? Select all that apply.

   A. Synthetic materials can replace all natural materials.

   B. Synthetic materials can help preserve food and are used in medicine.

   C. Synthetic materials can be less expensive alternatives to natural materials.

   D. All synthetic materials can be recycled.

Use the graph to answer Question 4.

4. Why does increasing the temperature of the water increase the rate of the chemical reaction shown in the graph?

   A. Faster moving particles will come into contact with each other less frequently.

   B. Faster moving particles will come into contact with each other more frequently.

   C. Changing the temperature does not change the motion of the particles.

   D. Warmer water contains more water particles.

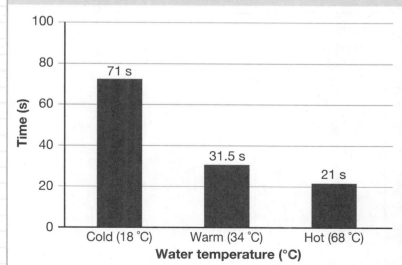

Effect of Temperature on Effervescent Tablets

This graph shows the time it takes for an effervescent tablet to finish reacting in water at different temperatures.

5. Complete the table by providing descriptions of how each of type of change relates to the properties of matter.

Properties of Matter	Physical Changes	Chemical Reactions	Changes in Energy
Arrangement of Atoms	During physical changes, the arrangement of atoms (molecular structure) of a substance remains the same.		
Physical Properties of Matter			
Chemical Properties of Matter			

Name: _____ Date: _____

Use the image and the molecular model to answer Questions 6–9.

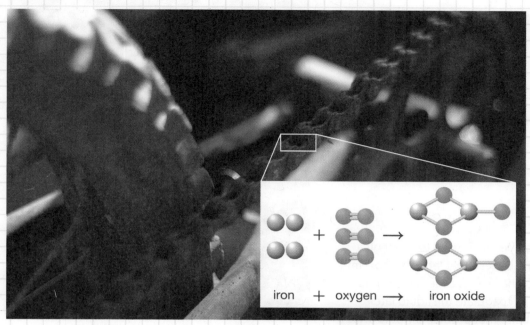

The rust forming on this bike is the product of a chemical reaction between iron and oxygen, as shown in the molecular model.

iron + oxygen ⟶ iron oxide

6. Describe how particles of iron (Fe) and oxygen (O_2) react to produce iron oxide (Fe_2O_3), also known as rust.

7. Write a balanced chemical equation based on the molecular model shown in the image. Describe the equation in a sentence.

8. The formation of iron oxide is a slow reaction that releases thermal energy. Describe what that means and explain the transfer of energy that is occurring.

9. Salt can act as a catalyst to the formation of iron oxide. What would happen if the bike were exposed to saltwater?

Use the image to answer Questions 10–12.

10. Rubber, which is made from latex, is very water resistant, slip proof, and durable. Describe some useful everyday applications for rubber.

11. A special tapping knife is used to shear off a thin layer of the bark so that latex can flow into a bucket. After the latex is collected, formic acid is added to coagulate the liquid latex into solid rubber. What problems would arise if synthetically-produced formic acid were not added to the natural latex?

Latex is collected from a rubber tree in Phuket Province, Thailand.

12. Rubber production influences the local people harvesting latex, the trees and environment from which it is harvested, and the land where rubber products are discarded. What are possible negative and positive effects of rubber production and disposal?

Name: Date:

Save the Sea Turtle Eggs!

As a marine biologist, you are responsible for transporting sea turtle eggs that may be in danger after a storm. It is important to keep the eggs at a safe temperature (approximately 27 °C to 33 °C) for the 30 minutes it takes to drive to the animal hospital. You have three possible combinations of materials available to create an egg warmer to maintain the proper temperature:

- ammonium nitrate crystals and a pouch of water
- fine iron powder, salt, and water
- sodium acetate solution and a small metal disc

The steps below will help guide your research to develop an egg warmer.

Engineer It

1. **Define the Problem** Clearly define the criteria and constraints associated with the design of the egg warmer.

Engineer It

2. **Conduct Research** Research each of the three possible material combinations you could use to make an egg warmer. Are you looking for a chemical process that releases or absorbs thermal energy?

3. **Analyze Data** Create a decision matrix to analyze each material option. Describe the strengths and weaknesses of each choice.

4. **Identify and Recommend a Solution** Based on your research, construct a written explanation describing which combination of materials would make the best egg warmer. How would you design the warmer to safely carry eggs?

5. **Communicate** Prepare a presentation of your recommendation explaining the best materials and design to make a portable egg warmer.

 **Self-Check**

	I identified the problem.
	I researched the three combinations of materials to determine how well they meet the criteria and constraints of the problem.
	I analyzed my research and data to create a decision matrix.
	My solution is based on evidence from research, data, and an analysis of my decision matrix.
	My recommended design was clearly communicated to others.

Go online to access the **Interactive Glossary**. You can use this online tool to look up definitions for all the vocabulary terms in this book.

Pronunciation Key

Sound	Symbol	Example	Respelling	Sound	Symbol	Example	Respelling
ă	a	pat	PAT	ŏ	ah	bottle	BAHT'l
ā	ay	pay	PAY	ō	oh	toe	TOH
âr	air	care	KAIR	ô	aw	caught	KAWT
ä	ah	father	FAH•ther	ôr	ohr	roar	ROHR
är	ar	argue	AR•gyoo	oi	oy	noisy	NOYZ•ee
ch	ch	chase	CHAYS	ōō	u	book	BUK
ĕ	e	pet	PET	ōō	oo	boot	BOOT
ĕ (at end of a syllable)	eh	settee lessee	seh•TEE leh•SEE	ou	ow	pound	POWND
ĕr	ehr	merry	MEHR•ee	s	s	center	SEN•ter
ē	ee	beach	BEECH	sh	sh	cache	CASH
g	g	gas	GAS	ŭ	uh	flood	FLUHD
ĭ	i	pit	PIT	ûr	er	bird	BERD
ĭ (at end of a syllable)	ih	guitar	gih•TAR	z	z	xylophone	ZY•luh•fohn
ī	y eye (only for a complete syllable)	pie island	PY EYE•luhnd	z	z	bags	BAGZ
îr	ir	hear	HIR	zh	zh	decision	dih•SIZH•uhn
j	j	germ	JERM	ə	uh	around broken focus	uh•ROWND BROH•kuhn FOH•kuhs
k	k	kick	KIK	ər	er	winner	WIN•er
ng	ng	thing	THING	th	th	thin they	THIN THAY
ngk	ngk	bank	BANGK	w	w	one	WUHN
				wh	hw	whether	HWETH•er

Index

Page numbers for key terms are in **boldface** type.
Page numbers in *italic* type indicate illustrative material, such as photographs, graphs, charts, and maps.

A

abiotic resource
    abundant, 374, 375
    limited, 372, *372*
abrasion, in weathering process,
    269, *269, 272, 273*
abundant resources
    abiotic, 374, 375
    biotic, 374, 375
    predicting effects of, 374–376
acetic acid, *113,* 114—115, 163
acid rain, 204, 218, *218,* 270
Act, 78, 167, 207, 349, 391
active volcano, 452, 474
    Kilauea, 455–456, *455, 456, 473,*
    473
    Mauna Loa, Hawaii, 474–475, *475*
Adélie penguin, 523
aggregate, 10, *10,* 13, *13,* 36, *36*
agricultural practices, soil impacts,
    349, *349*
agriculture, ecosystem
    disturbances caused by, 532
Aialik Bay, Alaska, 544, *544*
air, as matter, 54
airbag, 149–150, *149, 150*
airbag helmet, 28, *28*
air pressure, elevation changing,
    97, 103
Alaska, tectonic plates in, 333, *333*
algae
    as biofuel, 257, *257*
    for biomass fuel production, 211,
    211, 213, *213*
    as biotic factor, 372
    feeding relationships, 384, 385–
    387, *385*
    photosynthesis in, 256
    phototrophs, 243
    producer transform sun energy into
    food, 236, *236*

algal bloom, 374, *374*
    effects of, 550
    in Gulf of Mexico, 575
alligator, 364, *364,* 365
Alligator Rivers region, Australia,
    368, *368*
alluvial fan, 282, *282,* 432, *432*
aluminum
    life cycle of, 9, *9*
Amazon rain forest, 565
amino acids, 251
ammonia, 154, *154*
ammonium chloride, 183, *183,*
    185–186
amoeba, 366, *366*
amorphous silicon, 120, *120*
amphibolite, 297, *297*
analogy, 234
analysis
    of bicycle helmet designs, 30–31,
    30–31
    of biodiversity, 530–531
    of change of state, 88
    of chemical equations, 159–164
    of continental data, 320–323
    ecosystem energy flow, 402–406
    of habitat fragmentation, 572
    of impact of synthetic material,
    500–505, *500–505*
    of interactions within Earth system,
    428–431
    of molecules, 115
    natural hazard, historical data on,
    450–451, *450*
    of natural resources used to create
    synthetic materials,
    196–199
    of natural systems and chemical
    reactions, 138–139
    of ocean-floor data,
    324–327
    of states of matter, 73–74

    of substances before and after
    chemical reaction changes,
    146–148
    of synthetic material design,
    210–212
    of thermal energy used in chemical
    processes, 179–183
anemone, clownfish and, 389, *389*
anglerfish, 391, *391*
animal
    as biotic factor, 372
    competition among, 393, *393*
    consumers of, 237
    decomposition of dead, 237
    feeding relationship of, 385–387,
    385, 388, 394
    impact of resource use on, 15
    plastics impact on, 516, *516*
    sunlight as energy source for, 233–
    234, 256–257, *256*
anole lizard, 393, *393*
Antarctica, 523
anteater, 237, *237*
apple, 235, *235*
aquifer
    contamination, synthetic material
    production, 502, *502*
    groundwater, 347, *347,* 352
    model recharge and withdrawal
    from, 353–354, *353*
Aral Sea, shrinking, 352, *352*
Arches National Park, 284, *284*
Arctic, oil drilling in, 416, *416*
arctic ecosystem
    biodiversity in, 564
    disappearing sea ice in, 50, *50*
argument
    constructing, 537
    from evidence, 36, 255, 304, 375,
    387, 440, 569
    supporting, 231

Arizona
Barringer Meteorite Crater, 427, *427*, 487, *487*
meteorite crater, 427, *427*, 441, *441*
South Coyote Buttes Wilderness area, 268, *268*

Army Corps of Engineers, 37–38, *37–38*

Art Connection
Working with Wax, 126

ash tree, 577, *577*

Asian carp, 394, *394*

aspirin, 209, *209*

Assessment
Lesson Self-Check, 19–21, 39–41, 67–69, 81–83, 101–103, 123–125, 151–153, 171–173, 191–193, 215–217, 245–247, 263–265, 281–283, 305–307, 337–339, 357–359, 379–381, 397–398, 413–415, 441–443, 463–465, 489–491, 513–515, 541–543, 559–561, 585–587
Unit Performance Task, 47–48, 131–132, 223–224, 313–314, 421–422, 521–522, 593–594
Unit Review, 43–46, 127–130, 219–222, 309–312, 417–420, 517–520, 589–592

asteroid
Barringer Meteorite Crater, Arizona, 427, *427*, 487, *487*
biggest known Earth impacts, 488, *488*
impact prediction, 487–488, *487–488*
potentially hazardous asteroid (PHA), 487–488, *487–488*

Atlantic cod population, 536, *536*

atmosphere in Earth system, 429, *429*

atom
balanced chemical equation, checking, 166
bond to form molecule, 232, *232*
as building blocks of matter, 231–232
carbon as building block of living things, 251–252

in chemical formula, 156
in complex molecules, 115–117
compounds of, 109–110, *109*, *110*, 125, *125*
of elements, 108, *108*
law of conservation of matter, 165
mineral formation, 286
in molecules, 112
organisms and nonliving things made of, 104–120
particles of matter, 107, *107*
in simple molecules, 113
structure affected by connections of, 119

avalanche, prediction, 468, *468*

avocado, lipids in, 252, *252*

B

bacteria
as biotic factor, 372
exponential growth pattern, 377, *377*
nitrogen-fixing, 389
photosynthesis in, 256
phototrophs, 243
producer transform sun energy into food, 236, *236*

baking soda and vinegar chemical reaction, 144, *144*, 163

balanced chemical equation, 165, 166–168, 169–170

bamboo, renewable source, 202, *202*

bananas, 537, 586, *586*

Banff National Park, Canada, 426, *426*

Bangladesh, *553*

Barbary macaque, 528, *528*

Barringer, Daniel Moreau, 427, *427*

Barringer Meteorite Crater, Arizona, 427, *427*, 487, *487*

basalt
as igneous rock, 290, *290*
metamorphic rock formation, 297, *297*

bat, 59, *59*

beach erosion, 272, *272*

bear, *56*

beaver, 401, *401*, 413, *413*

bee
biodiversity of, 530, *530*
cross-pollination by, 390, *390*
importance of, 549

Bezeau, Robert, 23, *23*

bicycle
balanced equation for, 169
helmet design, 26, *26*, 27, *27*, 29, 30–31, 41, *41*
materials used to make, 206, *206*

biodiesel fuel, 213

biodiversity, 529
of bird species, 534, *534*
causes of loss of, 568–569
description of, 528–531, 543
ecosystem dynamics and, 523–594
ecosystem health indicated by, 526–538, 587
in ecosystem recovery, 533
evaluating loss of, 564–569
in Everglades, 563, *563*
human creativity preserving, 562, *562*
human influences on, 535–538
loss of affecting ecosystem health, 567–569
maintaining, 562–582
measuring, 530–531
monitoring and preserving, 538, 578, 587
negative impact on, 536–537
patterns in, 531
protecting, 537
solutions for maintaining, 578–582
strategies for maintaining, 570–577
types of, 529

biofuel, 213–214, *213*, *214*
algae as, 257, *257*

biomass, 201, 213, 347, *347*

biomass engineer, 213–214, *213*

biomimicry, 42, *42*

bioremediation, 240, *240*

biosensor, *576*

biosphere
Earth system, 6, 429, *429*
tabletop, 225

biotic resources
  abundant, 374, 375
  limited, 372–373
bird
  biodiversity of, 534, *534*
  oil spill impact on, 205, *205*, 501, *501*
bison, 536
bleaching, 570, *570*
blizzard, 449, *449*
boiling point, 89, *89*, *98*, 141
Bosch, Carl, 189–190, *189*, *190*
brainstorming, 25, *25*, 28, *28*
breccia, 292, *292*
bromine, 71, *71*, 81, *81*
Brown, Robert, 62
Brownian motion, 62
buckthorn, 536
bumblebee, 530, *530*
Burmese python, 536, *536*
burros, 532, *532*

C

calcite
  hardness of, 57
  in marble formation, 299, *299*
  as sedimentary cement, 292, *292*
calcium, 231, *231*
calcium carbonate
  limestone, 294, *294*, 295, *295*
  sedimentary rock formation, 59, *59*, 294, *294*
caldera, 439, *439*, 440, *440*
California
  Clear Lake wildfire, 444, *444*
  Griffith Park in Los Angeles, 524, *524*
  mountain meadow restoration, 580–581
  Oak Woodland Regeneration, 557–558, *558*
  San Francisco Bay, 126
  Sierra Nevada, 580
  Silicon Valley, 126
  Sonoran Desert, 532, *532*
  urbanization of, 579
  water levels in, 580
  Yosemite National Park, 291

canyon
  formation, 278, *278*, 285, *285*, 294, *294*, 305, *305*
  underwater, 318, *318*
Can You Explain It? 5, 19, 23, 39, 53, 67, 71, 81, 85, 101, 105, 123, 137, 151, 155, 171, 175, 191, 195, 215, 229, 245, 249, 263, 267, 281, 285, 305, 319, 337, 341, 357, 361, 379, 383, 397, 401, 413, 427, 441, 445, 463, 467, 489, 493, 513, 527, 541, 545, 559, 563, 585
carbon
  as building block of living things, 251–252
  carbon-based molecules in cells, 251–252, *252*
  carbon cycle, 408, *408*
  in complex molecules, 115, *115*
  in diamonds, 106, 116, *116*, 119, *119*
  in graphite, 119, *119*
  in humans, 105, *105*, 231, *231*, 232
  in propane, 105, *105*
carbon cycle, 408, *408*
carbon dioxide
  alcoholic fermentation, 261
  in cellular respiration, 258–259, *258*
  chemosynthesis, 243
  lactic acid fermentation, 261, *261*
  molecule of, 232, *232*
  photosynthesis producing, 236, *236*, 256, *256*
  plants using, 532, *532*
  removal of as ecosystem service, 7, *7*
  and water to form carbonic acid, 251, *251*
  from wood burning, 58
carbon fiber life cycle, 510
carbonic acid, 251, *251*
carbon monoxide, 113
carbon removal tower, 409, *409*
Careers in Engineering: Biomass Engineer, 213–214, *213*
Careers in Engineering: Civil Engineer, 37–38
Careers in Engineering: Materials Engineer, 511–512, *511*

Careers in Science: Ecotourism, 583–584
Careers in Science: Forensics, 99–100
Careers in Science: Restoration Ecologist, 539–540
carnivore, feeding relationships, 384, 385–387, *385*
Case Study
  Bicycle Helmet, 27, *27*
  Elephant Conservation in Thailand, 583–584
  Mountain Meadow Restoration, 580–581
  Reducing the Impact of Synthetic Fertilizers, 575
  Shark Bay Ecosystem, 576–577
cassiterite, 201, *201*
catalyst, in chemical reaction, 182, *182*
categories of matter, 55
cause and effect
  chain, 569
  constructing statements of, 527
  diagram, *376*
  relationship, 43, 359
  statement, 527
  table of, *44*, *393*
cave, ecosystem of, 59, *59*
cavefish, 59, *59*
Cave of Crystals, Mexico, 52, *52*
cell phone
  case for, 24
  design, 24, 26
  natural resources for, 6, *6*
  recycling, 504, *504*
  synthetic material life cycle example, 496–497, *496–497*, 500, *500*, 502, 506, *506*
cells
  carbon-based molecules in, 251–252, *252*
  energy production for, 248–265
  photosynthesis for energy production, 253–258

cellular respiration, 258
 for energy production, 258–260
 fermentation compared to, 261–262, *261*
 mitochondria, 258–259, *258, 259*
 oxygen used in energy production, 258–259, *258, 259*
cellulose, as natural resource, 197, *197*
cementation
 rock cycle model, 301–302, *301*
 sedimentary cement, 292, *292,* 294, *294*
ceramic, as synthetic material, 206
change of state, 86
 analyzing, 96
 classify and explain, 92, 103
 energy influences in, 86–88
 energy loss causing, 93–98
 gas to liquid, 94, *95*
 identifying, 88
 liquid to gas, 89–90
 liquid to solid, 94, *95*
 pressure affecting, 97–98
 solid to liquid, 89
Checkpoints, 20, 40, 68, 82, 102, 124, 152, 172, 192, 216, 246, 264, 282, 306, 338, 358, 380, 398, 414, 442, 464, 490, 514, 542, 560, 586
cheese, 261, *261*
chemical bond
 energy stored in molecular, 232, 250, 257
 in molecule, 232, *232*
 of molecules, 113, *113*
 photosynthetic energy storage, 256, 257
chemical cold pack design, 134, *134,* 184–188, *184*
chemical equation, 160
 analysis of, 159–164
 arrow in, 160, 162
 balanced, 160, 166–168, 169–170
 chemical reactions and, 162
 coefficient in, 160, 161, 166
 electrolysis of water, 160, *160*

 evaluate, 168
 identify, 164, *164*
 law of conservation of matter, 166–168
 to model chemical reactions, 154–173, 251, *251,* 252
 product in, 161, 251, *251,* 261
 reactant in, 251, *251,* 261
 subscript within, 160, 161, 166
chemical formulas, 156
 colored bricks as model for, 156, *156*
 using, 156–158, 160
chemical process
 chemical equations to model chemical reactions, 154–173, 251, *251,* 252
 energy analysis in, 179–183
 energy transformation through, 179–180, 181
 factors that affect thermal energy reaction rates, 182, *182*
 matter changes in chemical reactions, 136–153
 synthetic materials made from natural resources, 194–212
 thermal energy use in a device, 174–193
chemical property
 of elements, 107
 of matter, 58–59, 69, 141
 synthetic material, 209, *209*
chemical reaction, 144, 250
 in airbags, 149–150, *149, 150*
 analysis of, 148
 balanced chemical equations, 166–168
 carbon-based molecules in cells, 251–252, *252*
 cellular respiration for energy production, 258–260
 chemical equation to model, 154–173, 251, *251,* 252
 chemistry of cells, 250–252
 energy production for cells, 248–265
 evidence of, 146, 147
 law of conservation of matter, 165–168
 matter changing identity in, 136–153

 modeling, 160, 162, 165–168, 251
 photosynthesis for energy production, 253–258
 physical change compared to, 143–145
 product, 144, 159, 250
 rate variables, 182, *182*
 reactant, 144, 159, 250
 signs of possible, 146
chemical separation of substances, 106
Chemical Vapor Disposition (CVD) diamond, 500, *500*
chemical weathering, 270, *270*
chemists, 189–190
chemosynthesis, 243
chemotrophs, 243–244, *243*
chimpanzee, 24, *24*
chloroplast
 photosynthesis, 256, *256*
chloroplasts
 electron micrograph, 257, *257*
 light energy capture in, 257, *257*
cholera, 42
circle graph
 biofuel in United States, 214
citric acid
 as synthetic material, 211
civil engineer, 37–38, *37–38,* 65–66
claim
 evaluate, 569
 stating and supporting, 19, 39, 67, 81, 101, 123, 151, 171, 191, 215, 245, 263, 281, 305, 337, 357, 379, 397, 413, 441, 463, 489, 513, 541, 559, 585
climate, 449
 chemical weathering, 270, *270*
 ecosystem, 364
 freshwater distribution, 347, *347*
climate disasters, cost of, 461–462, *461, 462*
climate hazards
 described, 448, *448,* 449, *449,* 478
 historical data on, 478, 479
 monitoring, 480, *480*
 prediction, 477–481
 scientific understanding, 478
 worldwide data (1995–2015), 451, *451*

climate regulation, as ecosystem
service, 566, *566*
clownfish, 389, *389*
coal
fossil fuel distribution, 345, *345*
mining, 303–304, *303*
as nonrenewable resource, 201
coarse-grained igneous rock, 290
coastal mangrove forest, 564, *564*
coefficient
in balanced chemical equation, 166
in chemical equation, 160, 161
coffee plantation, 567, *567*
coffee plants, 567–568, *567*
cold pack design, 134, *134*, 184–188,
184
Collaborate, 18, 38, 66, 80, 100, 122,
145, 150, 170, 190, 214, 244, 262,
280, 304, 336, 356, 378, 396, 406,
412, 440, 462, 488, 512, 540, 558,
584
color
chemical reaction to change flower
petal color, 250, *250*
as physical property of matter, 141
as property of matter, 55, 57
colored bricks as model for
chemical formulas, 156, *156*
combustion
carbon cycle, 408, *408*
energy produced by reactant, 181
thermal energy and, 174, *174*
commensalism, 390
community, 365
as level of ecosystem organization,
365
compare and contrast
effects of disturbances, 551, *551*
elements and compounds, *111*
interior-to-edge ratios, 572
performance to costs, 120
competition for natural resources,
370–373, 392–394
competitive pattern of interactions
between organisms, predicting
effects, 392–394
complex molecule models, 115–117
component of bicycle helmets, 27,
27

composite material
dental, 210, *210*
described, 210
fiberglass, 209, *209*
formation of, 207
composition of matter, 118
compost, 313–314, *313*
compost bin, 238–239, *238*
compound, 109
extended molecule structures, 116,
116
computational thinking, 35, *35*
computer model, 34, *34*, 485
concentration in chemical reaction,
182, *182*
concrete, 6, *6*
critical building material, 12, *12*
production of, 10, *10*
condensation, 94, *94*, 95
water cycle, 407, *407*
conduction, 177, *177*, 178
conductivity
of elements, 107
of matter, 57
as physical property of matter, 141
coneflower, 536
conglomerate rock, 295, *295*
consequences
long-term, 203–204
negative, 203–204
positive, 203–204
short-term, 203–204
of using natural resources, 203–205
conservation
of elephants, 583–584
of Everglades, 563, *563*, 568, *568*,
585, *585*
individual species, 570–571, *571*
in Micronesia, 570
of natural water resources, 578
need for, 587
constraints
in addressing biodiversity loss, 579
of engineering problems, 25, *25*,
26, *26*
of fire alarms, 32, *32*
influences of, 4, *4*

consumer, 237
cellular respiration, 258
energy pyramid, 406, *406*
consumer use, 12, *12*, 15, *15*
synthetic material life cycle, 497,
497, 503, *503*, 508, *508*
container design, cold pack,
187–188
continental data analysis, 320–323
fossil data, 320–321, *320*, *321*
landform data, 322, *322*
continental shelf, 322, *322*
matching landform data across
Atlantic, 320, *320*, 323
ocean floor data, 324, *324*
contour plowing, 349, *349*
convection, 177, *177*, 178
convection current, 334
cooling in rock cycle, 301–302, *301*
copper
distribution of, 342, *342*, 343, *343*
electric conductivity of, 107
as natural resource, 197, *197*, 198
and silver nitrate chemical reaction,
155, *155*, 171, *171*
copper carbonate, 122, *122*
coral, 526, *526*, 528, 570, *570*
coral reef ecosystem, 526, *526*, 564,
564, 570, *570*
cost versus performance, 120
cougar, 524, *524*, 588
coyote
feeding relationships, 386–387, *386*
population and drought, 383, 397
coyotes, 529, *529*
crime scene, 99
criteria
of engineering problems, 25, *25*,
26, *26*
of fire alarms, 32, *32*
tradeoffs, 29, *29*

© Houghton Mifflin Harcourt Publishing Company

crop
    biodiversity lacking in, 537
    consumer use, 12, *12*
    demand on, 12, *12*
    from farming, 9, *9*
    production and distribution of, 10,
        10
    reintroducing wild genes in, 537
    resource availability, 200, *200*
    rotation of, 349, *349*, 575
cross-pollination by bees, 390, *390*
crude oil, 15, *15*
crystal, *286*
    mineral formation, 286, 287
    model formation of, lab, 289
    time scale, igneous rock formation,
        290, *290*
crystalline silicon, 120, *120*
crystals, 116, *116*
Cusatis, Ginluca, 65–66, *65*
Cynognathus, 320, *320*
cytoplasm, cellular respiration in,
        258
Czech Republic, 527, *527*

D

Dalton, John, 61
dam, hydroelectric, 347
data
    analyzing and interpreting, 35
    continental data, 320–323
    fossil data, 320–321, *320*, *321*, 323
    landform data, 322, *322*, 342, *342*,
        343, *343*
    from monitoring natural hazards,
        469, *469*, 471, 474–475, 480
    natural hazard, 450–451, *450*
    ocean-floor data analysis, 324–327
    tornado, interpreting patterns in,
        458–460
    volcanic, interpreting patterns in,
        452–457
dead zone, 589, *589*
decision matrix, 581
decomposer, 237, *237*, 533

decomposition
    bioremediation, 240, *240*
    as biotic factor, 372
    carbon cycle, 408, *408*
    cycle of energy and matter, 229,
        237–240, *237*, *238*, *239*
    ecosystem services of, 566, *566*
    by fungus, 236, *236*
    nitrogen cycle, 409, *409*
deep-ocean trenches, 324, *324*, 325,
        327
**Deepwater Horizon offshore drilling
        rig,** 501, *501*
deer, population change in, 375, *375*
deforestation, 349, *349*, 557
    for coffee plantations, 567, *567*
delta, river, 273, *273*, 435, *435*, 517,
        517
density
    measure of mass and volume, 64
    as physical property of matter, 141
density of matter, 57
deoxyribonucleic acid (DNA), 117
deposition, 272
    agents of, 272–275
    energy driving process of, 272–278
    gravity as agent of, 274, *274*
    ice as agent of, 274, *274*
    rock cycle model, 301–302, *301*
    time scale, 278, *278*
    water as agent of, 272–275, *273–275*
    wind as agent of, 272–274, *273*
desert
    ecosystem of, 364, 528
    sand in, 36, *36*
    water supply in, 56
desert locust, 545, 559, *559*
design, of synthetic materials,
        210–212
design problem. *See also*
        engineering problem
    defining constraints, 579
    defining criteria of, 579
    in real-life, 32, *32*
design process
    evaluate design solutions, 581
    identifying solutions, 2, *2*, 24, 36,
        522, 582
    solution tradeoffs, 582

desire
    identifying, 26, *26*
    met by synthetic materials, 495
Devils Tower, Wyoming, 291, *291*
diagram
    of airbag design, *150*
    of carbon-based molecules, *265*
    of carbon cycle, *408*
    cause and effect, *376*
    of cellular respiration and
        photosynthesis, *260*
    of chemical formulas of minerals,
        158, *166*
    of chemical reaction rate variables,
        182
    of cycling of matter, *410*
    of diamond structure, *116*
    of earthquake warning system, *336*
    of elements and compounds, *111*
    of engineering design process, 25,
        25
    of fish and crab relationships, *376*
    of food chain, *403*
    of formation of polyethylene, *207*
    of landfill exposure pathways, *520*
    of molecular models, *112*, *113*
    of ocean floor, *324*, *327*
    of pencil production, *45*
    of plate boundaries and surface
        features, *329*
    of plate movement, *334*
    of rock cycle, *301*, *307*
    of soil formation, *344*
    Venn diagram, *551*
    of volcanic hazards, *454*
    of water molecule, *124*, *157*
    of weathering and erosion, *342*
    of web design process, *46*
    of Yellowstone Caldera area, *440*
diamond, 116, *116*, 119, *119*
    chemical formula for, 158, *158*
    synthetic, 500, *500*
digestion, chemistry of, 218
dinosaur, 230, *230*
    matching fossil data across Atlantic,
        320–321, *320*, *321*
Dirzo, Rodolfo, 557–558, *557*

Discuss, 2, 6, 8, 16, 24, 50, 54, 57, 75, 86, 89, 98, 118, 138, 140, 143, 200, 203, 206, 226, 229, 230, 235, 241, 250, 253, 258, 271, 273, 278, 287, 288, 294, 296, 299, 301, 316, 320, 325, 342, 350, 362, 369, 374, 384, 392, 407, 424, 430, 431, 432, 446, 450, 473, 482, 495, 506, 508, 524, 546, 567

disease
  natural disasters and, 516, *516*
  as natural hazard, 448

disposable glove testing, 506, *506*

disposal
  of products, 16, *16*
  synthetic material life cycle, 496, *496*, 504, *504*, 508, *508*

dissolution
  mineral formation, 286, 294, *294*
  natural resource distribution, 342–343, *343*
  sedimentary rock formation, 294, *294*
  as thermal energy reaction rate factor, 182

distribution
  impact of, 15, *15*
  synthetic material life cycle, 497, *497*, 503, *503*, 507, *507*

disturbance, 548

disturbance in ecosystem, 532–533, *541*, 541, *543*, 543, 548–550, *548*, 561

diversity, types of, 529, *529*

dodder plant, as parasite, 391, *391*

dog, 390, *390*, 391

dolerite
  as igneous rock, 290, *290*

Doppler radar
  weather data, 458, *458*, 480

dormant volcano, 452

Do the Math, 74, 168, 405, 462, 530, 572
  Analyze Eruption Data, 457, *457*
  Analyze Groundwater Use, 354
  Analyze Land Reclamation in Singapore, 13, *13*
  Analyze Natural Resource Use, 199, *199*

Analyze Population Growth Data, 375, *375*
Analyze Relationships, 388, *388*
Analyze Size and Scale of Matter, 233
Analyze Temperature During a Change of State, 91
Analyze the Economics of Recycling, 505, *505*
Analyze Thermal Energy, 181
Assess Ecosystem Health, 534
Calculate Deposition, 293, *293*
Calculate Rate of Erosion, 272, *272*
Calculate Salinity, 60
Calculate the Amount of Material Needed, 28, *28*
Calculate the Rate of Sea-Floor Spreading, 326, *326*
Compare Costs and Benefits of Shade-Grown Coffee, 568
Compare Properties of Matter, 142
Compare Rates of Change, 434, *434*
Compare Rates of Renewal, 202, *202*
Compare Reactants and Products, 259
Explain Earthquake Probability, 476
Identify Factors That Change Populations, 553
Identify Ratios, 110
Interpret Natural Disaster Data, 451, *451*
Model the Scale of an Atom, 108
Stress-Strain Graph, 35, *35*

dragonfly, 362

Draw, 9, 95, 110, 116, 159, 187, 188, 278, 302, 319, 372, 410, 448, 499

drinking water, 12, *12*

drones (flying machine), 507, *507*

drought
  cost of, in U.S., 462, *462*
  coyote population, 383, *383*, 397
  desert locust swarms during, 545, *545*
  as natural hazard, 448, *448*
  as weather/climate hazard, 449, *449*
  worldwide data, 451, *451*

Dubai, 10, *10*

dunes, sand, 273, *273*
Dust Bowl, 349, *349*
dye, as natural resource, 197

E

eagle, 410, *410*
Earth interior, energy from, 431, *431*
earthquake
  data on U.S., 450, *450*
  deep-ocean trenches, 327, *327*
  distribution worldwide, 472, *472*
  as geographic hazard, 449, *449*, 472, *472*
  Haiti (2010), 472, *472*
  hazard areas in U.S., 450, *450*
  historic, in U.S., 450, *450*
  as natural hazard, 448, *448*
  natural hazard risk in U.S., 446, *446*
  practice drill, 424, *424*
  prediction, 475–476, *476*
  probability of major earthquake near Yellowstone National Park, 476, *476*
  tectonic plate boundaries and surface features, 329, *329*
  volcanic eruption, 452
  worldwide distribution, 472, *472*
  Yellowstone National Park, 439, *439*, 440, *440*

earthquake warning system, 335–336, *335*, *336*

Earth Science Connection
  cycling of resources, 416

Earths system
  distribution of natural resources in, 6, 7, *7*
  subsystems of, 6

Earth surface
  continental data analysis, 320–323
  explaining changes on, 432–438
  fossil data, 320–321, *320*, *321*
  geologic processes changing, 426–443
  geologic process impacts, 426–443
  human use of synthetic materials impact on, 492–516
  large-scale geologic changes to, 432–433, *432*

modeling Earth's surface, 328–332

natural hazard prediction and mitigation, 466–491

natural hazards as disruptive to, 444–465

ocean-floor data analysis, 324–327

small-scale geologic changes to, 432–433, *432*

tectonic plate movement, 318–339

time scale of changes to, 433–438, *435, 436, 437, 438*

Earth system, 428

analysis of interactions within, 428–431

atmosphere, 6, 429, *429*

biosphere, 6, 225, 429, *429*

cycle of energy and matter, 202, *202*, 229, 237–240, *237, 238, 239,* 430, *430*

cycles in, 138–139

cycling of matter in organisms, 228–247

distribution of natural resources in, 6, 7, *7*

Earth surface and plate movements, 318–339

ecosystem, 400–414

energy from Earth interior, 431, *431*

geosphere, 6, 429, *429*

human impact on, 202, 203–204

hydrosphere, 6, 429, *429*

igneous rocks related to, 288–291

inputs and outputs, 138–139

metamorphic rocks related to, 296–299

natural resource availability, 360–381

natural resource distribution, 340–359

patterns of interactions between organisms, 382–399

sedimentary rocks related to, 292–295

subsystem interactions, 429–430, *429, 430,* 431, *431*

time scale, 433

water on, 80

earthworm

as decomposer, 237

as food, 362, *362*

eastern gray squirrel, 551–552, *551, 552*

ecologist, 532

ecosystem, 362, 365, **528**

abiotic factors, 362

analysis of energy flow in, 402–406

biodiversity and dynamics of, 523–594

biodiversity indicating health of, 526–538

biodiversity influencing health of, 526–538, 567–569

biotic factors, 362

carbon cycle, 408, *408*

of caves, 52, *52,* 59, *59*

changes in, 546–550

of coral reefs, 526, *526*

cycling of matter in, 407–410

distribution of, 364

disturbances in, 532–533, 541, *541,* 543, *543,* 548, 561

within Earth system, 400–414

effects of change on, 549

energy pyramid, 406, *406*

energy transfer in, 402–406

eutrophication of, 548, *548*

Florida everglades, 364, *364,* 365

food chains and food webs, 403–404, *403, 404,* 406, *406*

forest, 363, *363,* 372, *372*

of forest floor, 546, *546*

habitat destruction of, 536, *536*

health of, 532, 564–569

human activity impact on, 535–538

human impacts on, 365

humans as part of, 535–538

humans' relying on, 564–567

impact of product disposal, 16, *16*

interactions in, 532, *532,* 573

keystone species in, 570–571

as level of ecosystem organization, 364, 365

levels of organization, 364–365, *365*

lionfish impact on local, 421–422, *421*

living environment, 362

living things and nonliving things in, 546–558, 561, *561*

maintaining, 562–582

natural resources from, 7, *7,* 14, *14,* 565, *565*

nitrogen cycle, 409, *409*

nonliving environment, *362*

parts of, 362–365

pond, 402, *402*

population changes in, 551–555, 561

production and distribution disrupting, 15, *15*

rain forest, 372, *372*

recovery from disturbances, 533, 550

restoration ecologist designing solutions for, 539–540

services provided by, 566, *566,* 578

society's relationship with, 16, *16*

stability of through disturbances, 532, 533, *533*

stabilization of, 544–556

water cycle, 352, 407, *407*

water distribution in, 56, *56*

wetlands, 400, *400*

ecosystem diversity, 529, *529*

ecosystem services, 7, *7*

ecotourism, 583–584

edge effect, 573

electrical energy, 120, *120*

electric conductivity of matter, 58

electromagnetic waves, 177, *177*

electron micrograph

chloroplasts, 257, *257*

mitochondrion, 259, *259*

element, 106

in chemical formula, 156

in human body, by mass, 231, *231*

properties of, 107

elephant

as consumer, 237

preservation of, *557,* 583–584

resources needed to survive, 366, *366*

Elephant Nature Park (ENP), 584

elevation

air pressure changing, 97–98, *97*

boiling point at, *98*

El Niño Southern Oscillation (ENSO), 478
El Niño weather cycles, 395–396, *395, 396,* 478
Elodea, 254–255, *254, 256*
Elton, Charles, 411–412, *411*
emerald ash borer, 536, 577, *577*
emergency preparation, 483, *483,* 484
encaustic painting, 126, *126*
Endangered Species Act, 570
energy, 233
  cells, production for, 248–265
  cellular respiration for, 258–260
  chemical reactions for cellular production of, 248–265
  collecting solar energy, 9, *9*
  consumers, 237, *237*
  cycle of matter and, Earth system, 202, *202,* 229, 237–240, *237, 238, 239,* 430, *430*
  decomposer and decomposition, 229, 237–240, *237–239*
  from Earth interior, 431, *431*
  flow of in ecosystem, 532, *532*
  kinetic energy, 76–77
  law of conservation of energy, 139, 241–242, 250
  loss of causing change of state, 93–98
  in molecular chemical bonds, 232, 250, 257
  in organisms, 233–234
  in organisms, sources of, 235–240
  photosynthesis for, 253–258
  photosynthesis production of, 253–258
  producers, 236, *236*
  pyramid of, food chain, 406, *406*
  renewable, 201
  sun as source for plants and animals, 233–234, *234*
energy flow
  chemical processes analysis, 179–183
  cycle of matter and, Earth system, 202, *202,* 229, 237–240, *237, 238, 239,* 430, *430*

deposition, 272–278
drives cycling of matter in organisms, 228–247
drives the rock cycle, 284–307
drives weathering, erosion and deposition, 266–283
ecosystem analysis, 402–406
erosion, 272–278
food chain, 403, *403,* 404, *404*
food webs, 403–404, *404*
matter in organisms, 230–233
model in ecosystem, 405
weathering, 268–271
energy in molecular chemical bonds, 232, 250, 257
energy pyramid of ecosystem, 406, *406*
energy transfer
  conduction, 177, *177,* 178
  convection, 177, *177,* 178
  in ecosystem, 402–406
  radiation, 177, *177,* 178
  types of, 177–178, *177, 178*
engineer
  science practices compared to, 8, *8*
  society role of, 8
  synthetic material disposal, 508, *508*
engineering
  careers in, 37–38, 65–66, 213–214, 511–512
  distribution networks, 10, *10*
  purpose of investigations by, 33–36, *33–36*
  relationship between science, resources and, 4–21, *4–21*
  role in synthetic material life cycle, 506–509, *506–509*
  and science, 1–48
  science, technology, and, 8, *8*
  science and, 1–48
  science practices compared to, 33–36, *33–36,* 41, *41*
  solving problems and developing solutions, 33
engineering design process
  analyze and interpret data, 35, 224, 522
  ask a question, 34, 41, 521
  brainstorm solutions, 25, *25,* 28

  choose and model solutions, 25, *25*
  communicate information, 36, 48, 224, 314, 422, 522, 593
  computational thinking, 35
  conduct research, 48, 224, 314, 422, 522, 593
  consider tradeoffs, 25, *25,* 29
  construct an explanation, 422, 593
  define the problem, 25, *25,* 26, 34, 41, 47, *47,* 223, 313, 421, 593
  design solutions, 2, 24–32, 36, 522
  develop and test models, 25, *25,* 30–31, 34, 314
  develop solutions, 24–32, 33
  engage in argument from evidence, 36
  engineering problems, 26–32
  evaluate data, 48, 224
  evaluate solutions, 25, *25*
  identify and recommend solutions, 48
  identifying criteria and constraints, 25, *25*
  identifying needs or desires, 26, *26*
  identify solutions, 2, 22, 48, 224
  implement solutions, 25, *25*
  iterative testing, 29, **29**
  make a recommendation, 314
  mathematical thinking, 35
  natural hazard mitigation, 486
  optimize solutions, 29, 41
  outline of, 25, *25*
  planning and carrying out investigations, 35
  recommend solutions, 2, 22, 48, 224, 422, 593
  refine solutions, 25, *25*
  solutions begin with, 24
  solve problems, 33
  test solutions, 25, *25,* 28, 29, 41
  using, 22–41
engineering model, 34
engineering problem
  brainstorming solutions, 28
  constraints of, 26
  criteria of, 26
  defining, 26–27
  developing and testing solutions, 28
  identifying solutions, 2

optimizing solutions, 29
precisely wording of, 26
solutions begin with, 24
testing solutions, 29
Engineer It, 7, 92, 145, 164, 211, 223,
277, 293, 333, 354, 421, 434, 456,
593
Analyze a Solution, 409, *409*
Analyze the Life Cycle of Carbon
Fibers, 510
Control Population Growth, 369
Designing a Landslide Warning
System, 471
Evaluate Cost vs. Performance, 120
Explore Bioremediation, 240
Explore Uses of Algae as Biofuel,
257
Forest Fire Control Policy, 556
Identify Patterns in Shape and
Volume, 74
Identify the Effects of an
Engineering Solution, 205
Maintaining Biodiversity and
Ecosystem Services, 562–587
Monitor and Preserve Biodiversity,
538
Performance Task, 47–48, 131–132,
223–224, 313–314, 421–422,
521–522, 593–594
Permeable Pavers, 588
Recommend a Material, 58
Reduce Erosion, 350
Use Competition to Control
Population Size, 394
Using the Engineering Design
Process, 22–41
Using Thermal Energy in a Device,
174–193
**Enhanced Fujita Scale (EF Scale) for
tornado,** 459–460, *459*, *460*, 464,
464
environment
changes in, 567–569
ecosystem disturbances in,
532–533
human use impacting, 12, *12*
Environmental Science Connection
acid rain, 218, *218*
oil drilling in the Arctic, 416, *416*

erosion, 272
agents of, 272–275, *273–275*
as ecosystem service, 566, *566*
energy driving process of, 272–278
gravity as agent of, 274, *274*
ice as agent of, 274, *274*
modeling, 276–278
natural control of, 7, *7*
obtaining resources causing, 14, *14*
reduction, 350
rock cycle model, 301–302, *301*
time scale, 278, *278*
water as agent of, 272–275, *273–275*
wind as agent of, 272–274, *273*
ethanol
as synthetic fuel, 206
as synthetic material, 211
ethylene, 574
in polyethylene formation, 207, *207*,
210
eucalyptus leaves, as koala food,
384, *384*
Eurasian red squirrel, 551–552, *551*,
552
European honeybee, 535, *535*
eutrophication of sediments, 548,
548
evaporation
of liquids, *89*
water cycle, 407, *407*
Everglades, 563, *563*, 568, *568*, 585
evidence
analyzing, 100
argument from, 36, *36*, 569
forensic scientist collecting, 99
supporting claims, 19, *19*, 39, *39*,
67, 81, 101, 123, 151, 171, 191,
215, 245, 263, 281, 305, 320, 337,
357, 379, 397, 413, 441, 463, 489,
513, 541, 559, 585
Evidence Notebook, 5, 12, 16, 19, 23,
26, 29, 34, 39, 53, 55, 60, 67, 71,
74, 76, 81, 85, 88, 91, 101, 105,
107, 109, 118, 123, 137, 141, 146,
151, 155, 164, 167, 171, 175, 178,
180, 191, 195, 207, 210, 215, 229,
237, 241, 245, 249, 253, 260, 263,
267, 270, 275, 281, 285, 287, 295,
301, 305, 319, 327, 328, 333, 337,
341, 344, 351, 357, 361, 369, 373,
379, 383, 388, 394, 397, 401, 404,
406, 408, 413, 427, 429, 433, 435,

441, 445, 449, 454, 458, 463, 467,
469, 475, 484, 489, 493, 499, 503,
510, 513, 527, 534, 537, 541, 545,
549, 555, 559, 563, 568, 577, 579,
585
Exploration
Analyzing Chemical Equations,
159–164
Analyzing Continental Data,
320–323
Analyzing Energy Flow in
ecosystem, 402–406
Analyzing Energy in Chemical
Processes, 179–183
Analyzing Feeding Relationships,
384–388
Analyzing How Energy Influences a
Change of State, 86–88
Analyzing Human Influences on
Biodiversity, 535–538
Analyzing Interactions Within the
Earth System, 428–431
Analyzing Natural Resources,
196–199
Analyzing Natural Systems, 138–139
Analyzing Ocean-Floor Data,
324–327
Analyzing Particles of Matter,
106–111
Analyzing Parts of an Ecosystem,
362–365
Analyzing Properties of Matter,
57–60
Analyzing Strategies for Maintaining
Biodiversity, 570–577
Analyzing Substances Before and
After a Change, 146–148
Analyzing the Chemistry of Cells,
250–252
Analyzing the Design of Synthetic
Materials, 210–212
Analyzing the Impact of Synthetic
Materials, 500–505
Analyzing the Life Cycle of Synthetic
Materials, 494–499
Comparing Engineering and
Science Practices, 33–36
Comparing Minerals and Rocks,
286–287

© Houghton Mifflin Harcourt Publishing Company

Comparing Physical Changes and Chemical Reactions, 143–145

Describing Biodiversity, 528–531

Describing Cellular Respiration, 258–260

Describing Changes in ecosystem, 546–550

Describing Matter and Energy in Organisms, 230–234

Describing Natural Hazard Mitigation, 482–486

Describing Natural Hazards and Natural Disasters, 446–451

Describing Natural Resource Use, 9–13

Describing the Cycling of Matter in ecosystem, 407–410

Describing the Impacts of Resource Use, 14–16

Designing a Cold Pack, 184–188

Developing Engineering Solutions, 24–32

Evaluating Biodiversity Loss, 564–569

Evaluating Ecosystem Health, 532–534

Evaluating How Pressure Can Affect Changes of State, 97–98

Evaluating Solutions for Maintaining Biodiversity, 578–582

Evaluating the Effects of Using Resources, 200–205

Explaining How Organisms Obtain Matter and Energy, 235–240

Explaining Human Impact on Natural Resource Distribution, 349–354

Explaining Patterns in Natural Resource Distribution, 342–348

Explaining Plate Motion, 332–334

Explaining States of Matter, 75–78

Explaining Symbiotic Relationships, 389–391

Explaining the Changes on Earth's Surface, 432–438

Exploring Agents of Erosion and Deposition, 272–275

Exploring Systems and Energy Flow, 176–178

Identifying Effects of Weathering, 268–271

Interpreting Patterns in Tornado Data, 458–460

Interpreting Patterns in Volcanic Data, 452–457

Investigating Photosynthesis, 253–257

Investigating Synthetic Materials, 206–209

Modeling Addition of Thermal Energy to a Substance, 89–92

Modeling Chemical Reactions, 165–168

Modeling Earth's Surface, 328–331

Modeling Matter, 61–64

Modeling Molecules, 112–117

Modeling Removal of Thermal Energy for a Substance, 93–96

Modeling the Rock Cycle, 300–302

Modeling Weathering, Erosion, and Deposition, 276–278

Observing Patterns in Matter, 54–56

Observing Properties of Matter, 72–74

Predicting Changes to Populations, 551–556

Predicting Effects of Abundant Resources, 374–376

Predicting Effects of Competitive Interactions, 392–394

Predicting Effects of Limited Resources, 370–373

Predicting Geologic Hazards, 472–476

Predicting Natural Hazards, 468–471

Predicting Weather and Climate Hazards, 477–481

Relating Cycling of Matter to Transfer of Energy, 241–242

Relating Engineering and the Life Cycle, 506–510

Relating Igneous Rocks to the Earth System, 288–291

Relating Metamorphic Rocks to the Earth System, 296–299

Relating Natural Resources to Science and Engineering, 6–8

Relating Resource Availability to Growth, 366–369

Relating Sedimentary Rocks to the Earth System, 292–295

Relating the Identity and Structure of Matter to Its Properties, 118–120

Using Chemical Formulas, 156–158

Using Properties to Identify Substances, 140–142

Explore First

Analyzing Food Labels, 228

Building Objects, 104

Categorizing State of Matter Changes, 84

Categorizing Substances, 194

Choosing Building Materials, 562

Classifying Events, 426

Constructing Puzzles, 318

Describing Properties of Objects, 52

Exploring Synthetics, 492

Identifying States of Matter, 70

Investigating Changes to Matter, 266

Investigating Plants, 248

Mapping Resources, 340

Measuring Changes in Energy, 174

Mining Clay, 4

Modeling a Cargo Boat, 22

Modeling a Flood, 466

Modeling a Sandstorm, 444

Modeling Ecosystem Change, 526

Modeling Rock Formation, 284

Modeling the Flow of Energy, 400

Observing Resource Use, 382

Planning a Terrarium, 360

Reorganizing Materials, 136

Thinking About Changes, 544

Writing Formulas, 154

Explore ONLINE!, 24, 62, 72, 76, 86, 93, 137, 144, 149, 151, 155, 175, 179, 180, 191, 229, 250, 256, 288, 319, 328, 332, 337, 361, 379, 410, 413, 430, 452, 484, 535, 546

exponential growth of population, 377, *377*, *378*, *378*

extended molecule structures, 116, *116*

extinction, 536, 570
  mass, 230

extinct volcano, 452

extrusive igneous rocks, 288

F

fabric, synthetic or natural, 194, *194*

farm
  obtaining resources, 9, *9*
  runoff from, 566, *566*, 567, 575
  synthetic fertilizer used on, 575, *575*

fat, in cells, 251–252, *252*

feeding relationship
  algae, 384, 385–387, *385*
  carnivore, 384, 385–387, *385*
  herbivore, 384, 385–387, *385*
  omnivore, 386
  pattern of interactions between organisms, 384–388
  plant, 384, 385–387, *385*
  and population size, 388
  predator and prey, 384, 385, 388, 394

fermentation, 261
  compared to cellular respiration, 261–262, *261*

fertility of soil, 344, *344*

fertilizer, 240, 503, 573

fiberglass, 209, *209*

fine-grained igneous rock, 290

fire
  alarm for, 32, *32*
  combustion, and thermal energy, 174, *174*
  non-matter, 54
  prevention, 556
  rates of energy transformation, 180

fireflies, 136

flameless heater, 175, *175*, 191, *191*

flamingo, food for, 384, *384*

flammability
  as chemical property of matter, 141
  of matter, 58

flea, as parasite, 391

flexibility of matter, 57

flood
  in Bangladesh, *553*
  causes, 480, 481
  cost in U.S., 462, *462*
  ecosystem affected by, 527, *527*, 541, *541*
  Houston park improvement, 521, *521*
  model of deposition, erosion and weathering, 276–277, *277*
  as natural hazard, 448, *448*
  New Jersey, 466, *466*
  prediction of, 480–481
  protection by wetlands, 316, *316*
  river, 435, *435*
  sudden changes from, 548
  from tropical cyclone (2015), 461, *461*
  as weather/climate hazard, 449, *449*
  worldwide, 451, *451*, 480, *480*

flood maps, 481, *481*

Florida
  everglades ecosystem, 364, *364*, 365
  sinkholes in, 519, *519*

Florida panther, 571

fluorite, 340, *340*

flying squirrel, 363, *363*

food
  biodiversity lacking in crop, 537
  molecular structure of, 252, *252*
  plant, 240
  producer transform energy into food, 236, *236*
  reintroducing wild genes in crop, 537
  as synthetic material, 211

food chain
  ecosystem energy transfer, 403, *403*, 404, *404*
  limited biotic resources, 372
  pyramid of numbers, 416, *416*

food warmer, flameless, 175, *175*, 191, *191*

food web
  ecosystem, 403–404, *404*, 406, *406*
  energy pyramid, 406, *406*
  nitrogen cycle, 409, *409*

forces, collision transferring, 97

forecasting
  natural hazards, 468, *468*
  tornado, 479, *479*
  weather hazards, 479, *479*

forensic scientist, 99–100

forest
  clear-cutting, consequences of, 203
  coniferous, 360, *360*
  ecosystem of, 528, 551
  harvesting, 498, 499
  inputs or outputs in, 139, *139*
  limited resource effects, 370, *370*
  wildfire, 361, *361*, 379, *379*, 423, *423*, 431, *431*
  wildfire hazard mitigation, 484, *484*

forest ecosystem, 363, *363*, 372, *372*
  fire prevention effects on, 556

forest fire, 548–549, *549*

forest floor ecosystem, 546, *546*

formulas
  interior-to-edge ratios, 572
  percentage, 530
  salinity, 60

fossil, 321

fossil data
  continental, 320–321, *320*, *321*
  matching across Atlantic, 320–321, *320*, *321*, 323

fossil fuel
  as ancient biofuel, 257
  natural resource distribution, 344–345, *345*, 346, 350–351, *351*
  nonrenewable, 16, 201, 350–351, *351*
  pollution from, 573
  reducing need for, 12, *12*
  refining, 226, *226*
  transportation of, 15
  use of, 535, 565, *565*

fracking (hydraulic fracturing), 14, *14*, 507, *507*

Fredrich Mohs, 57

freeze, cost in U.S., 462, *462*

freeze-thaw cycle
    chemical weathering, 270
    physical weathering, 269, *269*

freezing point, 94, *94*, 95

frequency, natural hazard data,
    450–451, *450*

freshwater
    natural resource distribution,
      346–347, *346, 347,* 352–354, *352*
    phytoplankton in ecosystem of, 249,
      249

frog, 258, *258*

fuel
    biofuel, 213–214, *213, 214*
    as synthetic material, 211, *211*

fungal disease, 537

fungus
    as biotic factor, 372
    as decomposer, 236, 237
    decomposition by, 236, *236*
    shelf fungi, 363, *363*
    soil formation, 344, *344*

G

gallium, 85, *85,* 101, *101*

game theory, 17

Garden by the Bay, Singapore, 562,
    562

gas, 74
    changing states of, 94, *95*
    chemical reaction production of,
      144, *144,* 146, 162, *162,* 172, *172*
    convection energy transfer, 177, *177*

gas chromatography (GC), 100, *100*

gases
    attraction of particles in, 78
    kinetic energy of, 97
    as state of matter, 55, 72, 83
    in volcanos, 49, *49*

gel electrophoresis, 131

genes, increasing variety of in
    crops, 537

genetic diversity, 529, *529*
    in crops, 537

geological processes
    igneous rock, 288, *288*
    metamorphic rock, 296, *296*
    sedimentary rock, 292, *292*

geologic hazard prediction
    earthquake prediction, 475–476,
      476
    timing and magnitude, 472, *472*
    volcanic eruption prediction, 472,
      472, 473–475

geologic hazards
    described, 448, *448,* 449, *449*
    predicting, 472–476

geologic hazard, volcanic eruption
    as, 452

geologic processes
    analysis of Earth system
      interactions, 428–431
    explaining changes on Earth
      surface, 432–438
    impacts on Earth surface, 426–443
    large-scale changes to Earth
      surface, 432–433, *432*
    small-scale changes to Earth
      surface, 432–433, *432*
    time scale of Earth surface changes,
      433–438, *435, 436, 437, 438*

geosphere
    Earth system, 6, 429, *429*
    igneous rock in, 290
    metamorphic rock in, 298, *298*
    rare earth elements (REE), 355–356,
      355
    sedimentary rock in, 294, *294*

geyser, 439, *439*

Gibbons, Doug, 335–336, *335*

ginseng, 536

giraffe, 233, *233*

GIS (Graphic Information System),
    485

glacier, 274, *274,* 548

glass, 6, *6*
    creating, 86, *86*
    liquid bioactive, medical, 511, *511*
    sand for, 6
    as synthetic material, 206, 210, *210*

glassworker, 86, *86*

Global Positioning System (GPS),
    474, *474, 475*

Glossopteris, 320, *320*

glove, testing disposable, 506, *506*

gluten-free foods, 308, *308*

gneiss, 296, *296,* 298, *298*

gold
    distribution of, 341, *341,* 342, *342,*
      343, *343*
    iron pyrite compared, 140, *140*
    as nonrenewable, 351, *351*
    panning for, 278–280, *279–280*
    weathering, erosion and deposition,
      278–280, *279–280*

gold particles, 62, 69, *69*

Gold Rush, 351, *351*

government, natural hazard
    mitigation, 483–484, *483, 484*

GPS (Global Positioning System),
    474, *474,* 475

gradual changes in ecosystem, 548

graduated cylinder, 72

Grand Canyon, formation of, 285,
    285, 294, *294,* 305, *305*

granite
    as igneous rock, 290, *290*
    as natural resource, 197, 198

graph
    of bird species biodiversity, 534, *534*
    of forest coverage, *553*
    Stress-Strain Graph, 35, *35*
    of temperature, 91

Graphic Information System (GIS),
    485

graphic organizer
    for key concepts, 3, 51, 135, 227,
      317, 425, 525
    Venn diagram, *551*

graphite, 119, *119,* 197, *197*

gravel, 36, *36*

gravity
    as deposition agent, 274, *274*
    as erosion agent, 274, *274*
    tectonic plate movement, 334
    water cycle, 407, *407*
    as weathering agent, 268

gray squirrel, 551–552, *551, 552*

Great Garbage Patch, 574

Great Lakes, glacial origin of, 274

Great Salt Lake, Utah, 523, *523*

greenhouse gas, nitrous oxide, 575

greenschist, 298, *298*

Griffith Park in Los Angeles, 524, *524*

grossular, chemical formula for, 158, *158*

groundwater

chemical weathering, 270, *270*

contamination, synthetic material production, 502, *502*

drilling for, 352

filtration and treatment of, 10

as freshwater resource, 346, *346*, 347, *347*, 352

groundwater, modeling, 562

growth, natural resource availability, 366–369

Gulf of Mexico

Deepwater Horizon oil spill impact, 501, *501*

Gulfport, Mississippi

Hurricane Isaac (2012), 447, *447*

gypsum crystal, 52, *52*, 286, 287

gyre, 574

H

Haber, Fritz, 189–190, *189*, *190*

Haber-Bosch reactor, 189–190, *190*

habitat

of cougar, 524, *524*

destruction of, 536, *536*, 568, 571

fragmentation of, 571–572, *571*

protecting and maintaining, 571–573

reducing loss of, 576–577

Haiti, earthquake (2010), 472, *472*

Half Dome, Yosemite National Park, 290, 291

halite

chemical formula for, 158, *158*

distribution of, 343, *343*

Halls Bayou, Houston, 521, *521*

Hands-On Labs

Analyze Visual Evidence, 436–437

Build a Structure Using Your Own Concrete, 11

Choose a Chemical Process, 185–186

Design a Bicycle Helmet Model, 30–31

Identify Factors That Influence a Population Change, 554–555

Investigate a Change of State, 87–88

Investigate Decomposition, 238–239

Investigate Effects of Limited Resources, 371

Investigate the Effect of Sunlight on *Elodea*, 254–255

Investigate the Influence of Decisions on Resource Use, 11

Make a Synthetic Material, 208

Measure Biodiversity, 530–531

Model Crystal Formation, 289

Model Energy Flow in an Ecosystem, 405

Model Erosion and Deposition, 277

Model Habitat Fragmentation, 572

Modeling Objects, 63

Model Molecules, 114–115

Model Particles in Objects, 63–64

Model Recharge and Withdrawal in an Aquifer, 353–354

Model the Movement of Continents, 330–331

Observe a Chemical Reaction, 163

Observe States of Matter, 73–74

Observe Substances Before and After a Change, 147

online, 1, 30, 63, 73, 87, 114, 147, 163, 185, 208, 238, 254, 277, 289, 330, 353, 371, 386, 405, 436, 455, 470, 509, 530, 554, 572

Simulate Feeding Relationships, 386–387

What Factors Influence a Population Change? 554–555

hand warmer

energy changes in, 179, *179*

harbor seals, 377, *377*

hardness, as characteristic of matter, 55

hartebeest, at watering hole, 392, *392*

Haupt, Anna, 28, *28*

Hawaii

Kilauea volcano, 455–456, *455*, *456*, 473, *473*

lava flows through, 288, *288*

lava rock formation, 438, 439

Mauna Loa volcano eruption data, 474–475, *474*, *475*

Health Connection

Cholera Today, *42*

Natural Disasters and Disease, 516, *516*

The Chemistry of Digestion, 218

The Gluten-Free Craze, 308, *308*

heater, flameless, 175, *175*

heat of combustion, 58

heat pack design, 133

hematite, chemical formula for, 158

herbivore, feeding relationships, 384, 385–387, *385*, *386–387*

Himalaya mountains, 332, *332*, 432, *432*

historical data

on hurricanes and tropical cyclones, 469, *469*

natural hazard, 450–451, *450*

natural hazard prediction, 469, *469*, 474, *474*

tornado, U.S., 446, *446*, 459, *459*, 460, *460*, 478, *478*

volcanic eruption, 474, *474*

weather monitoring, 480

Hoover Dam, 308, *308*

hotsprings, calcium-rich, 293, *293*

Houston, Texas, 521, *521*

Huacachina Oasis, Peru, 346, *346*

human

synthetic materials and society, 494–495, *495*

use of synthetic materials impact on Earth surface, 492–516

human activity

biodiversity influenced by, 535–538

ecosystem disturbances caused by, 532–533, 543, *543*

habitat destruction by, 568–569

protecting biodiversity, 537, 543, *543*

human behavior, modeling, 17

human habitation

ancient Italy, landslide or volcanic eruption, 445, *445*

hurricane damage, 447, *447*, 482, *482*

natural disaster risk, 447, *447*

wildfire, 444, *444*

human impacts

on ecosystem, 365

energy transfer in ecosystem, 402

on fossil fuel distribution, 350–351, *351*

on freshwater distribution, 352–354, *352*

population and demand for natural resources, 14

on resource quality and quantity, 368–369, *368*

on soil distribution, 349, *349*

human population, impact of, 14

hurricane

damage and deaths from U.S., 517, *517*

flood maps evacuation zones, 481, *481*

historical data on, 469, *469*

natural hazard risk in U.S., 446, *446*

prediction, 469, *469*

satellite image of, 447, *447*

as weather/climate hazard, 449

Hurricane Isaac (2012), 447, *447*

hydraulic fracturing (fracking), 14, *14*, 507, *507*

hydrochloric acid, 162, *162*, 172, *172*

hydroelectric energy, as renewable resource, 201, 347, 348, *348*

hydrogen, 61, *61*, 62

from chemically separated water, 106

electrolysis of water, 160, *160*

as element, 231

in human body, by mass, 231, *231*, 232

in humans, 105, *105*

in propane, 105, *105*

hydrogen chloride, 166

hydrogen peroxide, 164, *164*

hydrosphere, Earth system, 6, 429, *429*

hydrothermal vents, chemotrophs, 243–244, *243*

hyena, 373, *373*

I

ice

as deposition agent, 274, *274*

disappearing ecosystem of, 50

as erosion agent, 274, *274*

floating, 79–80

formation of, *93*

to model energy movement, 178, *178*

physical weathering, 269, *269*

as solid water, 70, *70*

ice chest as thermal system, 177, *177*

ice dam, Missoula Flood, 276, *276*

Iceland, Mid-Atlantic Ridge, 318, *318*, 325, *325*

igneous rock, 288

formation into metamorphic rock, 297, *297*, 301, *301*

formation of, and changes to, 291, *291*

geological processes, 288, *288*

in geosphere, 290

minerals in, 288, *288*, 290, *290*

related to Earth's systems, 288–291

time scale, 289, *289*, 438, 439

Indiana bat, 571

indigo dye, as natural resource, 197

individual

growth and natural resource availability, 367, 368

as level of ecosystem organization, 364, 365, *365*

infographic, 396

inputs and outputs

Earth's system, 138–139

system, 176

insulin, 209

interactions

in ecosystem, 532, *532*

feeding relationships, 384–388

between organisms, 382–399

Interactive Review, 21, 41, 69, 83, 103, 125, 153, 173, 193, 217, 247, 265, 283, 307, 339, 359, 381, 399, 415, 443, 465, 491, 515, 543, 561, 587

interior-to-edge ratios, 572

introduced species, 536, *536*, 573, *573*, 577, *577*

intrusive igneous rock, 288, *288*, 290

investigations

developing hypotheses, 531

recording data, 531

in science and engineering, 33–36

iron

chemical weathering, *270*

iron, chemical weathering, 270

iron ore

distribution of, *343*

iron pyrite, 140, *140*, 158, *158*

island, sudden formation of, 319, *319*, 337, *337*

Italy

ancient habitation, landslide or volcanic eruption buried, 445, *445*, 463, *463*

eroded rock formation, 275, *275*

Mount Vesuvius volcano, 457, *457*

iterative testing, 29

J

Japan, tsunami warnings, 469, *469*

Javan rhino, 588

jellyfish, 573

joule, 181

K

kayak, plastic, 195, *195*, 215

Kenai Fjord National Park, Alaska, 544, *544*

Kevlar©, 494, *494*

key concepts, graphic organizer for, 3, 51, 135, 227, 317, 425, 525

keystone species, 570–571, *571*

Khalili, Nadar, 42

Kilauea volcano, Hawaii, 455–456, *455*, *456*, 473, *473*

Kilhauea, 49, *49*

kinetic energy

energy of motion, 76–77

of gas particles, 97, *97*

of particles, 75, 76–77, 78, 79

thermal energy relating to, 89

kingfisher, 228, *228*
koala
  as consumer, 237
  eucalyptus leaves as food, 384, *384*
kudzu, 573, *573*
Kwolek, Stephanie, 494

L

lactic acid fermentation, 261, *261*
lahar, 453, *453*, 483, *483*
lake, ecosystem of, 528
land, biodiversity hotspots, 531, *531*
land bridges, 571, *571*
landfill
  disposal, 504, *504*
  exposure pathways, 520, *520*
landform data
  continental data analysis, 322, *322*
  mineral resource distribution, 342,
    342, 343, *343*
landforms, freshwater distribution,
    347, *347*
landslide, 274, *274*
  extreme, worldwide data, 451, *451*
  as geographic hazard, 472
  as natural hazard, 448, *448*
  predicting, 470–471, *471*
landslide warning system, 471
Language Development, 3, 51, 135,
    227, 317, 425, 525
Language SmArts, 9, 24, 77, 95, 148,
    162, 334, 346, 537, 552
  Analyze a Chemical Process, 183
  Analyze an Abundant Resource,
    376, *376*
  Analyze Rate of Environmental
    Change, 550
  Categorize Matter, 55
  Cite Evidence for Conservation of
    Matter and Energy, 242
  Cite Evidence for Plate Tectonics,
    334
  Compare Tornado Data, 460
  Determine Sources and Uses of
    Synthetic Materials, 212

Evaluate Agricultural Practices, 569
Evaluate Molecule Models, 117
Examine Changes over Time, 438
Explain Evidence of Competition,
    393
Explain Your Observations, 323
Find Evidence for Weathering, 271
Model the Cycling of Matter, 410
Model the Life Cycle, 499
Model the Rock Cycle, 302
Outline Design Steps, 36
Relate Photosynthesis and Cellular
    Respiration, 260
Use Flood Maps, 481
**large-scale geologic changes to
    Earth surface,** 432–433, *432*
latex, in rubber production, 222, *222*
lava, 75, 96, *96*, 452
  energy from Earth interior, 431, *431*
  as hazard, 138, *138*
  igneous rock formation, 288, *288*,
    290, *290*, 291, *291*
  mineral formation, 286
  rock formation, 438, 439
  sea-floor spreading, 325–326, *325*
  volcanic eruption, 452
  as volcanic hazard, 453
law of conservation of energy, 139,
    241–242, 250
law of conservation of matter, 165,
    250
  balanced chemical equations,
    166–168
  cycling of matter and energy
    transfers, 241–242
  modeling chemical reactions,
    165–168
  weathering, 268
law of definite proportions, 121, *121*
Laysan albatrosses, 574
lead, 121, *121*
lead iodide, 168
  lead nitrate and sodium iodide
    chemical reaction, *168*
lead sulfide, 121, *121*
leech, as parasite, 391

Lesson Self-Check, 19–21, 39–41,
    67–69, 81–83, 101–103, 123–125,
    151–153, 171–173, 191–193,
    215–217, 245–247, 263–265,
    281–283, 305–307, 337–339,
    357–359, 379–381, 397–399,
    413–415, 441–443, 463–465,
    489–491, 513–515, 541–543,
    559–561, 585–587
lianas vine, 236, *236*
lichen
  chemical weathering, *270*
life cycle
  of carbon fiber, 510
  impact of resource use through,
    14–16
  of products, 9–13
  synthetic material phases, 496–497,
    496–497, 500–505, *500–505*
Life Science Connection
  Effects of Plastics on Animals, 516,
    516
lightning
  as weather/climate hazard, 449
  as weather hazard, 448
lightning bugs, 136, *136*
limestone
  marble formation, 299, *299*, 300,
    300
  rock cycle, 300, *300*
  sedimentary rock formation, 294,
    294, 295, *295*
limestone cave, 59–60, *59*
limited resources
  abiotic, 372, *372*
  biotic, 372–373
  predicting effects of, 370–373
linear sea
  formation, *325*
lion
  limited resources, 373, *373*
  as predator, 384, *384*
lionfish, 536
  impact on local ecosystem,
    421–422, *421*

lipids
in avocado (food), 252, *252*
liquid, 74
attraction of particles in, 78, 79
changing states of, 89, *89, 90, 94, 95*
convection energy transfer, 177, *177*
gallium as, 85, 101, *101*
as state of matter, 55, 72, 83
liquid metal, 72, *72*
litter, 573
living things
decomposition of dead, 237
in ecosystem, 528, *528,* 546–558, 561
ecosystem disturbances affecting, 532
as matter, 54, 230
sunlight as energy source for, 233–234, *234,* 256–257, *256*
water use of, 56
location
chemical weathering, *270*
locust, 545, *545*
logistic growth, population, 377, *377, 378, 378*
long-term consequences, of using natural resources, 204–205
Los Angeles, 524, *524*
luster, 57, *57*
Lystrosaurus, 320, *320*

M

macromolecule, 117, *117*
magma, 452
deep-ocean trenches, 327, *327*
energy from Earth interior, 431, *431*
igneous rock formation, 288, *288,* 290, *290,* 291, *291*
mineral formation, 286
rock formation, 287, *287*
sea-floor spreading, 325–326, *325*
volcanic caldera, Yellowstone National Park, 439, *439,* 440, *440*
volcanic eruption, 452, 453, *453*
magma chamber, metamorphic rock formation, 296, *296*

magnitude, natural hazard data, 450–451, *450*
mahouts, 583, *583*
malachite, chemical formula for, 158, *158*
malleability, as physical property of matter, 141
manatee
conservation of, 563, *563,* 585, *585*
as herbivore, 385, *385*
marble, formation of, 299, *299*
Marco Antinous, *126*
marine debris, 574, *574*
marine ecosystem, 528, *528*
biodiversity hotspots, 531
biodiversity in, 536, *536*
marine ecosystem, phytoplankton in, 249, *249*
marine oil exploration, 573
Mars, 65
mass, 54
of atoms, 108
property of matter, 57, 83
mass extinction, 230
material
different properties from same, 105, *105*
recommending, 58
materials engineer, 511–512, *511*
mathematical model, 34
of matter, 62
matter, 54, 230
atoms as building blocks of, 231–232
categorization of, 55
changes in chemical reactions, 138–146
chemical properties, 141
chemical property of, 58–59
condensation of, 94
consumers, 237, *237*
cycle of energy and, Earth system, 202, *202,* 229, 237–240, 430, *430*
decomposer and decomposition, 229, 237–240, *237, 238, 239*
flow of, 532, *532*
mass and volume of, 54
modeling, 61–64
molecules composing, 232

observing properties of, 72–74
in organisms, 230–233
in organisms, sources of, 235–240
patterns in, 54–56, 69
physical properties, 141
producers, 236, *236*
properties of, 57–60, 118–120, 140–142
relating identity and structure to properties of, 118–120
states of, 55, 70–78, 83, 93–96, 103
structures of, 49–125
as tiny, moving particles, 75
matter, changes in chemical reactions
natural systems, analyzing, 138–139
physical changes compared to chemical reactions, 143–145
properties to identify substances, 140–142
substances before and after, analyzing, 146–148
Mauna Loa, Hawaii, volcanic eruption data, 474–475, *474, 475*
meadow plant, 581
mechanical engineers, 37–38, *37*
medicine, 573
aspirin, 209, *209*
insulin, 211
as synthetic material, 209, 211
melting, rock cycle model, 301–302, *301*
melting point, 89, *89,* 141
mercury, 64, *64*
Mesosaurus, 320, *320,* 321, *321*
metal
as natural resource, 197, *197*
thermal energy flow of hot metal in water, 176, *176*
metamorphic rock, 296
formation of, 296, 297, *297,* 298, 299, 301, *301*
geological processes, 296, *296*
in geosphere, 298, *298*
layers in, 296, *296,* 297, *297,* 298, *298,* 299, *299*
related to Earth's systems, 296–299
time scale, 298, *298*

metamorphism, 296

meteor, 487

meteorite

crater in Arizona, 427, *427*, 441, *441*

time scale of change, 433

meteorologist

natural hazard data, 450

tornado data, 459, *459*

methane, *113*

balanced chemical equation, 167

Micronesia, 570

microscopes, 108

Mid-Atlantic Ridge, 324, *325*, 434, *434*

mid-ocean ridge, 324–325, *324, 325*, 327, *327*

mineral, 286

formation of, 286

metamorphic rock formation, 296, *296*

resource distribution, 342, *342*, 343, *343*

within rock, 287, *287*

rock compared to, 286–287

rock formation, 287, *287*, 296, *296*

small-scale geologic changes to Earth surface, 432–433, *432*

mineral resources, 565

availability of, 6, *6*

chemical formulas of, 158, *158*

Mohs hardness scale for, 57

as nonrenewable resource, 201, 350–351, *351*

use of, *565*

minerals

in igneous rocks, 288, *288*, 290, *290*

natural resource distribution, 342–343, *342, 343*, 350–351, *351*

in sedimentary rock, 292, *292*

mining

coal, 303–304, *303*

impact on ecosystem, 14

mountaintop removal, 205, *205*

in United States, 7, *7*

Mississippi (state), Hurricane Isaac (2012), 447, *447*

Missoula Flood, 276, *276*

mitigation, 482

natural hazard, 482–486

mitigation plan, natural hazard, 482, 483, 485–486, *486*

mitochondrion, cellular respiration, 258–259, *258, 259*

model

balanced chemical equation, 167, *167*

chemical reactions, 160, *160*, 162, *162*, 165–168, 251

of chemical substances, 160

of deoxyribonucleic acid (DNA), 117, *117*

deposition, erosion and weathering, 276–277, *267*

developing and testing, 25, *25*, 30–31, 34

Earth's surface, 328–332

of ecosystem changes, 526

of elements and compounds, *111*

of matter, 61–64

mitigation planning, 485

of molecules, 112–117, *112*, 125, *125*

of objects, 63–64

Pangaea, 330–331, *331*

particles of solids, liquids, and gases, 76–77, *76*

of plastic polyvinyl chloride (PVC), 115

removal of thermal energy, 93–96

rock cycle, 300–302

of scale of atom, 108, *108*

testing solutions, 25, *25*

of thermal energy added to substance, 89–92

types of, 34

Mohs hardness scale, 57

mole (animal), 363, *363*

molecular structure, of food, 252, *252*

molecule

atoms bond to form, 232, *232*

carbon as building block of living things, 251–252

carbon-based molecules in cells, 251–252, *252*

chemical bonds in, 232, *232*

chemical equations and chemical reactions, 162

chemically bonded atoms, 109, 112

chemosynthesis, 243

coefficient in chemical equation, 160

compounds of, 109–110, *109, 110*

of deoxyribonucleic acid (DNA), 117, *117*

modeling, 112–117, *112*

particles of matter, 107, *107*

structures of, 118–120

mollusk, 528, *528*

monitoring

earthquake warning system, 335–336, *335, 336*

landslide warning system, 471

natural hazard, 469, *469*

volcano, 474–475, *474–475*

weather/climate hazard, 478, 480, *480*

monoxide, 118

moon in Earth system, 428

Morocco, 528, *528*

moss

chemical weathering, 270, *270*

resources needed to survive, 366, *366*

motion, of particles, 75, 76–77, 78, 90, *90*, 95

mountain, tectonic plate boundaries and surface features, 329, *329*

mountain ranges

matching landform data across Atlantic, 322, *322*, 323

volcanic, parallel to deep-ocean trenches, 327, *327*

mountaintop removal mining, 205, *205*

Mount Pinatubo volcanic eruption, 453, *453*, 472, *472*

Mount St. Helens volcanic eruption, 436–437, *436–437*, 453, *453*, 483, *483*

Mount Vesuvius volcano, Italy, 457, *457*

mudslide, lahar, 454, *454*, 483, *483*

mudstone, 292

muscle, lactic acid fermentation, 261, *261*

mushroom, as decomposer, 236, 237
mutualism, as symbiotic relationship, 390

N

nail, chemical properties of, 141, *141*
National Aeronautics and Space Administration (NASA), 42, 487
National Oceanic and Atmospheric Administration (NOAA), 478, 479, *479*
National Weather Service (NWS), 478
natural disaster, 447
    climate hazards, 449, *449*
    described, 447, *447*
    geologic hazards, 448, *448*, 449, *449*, 472–475
    types of, 446, *446*, 448, *448*, 449, *449*
    weather hazards, 448, *448*, 449, *449*
    worldwide data (1995–2015), 448, *448*, 451, *451*
natural disasters
    cost of, in U.S., 461–462, *461*, *462*
    disease and, 516, *516*
natural ecosystem disturbances, 532–533
natural gas
    fossil fuel distribution, 345, *345*
    as nonrenewable resource, 201
    propane, 105, *105*
natural hazard, 446
    climate, 449, *449*
    describing risk, 446–451
    as disruptive to Earth surface, 444–465
    geologic, 448, *448*, 449, *449*, 472–475
    historical data on, 450–451, *450*
    mitigation, 482–486, *482*, *483*, *484–485*, *486*
    monitoring data on, 469, *469*, 471, *474–475*, 474–475, 480, *480*
    prediction, 468–471, *468–471*

    risk in U.S., 446, *446*
    scientific understanding, 468, *468*
    tornado data, interpreting patterns in, 458–460
    types of, 446, *446*, 448, *448*, 449, *449*
    volcanic data, interpreting patterns in, 452–457
    weather, 448, *448*, 449
natural resource, 6, **196**, 340–359, 360–381
    analyzing, in creation of synthetic materials, 196–199
    availability of, 200–201, 360–381
    chemical makeup, 197, *197*
    competition for, 370–373, 392–394
    consequences of using, 203–205
    cycle of matter and energy, 202, *202*, 229, 237–240, *237*, *238*, *239*, 430, *430*
    distribution of, 6, 340–359
    ecosystem, parts of, 362–365
    evaluating the effects of using, 200–205
    factors that influence, 368–369, *368*
    fossil fuel, 344–345, *345*, 346, 350–351, *351*
    freshwater, 346–347, *346*, *347*, 352–354, *352*
    and growth, 366–369
    human impacts on, 349–354, 368–369, *368*
    life cycle of, 9–13
    limited resources, predicting effects of, 370–373
    living or nonliving, 196, 197, 202
    made from synthetic materials, 194–212
    management consequences, 203–204
    minerals, 342–343, *342*, *343*, 350–351, *351*
    nonrenewable, 16, 201, 350–351, *351*
    obtained in synthetic material life cycle, 496, *496*, 498, *498*, 501, *501*, 507, *507*

    obtaining, 9, *9*
    patterns of, 342–348
    potentially renewable, 201
    predicting effects of abundant resources, 374–376
    processing of, 10
    properties of, 197, *197*
    relationship between science, engineering and, 4–21
    renewable, 201, 202, 347, *347*
    soil, 344, *344*, 349, *349*
    sources of, 6, 196
    uses of, 6, 9–13, 21, 198–199
natural resources
    from ecosystem, 565, *565*
    properties of, 60
natural system
    changes in matter and energy, 139
    inputs and outputs, 138–139
    matter and energy in, 138–139
Nebraska, tornado data collection, 458, *458*
needs
    identifying, 26, *26*
    met by synthetic materials, 494, *495*
    resource use driven by, 8
    of society, 8, 15
negative consequences, of using natural resources, 203–204
New Jersey, flood, 466, *466*
New Zealand, tsunami warning signs, 467, *467*, 489, *489*
Nile River, 56, *56*
nitrogen-based fertilizer, 575, *575*
nitrogen cycle, 409, *409*
nitrogen dioxide, 110, *110*
nitrogen-fixing bacteria, 389
nitrogen, in human body, 231, *231*
nitrous oxide, 110, *110*, 575, *575*
NOAA (National Oceanic and Atmospheric Administration), 478, 479, *479*
nonliving things
    in ecosystem, 528, *528*, 546–558, 561
    ecosystem disturbances affecting, 532
    as matter, 54
    observing patterns in, 52–64

nonliving things, as matter, 230

nonnative species, 536, *536*, 573, *573*, 577, *577*

nonrenewable resource, 16, **201,** 350–351, *351*

North Carolina, tornado risk in, 477, *477*, 478, *478*, 479, *479*

nuclear power plants, 203

nucleic acids, 251

nutrient
in aquatic ecosystem, 550
decomposition releasing, 546, *546*
from forest fires, 556

NWS (National Weather Service), 478

nylon, 206, 209
rope, 498

O

Oak Woodland Regeneration, 557–558, *558*

ocean
chemotrophs, 243–244, *243*

ocean floor
age estimate, 326, *326*, 327, *327*
data analysis, 324–327
deep-ocean trenches, 324, *324*, 325, 327, *327*
mid-ocean ridge, 324–325, *324*, *325*, 327, *327*
sea-floor spreading, 325–326, *325*

octopus, 366, *366*

odor, as physical property of matter, 141

off-road enthusiasts, *582*

offshore oil drilling, 203, 205

Oglala Lakota Nation, 588

oil, 574
formation of, 345–346, *346*
fossil fuel distribution, 344–345, *345*, 346
plastic manufactured from, 195, *195*, 215

oil drilling
in the Arctic, 416, *416*
hydraulic fracturing "fracking," 14, 507, *507*
offshore, consequences of, 203, 205
offshore oil, 203, 205

oil spills
bioremediation, 240, *240*
impact of, 205, *205*, 501, *501*

OLED (organic light-emitting diode), 211, *211*

omnivore, feeding relationships, 386

online activities
Explore ONLINE! 24, 62, 72, 76, 86, 93, 137, 144, 149, 151, 155, 175, 179, 180, 191, 229, 250, 256, 288, 319, 328, 332, 337, 361, 379, 410, 413, 430, 452, 484, 535, 546
Hands-On Labs, 11, 30, 63, 73, 87, 114, 147, 163, 185, 208, 238, 254, 277, 289, 330, 353, 371, 386, 405, 436, 455, 470, 509, 530, 554, 572
Take It Further, 17, 37, 65, 79, 99, 121, 149, 169, 189, 213, 243, 261, 279, 303, 335, *355*, 377, 395, 411, 439, 461, 487, 511, 539, 557, 583
Unit Project Worksheet, 2, 50, 134, 226, 316, 424, 524
You Solve It, 1, 49, 133, 225, 315, 423, 523

ore, 343

organic light-emitting diode (OLED), 211, *211*

organic matter, soil formation, 344, *344*

organism
atoms making, 104–120
observing patterns in, 52–64

organisms
chemotrophs, 243–244
consumers, 237, *237*
decomposer and decomposition, 229, 237–240, *237*, *238*, *239*
energy in, 233–234
energy sources for, 235–240
matter in, 230–233
matter sources for, 235–240
phototrophs, 243, 244
producers, 236, *236*

organisms, patterns of interactions between, 382–399
feeding relationships, 384–388
predicting effects of competitive, 392–394
symbiotic relationships, 389–391

outputs
Earth's system, 138–139
system, 176

overharvesting, 536, 537, 570

owl, 411, *411*

oxygen
biotic resources, 372–373, 374, 375
in cellular respiration, 258–259, *258*, *259*
from chemically separated water, 61, *61*, 62, 106
chemical reaction from, 58
in ecosystem, 528
electrolysis of water, 160, *160*
as element, 231
in human body, by mass, 231, *231*
in humans, 105, *105*
hydrogen peroxide breakdown, 164, *164*
molecular structure of, 118, *118*
molecule of, 232, *232*
as monoxide, 118
in propane, 105, *105*

ozone, molecular structure of, 118, *118*

P

Pacific bluefin tuna, 570–571, *571*

Pacific Remote Islands Marine National Monument, 203, *203*

packing peanuts, 508

Palau, Italy, eroded rock formation, 275, *275*

Panama disease, 537

panda, as consumer, 237

Pangaea
fossil data as support for, 320–321, *320*
landform data to support, 322, *322*
model, 330–331, *331*
tectonic plate movement, 328, 331, *331*

paper, consequences of using, 203

parasitism, as symbiotic relationship, 391, *391*

parentheses, in chemical formula, 157

© Houghton Mifflin Harcourt Publishing Company

parent rock, soil formation, 344, *344*
particle
    affecting properties of matter, 64, *64*
    density of in ice, 80
    energy of, 75–78, 83
    modeling, 63–64
    movement of, 75, 76–77, 78, 83, 90, *90*, 95
    of solids, liquids, and gases, 76–77, 90, *90*
    types of, 107
    of water, 107, *107*
particle theory of matter, 62, *62*, 69
passenger pigeon, 201, *201*
pattern
    in matter, 54–56, 57, 69
    in organisms and nonliving things, 52–64, *52*
    in resource distribution, 56, *56*
    scientist using, 56
    in shape and volume, 74
pattern of interactions between organisms, 382–399
    feeding relationships, 384–388
    predicting effects of competitive, 392–394
    symbiotic relationships, 389–391
pelican, oil spill impact on, 501, *501*
penguin, 70, *70*, 104, *104*
People in Engineering: Cochran, Elizabeth Dr., 516
People in Engineering: Cusatis, Gianluca, 65
People in Engineering: Sultana, Mahmooda, 218
People in Science: Balmonte, John Paul, 588
People in Science: Belnap, Jayne Dr., 308
People in Science: Bosch, Carl, 189–190
People in Science: Dirzo, Rodolfo, 557–558
People in Science: Elton, Charles, 411–412, *411*
People in Science: Gibbons, Doug, 335–336, *335*
People in Science: Haber, Fritz, 189–190

People in Science: Hodgkin, Dorothy, 126
People in Science: Khalili, Nader, 42
People in Science: Proust, Joseph, 121–122, *121*
People in Science: Sundaram, Shrevas, 17
People in Science: Wegener, Alfred, 416, *416*
performance, cost versus, 120
permeable paver, 588, *588*
Peru, Huacachina Oasis, 346, *346*
pesticide, 573
petroleum
    as natural resource, 197
    as nonrenewable resource, 201
PHA (potentially hazardous asteroid), 487–488
phases of matter, 72
phenomena, science investigating, 33
philosophical models of matter, 62
phosphorus, in human body, 231, *231*
photosynthesis, 256
    carbon cycle, 408, *408*
    changes in matter and energy, 139, *139*
    chemical bond for energy storage, 256, 257
    chloroplasts for, 257, *257*
    as Earth system, 138–139
    for energy production, 253–258
    light energy capture in chloroplasts, 257, *257*
    modeling chemical reactions, 165, *165*
    phototrophs, 243
    of phytoplankton, 566, *566*
    producers, 253
photosynthetic algae, 570, *570*
phototrophs, 243, 244
photovoltaic cells, 120, *120*
phyllite, metamorphic rock formation, 297, *297*

physical change
    analysis of, 148
    chemical reaction compared to, 143–145
    described, 143
    law of conservation of matter, 165
physical damage, from obtaining resources, 14
physical model, 34
physical properties
    of matter, 141
    synthetic material, 209, *209*
physical properties of elements, 107
physical properties of matter, 57–58, 69
Physical Science Connection
    Energy Transformation, 308, *308*
physical weathering, 269, *269*
phytoplankton, 249, *249*, 566, *566*
Pinatubo volcanic eruption, 453, *453*, 472, *472*
pine marten, 552
pine tree, 581
    rates of renewal, 202
planning, natural hazard mitigation, 482, 483, 485–486, *486*
planning and carrying out investigations, 114–115
    ask questions, 132
    communicate information, 132
    conduct research, 131
    construct an explanation, 132
    develop a model, 132
plant. *See also* **photosynthesis**
    availability of crop resources, 200, *200*
    as biotic factor, 372
    consumers of, 237
    decomposition of dead, 237
    Elodea, 254–255, *254*, 256
    energy for the sun, 532, *532*
    feeding relationships, 384, 385–387, *385*
    fertilizers, 240, 503
    matching fossil data across Atlantic, 320, *320*

nitrogen cycle, 409, *409*

phototrophs, 243, 244

physical weathering, 269, *269*

producer transform sun energy into food, 236, *236*

as renewable resource, 16

sugar stored in, 252, *252*, 257

sun as energy source for, 233–234, *234*

sunlight as energy source for, 233–234, *234*, 256–257, *256*

plant material

for biomass fuel production, 211, *211*, 213

as natural resource, 197, *197*

plastic

impact on animals, 516, *516*

as synthetic material, 206, 210

plastic bag, 502, *502*, 573, *573*, 574

plastic bottle, recycling of, 23, *23*, 39, *39*, 493, *493*, 513, *513*

Plastic Bottle Village, 23, *23*, 39, *39*

plastic microbead, 574

plastic polyvinyl chloride (PVC), 115, *115*

plate tectonics, 333–334, *333–334*

platypus, as carnivore, 385, *385*

plesiosaurs, 230, *230*

pollen, *61*, 62

pollination

cross-pollination by bees, 390, *390*

as ecosystem service, 7, 566, *566*

from obtaining resources, 14

pollinator, role in ecosystem recovery, 533, *533*

pollution

reducing, 573, *573*, 576–577

from synthetic materials, 501–504

polyester, 209, *209*

polyester fabric, 493, *493*, 495, *495*, 513, *513*

polyethylene, formation of, 207, *207*, 210

polymer, 210, **210**

pond ecosystem, 402, *402*, 548, *548*

population, 365

in community, 365

competition, to control size, 394, *394*

dependent on disturbances, 556

effects of ecosystem changes on, 553–555

exponential growth pattern, 377, *377*, 378, *378*

factors influencing, 554–555

growth and natural resource availability, 367, *367*, 369, 373, *373*, 375

as level of ecosystem organization, 365

logistic growth pattern, 377, *377*, 378, *378*

predicting changes in, 551–556

size of, and feeding relationships, 388

symbiotic relationships, predicting changes, 391, *391*

Port Campbell National Park, 267, *267*, 281, *281*

positive consequences, of using natural resources, 203–204

potentially hazardous asteroid (PHA), 487–488, *487–488*

potentially renewable resource, 201

Praia do Camilo region, Portugal, 266, *266*

prairie ecosystem, 530

precipitate

chemical reaction production of, 146

copper sulfate and ammonia, 154, *154*

defined, 146

precipitation

El Niño cycles, 395–396, *395*, *396*

water cycle, 407, *407*

predator

feeding relationships, 384, *384*, 385, *385*, 388, *388*, 394, *394*

lion as, 384, *384*

role in ecosystem recovery, 533

prediction

asteroid impacts, 487–488, *487–488*

of change of state, 87–88

of climate hazards, 477–481, *477–481*

flood, 480–481, *480–481*

of geologic hazard, 472–476

hurricane, 469, *469*

of landslide, 470–471, *471*

of natural hazard, 468–471, *468–471*, 469, *469*, 474, *474*

of population changes, 551–556

of volcanic eruption, 472, *472*, 473–475, *473–475*

of weather hazard, 477–481, *477–481*

preparation, natural hazard mitigation, 483, *483*, 484

preservative, as synthetic material, 211

pressure

affecting change of state, 97–98, 103

to form diamonds, 119

metamorphic rock formation, 296, 297, *297*, 298, *298*, 301, *301*

mineral formation, 286

rock cycle, 301, *301*

rock cycle model, 301–302, *301*

rock formation, 287, *287*

sedimentary rock formation, 292, 293, *293*, 294, *294*

prey, feeding relationships, 384, 385, 388, 394, *394*

primary productivity, 253, *253*

problem, in science and engineering, 34. *See also* **engineering problem**

producer, **236**, *236*

cellular respiration, 258

energy pyramid, 406, *406*

photosynthesis, 253

primary productivity, 253, *253*

product, 144

in balanced chemical equations, 166, 167

cellular respiration, 258, *258*

in chemical equation, 161, 251, *251*, 261

in chemical reaction, 144, 159, 250
life cycle of, 9–13
photosynthesis, 256, *256*
synthetic material, 207

production
impact of, 15
processing resources, 10, 15
synthetic material life cycle, 497,
502, *502*, 507, *507*

progesterone crystal synthesis, 133,
133
propane, 105, *105*
properties of matter, 57–60, 69
chemical properties, 58–59
physical properties, 57–58

property
of natural resources, 60
of objects, 52

protein
carbon-based molecules in cells,
251–252, *252*
molecules of, 126
in salmon (food), 252, *252*

prototype, 34
Proust, Joseph, 121–122, *121*
pumice, 290, 291
pure substance, 111, 118, 119–120,
125, *125*
**P-waves, earthquake warning
system,** 335–336, *335, 336*
pyramid of numbers, 411, 416, *416*
pyroclastic flow, 452, 453, *453*

Q

quartz
hardness of, 57
as sedimentary cement, 292, *292*
questions
asking questions, 34, 41, 132, 521
in science and engineering, 34

R

rabbit, feeding relationships,
386–387, *386*
radiation
as energy transfer, 177, *177*, 178
nuclear power plants, 203

Rainbow Mountains, China, 295, *295*
rain forest ecosystem, 372, *372*
rain forest, water supply in, 56, *56*
rare earth elements (REE), 355–356,
355
**rates of thermal energy
transformation,** 180, 182
raw materials
obtaining, 9, *9*, 14
processing of, 10
reactant, 144
in balanced chemical equations,
166, 167
cellular respiration, 258, *258*
in chemical equation, 161, 251, *251*
in chemical reaction, 144, 159, 250
energy produced by combustion,
181
photosynthesis, 256, *256*
synthetic material, 207
reactivity, of matter, *58,* 141
real-life design problem, 32
recovery, natural hazard mitigation,
484–485, *484–485*
recycling
cell phone, 504, *504*
disposal of synthetic materials, 504,
504, 508, *508*
plastic bottle into polyester fabric,
493, *493,* 513, *513*
product disposal, 504, *504,* 508, *508*
of products, 12, 16, 23, *23*
resources obtained in synthetic
material life cycle, 496, *496,* 498,
498, 501, *501,* 507, *507*
sorting machine for, 509, *509*
recycling product, 576
red clover, feeding relationships,
386–387, *386*
REE (rare earth elements), 355–356,
355
relationship
feeding, 384–388, *385, 385–387,*
394
local ecosystem and lionfish,
521–522
science, engineering, and
resources, 4–21
society and ecosystem, 16

remora, on whale shark, 390, *390*
renewable resource, 16, **201,** 202,
347
natural resource distribution, 347
of natural resources, 16
resource. See also natural resources
cycling of, 416
discarding, reusing, or recycling, 12
disposal of, 12, *12*
distribution of, 10
impact of using, 14–16, 21
life cycle of, 9–13
obtaining, 14–16
relationship between science,
engineering and, 4–21
respiration, carbon cycle, 408,
408
**response, natural hazard
mitigation,** 484, *484,* 485
restoration ecologist, 539, *539*
reusing product, 12, 16
review
Interactive Review, 21, 41, 69, 83,
103, 125, 153, 173, 193, 217, 247,
265, 283, 307, 339, 359, 381, 399,
415, 443, 465, 491, 515, 543, 561,
587
Unit Review, 43–46, 127–130,
219–222, 309–312, 417–420,
517–520, 589–592
rhino, 236, *236*
rift valley, formation of, 325, *325*
river
canyon formation, 278, *278,* 285,
285, 294, *294,* 305, *305*
canyon underwater, 318, *318*
delta formation, 273, *273,* 435, *435,*
517, *517*
erosion and weathering, 273, *273*
flood, 435, *435*
river sand, 36, *36*
road construction, 204, *204*
robin, 362, *362*
rock
chemical weathering, 270, *270*
formation of, 286
igneous rocks related to Earth's
systems, 288–291
metamorphic rocks related to
Earth's systems, 296–299

mineral compared to, 286–287

physical weathering, 269, *269*

sea-floor spreading based on age of, 326, *326*

sedimentary rocks related to Earth's systems, 292–295

small-scale geologic changes to Earth surface, 432–433, *432*

weathering, 268–271

rock cycle

energy flow driving process of, 284–307

modeling, 300–302

Rocky Mountains

intrusive igneous rock, 290

wildfire in, 423, *423*

roller coaster design, 24

rooftop garden, 538, *538*

root of plant, sugar stored in, 252, *252*, 257

rubber production, 222, *222*

runoff, water cycle, 407, *407*

rust

chemical property of matter and, 141

chemical weathering, 270, *270*

formation, 221, *221*

thermal energy produced by, 180, 181

S

salinity, calculating, 60

salmon, *56*

salmon (food), 363, *363*

protein in, 252, *252*

salt (table), distribution of halite, 343, *343*

salt deposits, 523

salt marsh, ecosystems of, 528

salts, sedimentary rock formation, 294, *294*

sample area, 538, *538*

sand

distribution of, 10, *10*

in hydraulic fracturing, 14, *14*

mining for, 9, *9*

as natural resource, 6, *6*

rock formation, 287, *287*

sand dune, 273, 278

sandstone, 293

San Francisco Bay, 126

satellite, launch of weather, 480, *480*

satellite images

of hurricanes, 447, *447*

of Mississippi River dead zone, 575, *575*

saw mill, 199, *199*

Scablands, Missoula Flood, 276, *276*

scale. *See also* time scale

Enhanced Fujita Scale (EF Scale) for tornado, 459–460, *459*, *460*, 464, *464*

Volcanic Explosivity Index (VEI), 453, *453*

scale (proportion)

of atoms, 108, *108*

scanning tunneling microscope, 62

schist, 298, *298*

science, 41. *See also* **People in Science/Engineering**

analyzing and interpreting data, 35

asking questions, 33, 34, 132, 521

communicate information, 36, 48, 224, 314, 422, 522

constructing explanations, 36

defining problems, 34

developing and using models, 34

developing explanations, 33

engage in argument from evidence, 36

engineering, technology, and, 8

engineering and, 1–48

engineering practices compared to, 8, 33–36, 41

People in Science, 17–18

planning and carrying out investigations, 35

purpose of investigations by, 33–36

recognizing patterns, 56

relationship between engineering, resources and, 4–21

scientific knowledge

natural hazard mitigation, 486

scientific research

recognizing patterns, 56

scientific understanding

climate hazards, 478

natural hazards, 468, *468*

volcanic eruption, 473, *473*

weather hazards, 478

scientist

monitoring biodiversity, 578

monitoring ecosystem, 576–577, 578

society role of, 8

sea cow, 576

sea-floor spreading, 325–326, *325*

seagrass, 576

seagrass ecosystem, 576–577

sea level, rising, 570

sea otter, 570–571, *571*

season

ecosystem changes in, 547, *547*

sea star, 528, *528*

sea turtle, 573, *573*, 576

sediment, 268

buildup of, 548, *548*

erosion and deposition, 273, *273*, 274, *274*

rock formation, 287, *287*, 292, 293, *293*

soil formation, 344, *344*

sedimentary cement, 292, *292*, 294, *294*

sedimentary rock, 292

in caves, 59–60, *59*

coal as, 345, *345*

coal mining, 303–304, *303*

formation into metamorphic rock, 297, *297*, 301, *301*

formation of, and changes to, 287, *287*, 292, *292*, 293, *293*, 295, *295*

geological processes, 292, *292*

geosphere, 294, *294*

layers in, 292, *292*, 294

related to Earth's systems, 292–295

time scale, 294, *294*

seed bank, 537

seismometer

to monitor volcanos, 474, *474*

Self-Check, 48, 132, 224, 314, 422, 522, 594

sequoias, 556, *556*

services, ecosystem providing, 566, 566

shade-grown coffee, 567–568, 567

shale, metamorphic rock formation, 296, 296, 297, 297

shared resource, 17

shark, 203, 237, 390, 390, 395–396, 396, 568, 568, 569, 576–577, 576, 582

sheep, 53, 53, 67, 67

shelf fungi, 363, 363

shellfish, 576

shield volcano, 474, 474

shipping, product distribution, 503, 503

shooting stars, 487

short-term consequences, of using natural resources, 204–205

Shreyas Sundaram, 17–18, 17

shrimp, oil spill impact on, 501, 501

Siamese crocodile, 588

Sierra Nevada, 580

Sierra Nevada Mountains, 344, 344

silica, 6, 6, 36

silicon
 atoms of, 108, 108
 in solar panels, 120, 120

silicon dioxide, 36

silicon chips, 6, 6

Silicon Valley, 126, 126

silver nitrate, 155, 155, 171, 171

simple molecule models, 113

Singapore, 562, 562
 reclaiming land, 13

sinkhole
 in Florida, 519, 519
 as geographic hazard, 449, 449, 472

slate, metamorphic rock formation, 297, 297

slug, as decomposer, 237, 237

small-scale geologic changes to Earth surface, 432–433, 432

smoke, 58

snail, as decomposer, 246, 246

society. *See also* **human impacts**
 demands of, 15
 ecosystem's relationship with, 16
 natural resources and, 6
 needs of, 8, 15
 role of engineers and scientists in, 8
 synthetic materials and, 494–495, 495

sodium azide, 150, 150

sodium chloride, 110, 110

sodium hydroxide, 156, 156

soil
 formation of, 344, 344
 natural resource distribution, 344, 344, 349, 349
 sediment in, 268

solar energy
 collecting, 9, 9
 as renewable resource, 16, 201, 347, 348, 348

solar panel, 12, 12, 120, 508, 508

solar-powered Supertrees, 562, 562

solid, 74
 attraction of particles in, 78
 changing states of, 89, 89, 90
 conduction energy transfer, 177, 177
 gallium as, 85, 101, 101
 as state of matter, 55, 83

solubility, as physical property of matter, 141

solution
 begin with design problems, 24
 brainstorm, 25, 28
 choose and model, 25, 25
 design, 2, 24, 36, 522
 develop, 24–32, 33
 evaluate and test, 25, 25, 581
 for habitat loss, 576–577
 identify, 2, 22, 26, 48, 224, 582
 implement, 25, 25
 for maintaining biodiversity, 578–582
 optimize, 29, 41
 for pollution, 576–577
 recommend, 2, 22, 48, 224, 422
 refine, 25, 25
 to solve problems, 33
 test, 25, 25, 28, 29, 41
 tradeoffs, 582

songbird, 552

Sonoran Desert, 532, 532

sorting machine for recycled materials, 509, 509

South Carolina, tropical cyclone flooding (2015), 461, 461

South Coyote Buttes Wilderness area, Arizona, 268, 268

space, energy transfer in, 177–178, 178

species, 365
 extinction of, 536, 536
 introduced, 536, 536
 nonnative (introduced), 536, 536, 573, 573, 577, 577
 overharvesting of, 536, 536
 protecting individual, 570

species diversity, 529, 529

Sphinx, Egypt, 278, 278

spider, as carnivore, 385, 385

spork, 29, 29

squid, 574

squirrel, 551–552, 552
 flying, 363, 363

squirrel pox, 552

stabilization of ecosystem, 544–556

stalactite, sedimentary rock formation, 294, 294

state change, as thermal energy reaction rate factor, 182

state of matter, thermal energy causing changes in, 84–98

states of matter, 70–78

steel, 176, 176

steel wool, thermal energy produced by rust, 180, 181

stem of plant, sugar stored in, 252, 252, 257

storm
 cost in U.S., 462, 462
 as natural hazard, 448, 448
 as weather/climate hazard, 449
 worldwide data, 451, 451

Stress-Strain Graph, 35, 35

structural engineer, 65

structures, of matter, 49–125

subscript
in balanced chemical equation, 166
within chemical equation, 160, 161
in chemical formula, 157
subsystem interactions, Earth,
429–430, *429*, *430*, 431, *431*
subunits, 116
sudden changes in ecosystem,
548–549
sugar
carbon-based molecules in cells,
251–252, *252*
in cellular respiration, 258–259, *258*
molecule structure of, *116*
plants making, 532, *532*
producer transform sun energy
into, photosynthesis, 236, *236*,
256–257, *256*
and sulfuric acid chemical reaction,
137, *137*, 151, *151*
sugarcane, 106, *106*
sulfur, 121, *121*
using on Mars, 65
sulfur dioxide, 110, *110*
sulfuric acid
chemical formula for, 157
and powdered sugar chemical
reaction, 137, *137*, 151, *151*
sulfur trioxide, 110, *110*
sun, light energy capture in
chloroplasts, 257, *257*
sunfish, 574
sun-grown coffee, 567–568, *567*
sunlight. *See also* **photosynthesis**
as energy source, 532, *532*
as energy source for plants and
animals, 233–234, *234*, 256–257,
256
phototrophs, 243, 244
producer transformation into food,
236
rain forest ecosystem, 372, *372*
as renewable resource, 16, 201,
347, 348, *348*
supercell, tornado formation, 458
Supertree, 562, *562*
surface area
as chemical reaction rate variables,
182, *182*
weathering, 268

S-waves, earthquake warning
system, 335–336, *335*, *336*
symbiotic relationship
commensalism, 390
mutualism, 390
parasitism, 391, *391*
pattern of interactions between
organisms, 389–391
population changes, predicting,
391, *391*
symbols
chemical formula, 156
in parentheses, chemical formula,
157
synthetic fuels, 206
synthetic magnet, 49
synthetic material, 206
analysis of impact of, 500–505,
500–505
analysis of natural resources used to
make, 196–199
analysis the design of, 210–212
evaluating the effects of using
natural resources to make,
200–205
foods, 211
formation of, 207, *207*
fuel, 211, *211*
human use impact on Earth surface,
492–516
investigating, 206–209
life cycle phases of, 496–497,
496–497, 500–505, *500–505*
materials for products, 211
medicine, 209, 211
natural resources used to make,
194–212
pollution and waste, 501–504,
501–504
properties of, 207
recycle as disposal of, 504, *504*, 508,
508
recycle for resources, 496, *496*, 498,
498, 501, *501*, 507, *507*
reducing impact of, 574–575
reuse or recycle, 498
society and, 494–495, *495*
types of, 210–211
uses, 209

synthetic material life cycle, 496–497,
496–497, 500–505, *500–505*
analysis of impact of, 500–505,
500–505
cell phone as example, 496–497,
496–497, 500, *500*, 502, 506, *506*
consumer use, 497, *497*, 503, *503*,
508, *508*
disposal, 496, *496*, 504, *504*, 508,
508
distribution, 497, *497*, 503, *503*,
507, *507*
economic impact of, 505
engineering role in, 506–509,
506–509
production, 497, *497*, 502, *502*, 507,
507
recycle, 496, *496*, 498
resources obtained for, 496, *496*,
498, *498*, 501, *501*, 507, *507*
system, 428. *See also* **Earth's system**
described, 176
energy flow in, 176–177
inputs and outputs, 176

T

table
of cause-and-effect, *44*, *393*
comparing coffee plants, *568*
of criteria and constraints, 31, 32,
580
decision matrix, *581*
of electrical conductivity and
reactivity of matter, *58*
of living and nonliving things, *528*,
547
of observations, *73*, *87*
of particles of solids, liquids, and
gases, *77*
of patterns, *55*
of population changes, *554*
of pure substances, *111*
of salinity, *60*
of states of matter, *83*

Take It Further

Analyzing Types of Population Growth, 377–378

Balancing a Chemical Equation, 169–170

Careers in Engineering: Biomass Engineer, 213–214

Careers in Engineering: Civil Engineering, 37–38

Careers in Engineering: Materials Engineer, 511–512

Careers in Science: Ecotourism, 583–584

Careers in Science: Forensics, 99–100

Careers in Science: Restoration Ecologist, 539–540

Chemistry and Engineering: Airbags, 149–150

Chemotrophs, 243–244

Coal Mining, 303–304

Cost of Natural Disasters, 461–462

Environmental Changes and Interactions, 395–396

Fermentation, 261–262

Geologically Active Yellowstone, 439–440

Gold Rush, 279–280

People in Engineering: Cusatis, Gianluca, 65–66

People in Science: Bosch, Carl, 189–190

People in Science: Dirzo, Rodolfo, 557–558

People in Science: Elton, Charles, 411–412

People in Science: Gibbons, Doug, 335

People in Science: Haber, Fritz, 189–190

People in Science: Proust, Joseph, 121–122

People in Science: Shreyas Sundaram, 17–18

Predicting Asteroid Impacts, 487–488

Rare Earth Elements (REE) and Technology, 355–356

Why Does Ice Float? 79–80

tall-grass prairie ecosystem, 530, *530*

tapeworm, as parasite, 391

technology

development of through engineering and science, 33

impact of on natural resources, 14, 21

rare earth elements (REE) in, 355–356, *355*

reducing emissions, 575, *575*

role in natural hazard mitigation, 485–486, *486*

science, engineering, and, 8

Technology Connection

Biomimcry, 42

Camera Traps in Wildlife Research, 588

Silicon Valley, 126, *126*

tectonic plate, 328

cause of plate movement, 334, *334*

continental data, 320–323

earthquake and volcano distribution worldwide, 472, *472*

Earth surface impacts, 318–339

large-scale geologic changes to Earth surface, 432–433, *432*

model Earth's surface, 328–332

motion and movement, 328–334

movement explained, 332–334

ocean-floor data, 324–327

plate boundaries, 329, *329*, 342, *342*

surface features, 329, *329*

theory of plate tectonics, 333–334

temperature, 89

ammonium chloride and water, as chemical reaction, 183, *183*

during changes in states of matter, 91

changing states of matter, 84, *84* , 89–96, *89–96*

as chemical reaction rate variable, 182, *182*

extreme, as weather/climate hazard, 449, *449*

extreme, cost in U.S., 462, *462*

extreme, worldwide data, 451, *451*

extreme as natural hazard, 448, *448*

to form diamonds, 119

of lava, 96, *96*

metamorphic rock formation, 296, 297, *297*, 298, 301, *301*

mineral formation, 286

physical weathering, 269, *269*

rock cycle, 301, *301*

rock cycle model, 301–302, *301*

rock formation, 287, *287*

sedimentary rock formation, 292

thermal energy increasing, 89, *89*

tensile strength testing, 34, *34*, 35, *35*, 41, *41*

termites, *Trichonympha* **mutualism,** 390

Texas, Houston flooding and park improvement, 521, *521*

texture, as physical property of matter, 141

theory of plate tectonics, 333–334, *333–334*

thermal conductivity, cold pack container design, 188

thermal energy, 89

airbags, 150

changing states of matter, 84–98, 103

in chemical processes, 179–183

cold pack design, 184–188, *184*

energy analysis in chemical processes, 179–183

energy transfer types, 177–178, *177, 178*

factors that affect reaction rates, 182, *182*

Haber-Bosch reactor, 189–190, *190*

increasing particle movement, 90, *90*

modeling adding to substance, 89–92

model movement, 178, *178*

modeling removing from a substance, 93–96

rates of energy transformation, 180, 182

systems and energy flow, exploring, 176–178

use in a device, as chemical process, 174–193

volcanic eruption as, 138, *138*

thorny devil, 414, *414*

thunderstorm

tornado formation, 458, *479*

as weather hazard, 448, 449, 477, 478

tick, 390, *390*, 391

tiger shark, 395–396, *396*, 576–577, *576*

tiltmeter, to monitor volcanos, 474, *474*

time scale

deposition, 271, 278, *278*

of Earth surface changes, 433–438, *435, 436, 437, 438*

Earth system, 428

erosion, 278, *278*

igneous rock, 289, *289*

metamorphic rock, 298

sedimentary rock, 294, *294*

weathering, 271, 278, *278*

tool

engineers designing, 8, 24

gas chromatography (GC), 100, *100*

graduated cylinder, 72

microscopes, 108

scanning tunneling microscope, 62, 108

scientist using, 8

technological advances of, 8

tiltmeter, 474, *474*

tornado, 548, *548*

average annual number in U.S., 459, *459*

average monthly number in U.S., 460, *460*

classification, 459, *459*

data, interpreting patterns in, 458–460, *458–460*

EF Scale (Enhanced Fujita Scale), 459–460, *459, 460,* 464, *464*

forecasting, 479, *479*

formation, 458

hazards, 459, *459*

historical data on U.S., 446, *446, 459, 459,* 460, *460,* 478, *478*

natural hazard risk in U.S., 446, *446*

by season in U.S., 478, *478*

warning, 477, *477*

as weather/climate hazard, 449

as weather hazard, 448

worldwide risk of, 477, *477*

Tornado Alley, U.S., 458, 459, *459*

tornado season, 458, *458*

toxicity of matter, 58

tradeoffs, 25, *25,* 29, 204

Trans-Alaska pipeline, 15

transportation system, impact of, 15, 204, *204*

tree

changes in matter and energy, 139, *139*

conservation of matter and energy, 241–242, *241*

decomposition by fungus, 236, *236*

as natural resource, 198, *198,* 199, *199*

trees

clear-cut harvesting, consequences of, 203

rates of renewal, 202

trenches, deep-ocean, 324, *324,* 325, 327, *327*

Trichonympha, **termite mutualism,** 390

tropical cyclone

cost of, in U.S., 461–462, *461, 462*

historical data on, 469, *469*

tropical storm, as weather hazard, 448

tsunami, 452

as geologic hazard, 449, *449,* 472, 486

as natural hazard, 448, 469, *469,* 475

volcanic eruption, 452, 469

warnings, Japan, 469, *469*

warning signs, 467, *467,* 489, *489*

Turkey, calcium-rich hotsprings, 293, *293*

turtle

algae on sea turtle shell, 382, *382*

competition, 370, *370*

saving sea turtle eggs, 223–224, *223*

U

United States Forestry Service, 556

United States National Park Service, 556

Unit Performance Task

How do lionfish affect relationships in local ecosystems? 421–422

Molecular Clues! 131–132

Save the Sea Turtle Eggs! 223–224

Should your school use vermicomposting? 313–314

What is the best plan to improve a park? 521–522

What is the best way to prevent shoreline erosion? 593–594

Which is the better water filtering solution for a village? 47–48

Unit Project Worksheet

Analyze the Impacts of Resource Use, 316

Design a Chemical Cold Pack, 134

Develop a Natural Hazard Mitigation Plan, 424

Develop a Solution, 2

Explore Disappearing Arctic Sea Ice, 50

Evaluate Biodiversity Design Solutions, 524

Investigate Fossil Fuels, 226

Unit Review, 43–46, 127–130, 219–222, 309–312, 417–420, 517–520, 589–592

uplift, 290, 294, 298, 342–344

uranium, as nonrenewable resource, 201

urban forest, 579

V

values, met by synthetic materials, 495, *495*

vanilla, synthetic, 212

Vanuatu islands, 332, *332*

vegetable farm, 9, *9*

VEI (Volcanic Explosivity Index), 453, *453*

Venn diagram, *551*

vermicomposting, 313–314, *313*

vinegar, 144, *144*, 163, 180, *180*, 186–187

volcanic ash
    energy from Earth interior, 431, *431*
    as hazard, 138, *138*, 452, 454, *454*

volcanic eruption, 452, 548–549, *549*
    deep-ocean trenches, 327, *327*, 332, *332*
    energy from Earth interior, 334, *334*, 431, *431*
    as geologic hazard, 452
    hazards associated with, 452, *452*, 454, *454*, 472, *472*
    historical data, 474, *474*
    Mauna Loa data, 474–475, *474*, *475*
    Mount Pinatubo, 453, *453*, 472, *472*
    Mount St. Helens, 436–437, 453, *453*, 483, *483*
    as natural hazard, 448, *448*
    prediction, 472, *472*, 473–475, *473–475*
    scientific understanding, 473, *473*
    sea-floor spreading, 325–326, *325*
    tectonic plate boundaries and surface features, 329, *329*
    tectonic plate motion, 329, *329*, 332, *332*, 333, *333*, 472, *472*
    volcano monitoring, 474–475, *474–475*
    Yellowstone National Park, 439–440, *439–440*

Volcanic Explosivity Index (VEI), 453, *453*

volcanic processes
    eruption, 138, *138*
    igneous rock formation, 288, *288*, 290, *290*

volcano
    caldera, 439, *439*, 440, *440*
    distribution worldwide, 472, *472*
    as geologic hazard, 448, *448*, 452–457, *452–457*, 464, *464*, 472–475, *472–475*, 490
    hazards, 452, 454
    hot gases and liquid molten material in, 49, *49*, 454, 472, *472*
    Kilauea, Hawaii, 455–456, *455*, *456*, 473, *473*
    lava from, 96, *96*, 332, *332*, 452, *452*, 454, *454*
    monitoring, 474–475, *474–475*
    types of eruptions, 452–453, *452*
    worldwide distribution, 472, *472*

volcano data, interpreting patterns in, 452–457, *452–457*, 473–475, *473–475*
    building site assessment, 455–456, *455*, *456*
    eruptions, 452–457, *452–457*, 473–475, *473–475*, 490
    volcanic hazards, 452, 454
    volcano classification, 452–453, *453*

volcano eruptions, data, 452–457, *452–457*, 473–475, *473–475*, 490

vole, as prey, 411, *411*

volume, 54
    measuring, 72
    patterns in, 74
    as property of matter, 57, 72, 83
    of solid, liquid, and gas, 73–74

volunteer, 582

W

Wallula Gap, Missoula Flood, 276, *276*

warning
    tornado, 477, 479, 486
    tsunami signs, 467, *467*, 484, 486, *486*, 489, *489*

warning system
    earthquake, 335–336, *335*, *336*
    landslide, 471

Washington, Mount St. Helens volcanic eruption, 436–437, *436–437*, 453, *453*, 483

waste
    decomposition of, 237, 313–314, 344, 402
    synthetic materials, 501–504, *501–504*

water
    and ammonium chloride, as chemical reaction, 183, *183*, 185–186
    carbon dioxide and, 251, *251*
    in cellular respiration, 258–259, *258*
    chemical formula for molecule of, 157, *157*
    chemical separation of, 61, *61*, 106, 160, *160*
    contamination, synthetic material production, 502, *502*
    cycle of, 138, 202, 349, 352, 407, *407*, 430, *430*
    as deposition agent, 272–275, *273–275*
    distribution of, 10, 56, *56*
    drinking water extraction, 9, *9*, 565, *565*
    on Earth, 80
    electrolysis, 160, *160*
    filtering solution for, 2, 47–48, *47*
    gravity as agent of erosion, 274, *274*
    hydrogen peroxide breakdown, 164, *164*
    molecule, 110, *111*, 112, *113*, 232, *232*
    monitoring quality of, 578, *578*
    natural filtration of, 566, *566*
    as physical weathering agent, 269, *269*
    pollution of, 573, 575
    producer transform sun energy into, photosynthesis, 236, *236*, 256, *256*
    states of, 75
    thermal energy flow from hot metal, 176, *176*
    as weathering agent, 268

water energy
    as renewable resource, 201, 347, 348, *348*

waterfall, 274, *274*

water molecule, 110, *111*, 112, *113*, 232, *232*

watershed-protection, 578

water vapor
    condensation of, 88, *88*, 94
    formation of, 89, *89*

waves, erosion and weathering, 267, 272–273, *273*, 277, 281, *281*

weather, 449

El Niño cycles, 395–396, *395,* 478

weather and climate disasters, cost of, 461–462, *461, 462*

weather hazards

described, 448, *448,* 449, *449,* 477

flood prediction, 480–481, *480–481*

historical data on, 478, 479, 480

monitoring, 469, *469,* 478, 480, *480*

prediction, 477–481, *477–481*

scientific understanding, 468, 478

worldwide data (1995–2015), 451, *451*

weathering, 268

chemical, 270, *270*

energy driving process of, 268–271

gravity as agent of, 268

law of conservation of matter, 268

modeling, 276–278

physical, 269, *269*

time scale, 271, 278, *278*

weather stations, 480

Wegener, Alfred, 416, *416*

Western Australia's Shark Bay, 576–577, *576*

West Mata volcano, 332, *332*

wetland

as ecosystem, 364, *364,* 400, *400*

flooding protection by, 7, *7,* 204, 365, 483, *483,* 501, 586

natural hazard mitigation, 204, 483, *483*

oil drilling impact on, 501, *501*

whale, 573

whale shark, remora on, 390, *390*

White Cliffs of Dover, England, 295, *295*

WHO (World Health Organization), 42

wildebeest, 406, *406*

wildfire

cost in U.S., 462, *462*

forest, 361, *361,* 379, *379,* 423, *423,* 431, *431*

human habitation and, 444, *444*

as natural hazard, 446, 448, *448,* 451, *451*

natural hazard mitigation, 484, *484*

wildlife corridor, 537

wind

as deposition agent, 267, *267,* 272–274, *273,* 277–278, *278,* 281, *281,* 433

as erosion agent, 272–274, *273*

as renewable resource, 6, 15, 201, 203, 204, *204,* 347

tornado EF Scale (Enhanced Fujita Scale), 459–460, *459, 460,* 464, *464*

as weathering agent, 268

wolf

ecosystem reintroduction and beaver population, 401, *401,* 413, *413*

population changes in, 554–555

wood

changes in matter and energy, 139, *139*

as matter, 57, 58, *58*

physical change to, 143, *143*

wool, 53, *53,* 67, *67*

world biodiversity hotspots, 531, *531*

World Health Organization (WHO), 42

worldwide, natural disaster data (1995–2015), 448, *448,* 451, *451*

worms, vermicomposting, 313–314, *313*

Write, 32, 370, 438, 499

Wyoming, Devils Tower, 291

Y

yeast, alcoholic fermentation, 261

Yellowstone National Park

as geologically active, 439–440, *439–440*

probability of major earthquake near, 476, *476*

volcanic explosivity, 453, *453*

wolf reintroduction and beaver population, 401, *401,* 413, *413*

yogurt, lactic acid fermentation, 261

Yosemite National Park, 580

Yosemite National Park, California, 291, *291*

You Solve It, 1, 49, 133, 225, 315, 423, 523

Z

zebra, at watering hole, 392, *392*

zinc, 162, *162,* 172, *172*